Extraterrestrials and the
American Zeitgeist

Extraterrestrials and the American Zeitgeist

*Alien Contact Tales
Since the 1950s*

AARON JOHN GULYAS

McFarland & Company, Inc., Publishers
Jefferson, North Carolina, and London

ISBN 978-0-7864-7116-4
softcover : acid free paper ∞

LIBRARY OF CONGRESS CATALOGUING DATA ARE AVAILABLE

BRITISH LIBRARY CATALOGUING DATA ARE AVAILABLE

Cover illustration by Mark Durr

Manufactured in the United States of America

*McFarland & Company, Inc., Publishers
Box 611, Jefferson, North Carolina 28640
www.mcfarlandpub.com*

For Cindy, who thought it was a good idea; and
Matthew, who I think would very much
like to meet a Space Brother.

Table of Contents

Acknowledgments

No one completes a project like this by himself. At the risk of leaving someone out, I'd like to publicly thank the following people, organizations, and entities for their help and support during the research and writing of this book.

First, I need to thank Cindy and Matthew for putting up with all the extra time I spent working on this project, especially during the summer months; the team at CR (especially Doug, Jimmy, and Hiram); too many supportive friends to safely mention; my and Cindy's parents, as well as Anne, Greg, and Stephen. Cindy and Anne also helped out by reading and critiquing early drafts of the book.

This project probably would not exist if not for the encouragement and criticism of my advisor and mentor Annie Gilbert Coleman when it began life as a MA thesis (with a much more limited scope) for the history department at Indiana University-Purdue University at Indianapolis. Going back even further, Dr. Daniel Murphy at Hanover College deserves credit — or perhaps blame — for helping the college's history club bring historian and alien abduction researcher David M. Jacobs to campus in the spring of 1997, which planted in my head the idea that scholarly writing and writing about flying saucers were not necessarily, mutually exclusive.

My colleagues at Mott Community College have been putting up with me talking about flying saucers for the last few years and I'm sure they hope this book has emptied my brain of the topic. In particular, Brian Harding, Krista Black, Jennifer Fillion, Terrence Stewart, Brenda Zicha, and Joshua Sauvie have all been valuable sounding boards throughout this process. Paul Kimball and the late Mac Tonnies are (like myself) outside of the mainstream of those who consider themselves "paranormal investigators" but who have been — at various times — deeply interested in its culture, whose ideas, theories, and musings made me want to look into contact culture again. Thanks especially to Paul Kimball and Greg Bishop for having me on their radio shows and podcasts, *The Other Side of Truth* (http://tosot.podbean.com) and *Radio Misterioso* (http://www.radiomisteroso.com), respectively. Writer and taste-maker Warren Ellis (http://www.warrenellis.com) featured a short piece I wrote on the space brothers on his website in June 2012 which brought a lot of eyeballs my way, and I thank him for that, if even as few as one pair of those eyeballs is reading this now. Numerous connections on Twitter have been great, motivating fellow-writers and teachers; and, of course, thanks to the countless acquaintances who kept me accountable for deadlines ("Did you write today, Gulyas?" they would ask, menacingly).

The library staff here at Mott Community College deserve thanks for interlibrary loan work and help locating various resources; David Houchin at the Gray Barker collection was a great host when I was there in March 2012, full of great information about some of the key figures in the earliest days of the flying saucer craze; Glenn Steckling at the George Adamski Foundation and Oscar E. Leon at the Aetherius Society were both invaluable in locating and clearing photos related to Adamski and George King; Greg Bishop's *Radio Misterioso* radio show/podcast was very helpful in presenting incredibly useful interviews and information about the contactee movement's beginnings. I particularly want to thank him for making available a rare tape-recorded presentation by Albert K. Bender (of Men in Black fame) from 1967. Anthropologist Megan McCullen was a great help in checking out suspiciously fake-appearing or misused Native American words and concepts (which appeared distressingly often), and also a willing participant in writing sprints via Twitter.

Introduction: Meeting the Saucer People

This is not really a book about flying saucers. This is not really a book about aliens or abductions, or about the alleged UFO crash at Roswell or faces on Mars, or any of the other cultural trappings of the paranormal.

This is really a book about stories and how people have used stories in an attempt to understand and reshape the world around them. Humans have always used stories in this way, with storytellers presenting their view of the world through their words and pictures. In this case, the stories tell of physical or psychic encounters with extraterrestrial entities. Still, this is not a book about friendly (and, sometimes, unfriendly) human-like aliens so much as it is a book about people who thought that relating stories about such aliens would be a useful means through which to convey messages on politics and society, ethics and religion, war and peace.

An often unsubtle subtext has run through these tales, telling of a better world for humanity and calling for change in politics, society, religion and other areas. Through stories of space brothers and space sisters, people like George Adamski, Truman Bethurum, Elizabeth Klarer, and Albert Bender showed readers the late 20th century through a different lens from that of the dominant media. These storytellers exist on a parallel track to the Beats, the counterculture of the sixties, the New Age movement of the 1970s, and the ennui and paranoia of the 1980s and 1990s.

Even in the 21st century, more than six decades after the phrase "flying saucer" was first uttered, the paranormal remains popular. Documentaries fill cable and satellite channels; Amazon.com carries over 32,000 books that fall under the broad umbrella of the paranormal, ranging from scientific investigations of ESP to paranormal romances featuring sexy werewolves and randy vampires. Even narrowing the field to various flavors of extraterrestrial visitation ideas — leaving out ghosts, vampires, ESP, and so on — the amount of extant material is staggering. The Internet, unsurprisingly, is full of paranormal resources of varying utility. A Google search for the term "alien abduction" produces about 5.2 million hits. A search for a specific, isolated incident — "Roswell UFO" — delivers 696,000 results. Getting more generic, "flying saucer" and "UFO" produce 5.8 million and 48.1 million items, respectively. A Google search for the term "contactee," however, results in a *relatively* meager 477,000 hits.

Narrowing the investigation down to a single popular book, *Alien Agenda: Investigating the Extraterrestrial Presence Among Us* is a popular book by Jim Marrs, a journalist who specializes in paranormal and political conspiracy stories. First published by HarperCollins in 1997, appearing in hardcover and numerous paperback editions, it is one of the most recent comprehensive overviews of UFOs, flying saucers, and alleged extraterrestrial encounters. The 1998 paperback edition stretches to nearly 650 pages. Contactees and their claims take up only 9 of those pages. Even this, one of the more credulous histories of the flying saucer phenomenon, is generally dismissive of contactee claims.

Even the most paranormally and pop culturally aware readers may, after reading that paragraph, ask a simple question: "What's a 'contactee'?" Abductions, Roswell, and the concept of mysterious lights in the sky are familiar to people of the 20th and 21st centuries. The contactees, however, despite their longevity (the first contactee story surfaced in the early 1950s), have faded from public view, little noticed or considered even by the most rabid devotee of extraterrestrial theories.

The contactees were (and are still today) people who claim to have had physical or psychic contact with extraterrestrial beings. The extraterrestrial beings in their stories are stereotypically human in appearance and often — but not always — hail from one of the planets in Earth's solar system. These beings, through their human representatives, the contactees, convey messages of universal brotherhood and warnings that Earth is in danger of destruction from humanity's warlike tendencies. One enduring stereotype of the phenomenon is that the contactee movement fizzled out by the end of the 1960s. While the contactee phenomenon had its birth and peak in the 1950s and declined after the mid–1960s, the story of the contactees is more nuanced and has greater longevity than most know. It is my goal in this book to tell the story of extraterrestrial contact culture and narratives since the 1950s in a way that demonstrates their breadth beyond the stereotypes and — crucially — connect this genre of paranormal writing to the broader trends of extraterrestrial belief during the past 60 years, as well as the broader story of western culture and history during that time period. One of the key ways in which to do this is to study the written accounts through which contactees of the past six decades have used to promulgate their views — both on the intentions of the their space brothers and sisters, and on more politically, socially, and culturally relevant issues of their particular times and places.

The contactees' largely literary, textual presence, as opposed to a massive visual presence in the media, has helped ensure that their story has, in many ways, remained below the radar of the mass media, particularly in the United States. While an array of magazines, books, conferences and conventions have shaped the views of flying saucer aficionados, mass media have shaped the average American's image of flying saucers (or UFOs). Similarly, the media has also shaped the ways in which Americans perceive those who *believe* in flying saucers. Late 20th and early 21st century television shows and films such as *The X-Files* (and its short-lived spin-off *The Lone Gunmen*), *Dark Skies*, and *Threshold* often presented a vision of extraterrestrial visitors as malevolent. Indeed, the aliens in these shows were rarely human in any fundamental way and — with few exceptions — were focused on the visitors' subjugation of humanity. People in shows such as these who believe in the existence of these creatures are usually characterized as obsessive and paranoid; these characters are unable to function without the support of their "UFOlogical" belief system.

Similarly, the popular image of "alien" visitors from the 1990s to the present is that of the "gray" — a slight body with large head tapering to a pointed chin and large, blank, black eyes. The term "abduction" often comes to mind, complete with disturbing imagery of clinical, reproductive-focused experimentation, anal probes, mysterious implants, and other forms of violation. If these extraterrestrial creatures appear human, it is only an appearance, designed to deflect attention from them while they plot the destruction or enslavement of the human race.

Portrayals of extraterrestrials — both fictional and those which purport to be real — were not always so one-dimensional. Beginning in the 1950s and '60s, continuing into the 1970s and '80s, '90s, and into the 21st century, there is a culture of contact between humans and extraterrestrial visitors who are — in all significant ways — human. While scholars have extensively written about the imagery and significance of the abduction phenomenon of the late 20th and 21st centuries, more benign contacts have taken a back seat. These contact narratives, however, are intricately woven into the fabric of modern flying saucer myth.

From the first modern reported sighting in 1947, the concept of crewed craft from other planets visiting Earth has provided fodder for thousands of books, magazines, articles, websites, documentaries, and pieces of fiction. The issue of whether or not humanity is alone in the universe and, if not, what form extraterrestrial life might take, resonates with people. It forces us to consider our place in the universe. For some, however, the answers to these questions are clear: we are not alone, and those Extraterrestrials not only visit us, they are *like* us. They love us. They worry about us. They have a message that we need to hear. They are, in both a figurative and a literal sense, our brothers and sisters from space. For a fringe of devotees, the lights in the sky are less important than those who travel in the craft that shine those lights. This fringe represents a fascinating slice of culture and thought that gives insight into the late 20th and 21st centuries. While flying saucers may be interesting, flying saucer *believers* are important. The most important of all are the contactees — those who allege contact and conversation with benevolent, human-like extraterrestrials.

Why Contactees?

Of all the many interesting and significant aspects of paranormal belief, why would I choose to examine contactees? The History Channel, the National Geographic Channel, and other cable networks have broadcast several series on UFOs and other paranormal topics. They generally have focused on Roswell, alien abductions, "ancient aliens," and the like. Men and women who claim to have communicated with human-like extraterrestrials rarely get airtime. As I developed an interest in these topics as an undergraduate (thanks to the nascent Internet), I was overwhelmed with the intricate conspiracy theories that dominated (and still dominate) the paranormal landscape. In some of the postings on various Usenet newsgroups, I saw a mention of George Adamski. As I tracked down his initial contactee tales from the 1950s, I was struck by the blithe, guileless tone and the overt use of the story to make claims about the Cold War. I was surprised by the vast number of contactees during the Cold War and that their tradition continued into the present day, overshadowed by the dark conspiracy theories prevalent in the 1990s.

There exist — and have existed for decades — numerous clearinghouses for organizing and investigating the claims of those from around the world who have witnessed unidentified flying objects. The focus on UFO research is still largely on the investigation of sightings of strange objects in the sky. There is not a similar system for reporting claims of contact with the beings supposedly inside those UFOs. These stories, however, have been a part of the UFO phenomenon nearly as long as it has existed. The tales of contact with otherworldly beings reflect the fears and ambitions of people living in the modern age both in the United States and elsewhere.

Among the array of lurid stories of sinister abductions, cattle mutilations, government conspiracies, and crashed UFOs carrying technology from beyond, the public tends to overlook the equally fascinating stories of personal visits from friendly, loving space people with a positive message for humanity. Yet, from the 1950s to the present one of the most consistent (if not most numerous or popular) aspects of the UFO/flying saucer/extraterrestrial phenomenon has been the motif of individual humans coming into personal contact with beings that look — to varying degrees — like us, but claim to be from elsewhere.

This book seeks to explore the genre of extraterrestrial contact tales as changing expressions of American culture and society. From the November 1952 meeting of George Adamski and a blond Venusian man named Orthon to present-day reports of contact with ascended interplanetary masters, alien contact narratives have served to promulgate a variety of political, religious, and social viewpoints. These contactees often express views that are at odds with conventional politics and religion, camouflaging their critiques of contemporary society within outlandish stories of extraterrestrial encounters. While most contact-type stories have been positive, over time some have become more menacing. The human-appearing extraterrestrial trope is not, however, entirely positive and benevolent. If we acknowledge that narratives of extraterrestrial contact have a spiritual element to them, then we must also acknowledge that many spiritual traditions possess both light and dark aspects. If the "space brothers" represent angelic companions and guardians, then figures such as the "Men in Black" and other, more overtly demonic figures serve a role of tricksters and agents of disruption. These encounters, no less than their friendlier counterparts, also explicate the concerns and aspirations of society.

From Cold War–era denunciations of nuclear war and capitalism to present-day lamentations about environmental degradation and the dangers of mandatory vaccination, contact narratives represent a current of countercultural thought that has largely been unexamined by historians and scholars. Tales of otherworldly contact range from antiwar sentiments to evangelical Christianity and from clandestine meetings with space brothers at soda fountains to bizarre ET seductions in South America. This modern mythology has a place within the historical and cultural context of the western world from the era of the Cold War to the present day.

But why is the Cold War world, and beyond, a fruitful area for study? Stories of contact between humans and purported non-humans are nearly as old as humanity itself. Mythic tales of meetings between gods and mortals appear extensively in the early writings of humanity. What, then, makes the tales of alien contact that began after the Second World War significant? Why should those concerned with history and culture bother paying attention to those claiming interaction with benevolent space brothers, sinister Men in Black, or sultry women from the stars? The significance of late 20th-century contact culture stems from the intersection of these stories with the larger cultural trends of the time. The importance of these intersections lies in their context, connections, and continuity.

Context

The 20th century contact phenomenon dawned and developed during a period of phenomenal change. From the Cold War to the Global War on Terror and all the concomitant social, cultural, and political changes along the way, tales of contact persisted, adapting their messages to the messengers' perception of what humanity needed to hear. When we study contact stories and those who tell them, we unravel one of the many threads that run through history; the words and ideas of the contactees reflected the fears and aspirations of the societies from which they came. These modern tales of contact (as opposed to earlier mythic encounters with gods, fairies, devils and the like) coincided with and fed off the space race. Just as the religious and spiritual context of the fairies, demons and witches informed the tales common in the ancient, medieval, and early modern worlds, supersonic flight, artificial satellites, and space travel informed the tales of those claiming contact with the extraterrestrial. After the end of the space age, into the 1970s and beyond, the concerns of the New Age tended to dominate contactees' writings. Personal enrichment and spiritual development moved to the fore.

Connections

The topic contactees addressed were not unique to those who watched the skies and believed in extraterrestrial visitation. Social justice, nuclear proliferation, the destruction of Earth's environment, race relations, and other issues make appearances in contactee tales. Despite the often outlandish and unbelievable nature of their stories, contactees' concerns were in line with the concerns of other activist groups. Contactees have always been a part of larger conversations about reform. This reforming aspect of contactee culture is particularly striking in the 1950s when the consensus culture largely frowned on political dissent, particularly when such dissent targeted distinctively American ways of life, including issues such as capitalism, race, and military belligerence. As the Cold War world entered a period of détente in the 1970s, the issues addressed by contactees shifted accordingly. Concerns of the contactees once again mirrored concerns and interests of the time, ranging from ecology and the environment to personal enrichment, meditation and the spiritual aspects of what Bruce J. Schulman calls "the Third Great Awakening." This parallelism between the concerns of contactees and other reform-minded groups continued after the Cold War and into the 21st century.

Continuity

In addition to being a fascinating part (though little known or regarded) of reform conversations, the cultural phenomenon of extraterrestrial contact narratives represent a strand of the very long tradition of American and Western mysticism and religious or quasi-religious thought. Indeed, at times contactees directly addressed mystical and religious topics, critiquing mainstream spiritual thought or engaging in methods of contact that were mystical in nature, such as channeling or automatic writing. As the New Age and personal awareness movements grew in popularity in the 1970s and '80s, contactees responded by cloaking themselves in the language of this new constellation of belief. Schulman describes "New Age" as an "amorphous term, encompassing a broad range of beliefs and activities. It included non–Western spiritual traditions ... and a variety of supernatural phenomena and belief systems (channeling, Wicca, neopaganism, harmonic convergence, crystals.)"[1] It is not difficult to see how belief in otherworldly visitors could fit into such a worldview. In 1981 Marilyn Ferguson wrote *The Aquarian Conspiracy*, a manifesto for New Age thought and the "Bible" for the New Age Movement.[2] In the first chapter she describes what was happening:

> Broader than reform, deeper than revolution, this benign conspiracy for a new human agenda has triggered the most rapid cultural realignment in history. The great shuddering, irrevocable shift overtaking us is not a new political, religious, or philosophical system. It is a new mind — the ascendance of a startling worldview that gathers into its framework breakthrough science and insights from earliest recorded thought.[3]

As we will see, this vision of, and desire for, a massive, nearly universal paradigm shift is similar to the visions promulgated by contactees from the 1950s to the present.

That is not, however, unique. The story of the post–World War II world is one of increasing citizen involvement. Since 1945, millions of people around the world have written books, published magazines, and taken to the streets, agitating for change and progress, and urging humanity to think and act differently. That contactees have done so via stories of extraterrestrial visits and personal experiences traveling in flying saucers is extraordinary and worthy of investigation in its own right.

Defining Terms and Scope

Narrowing down the scope of an investigation into the history of any topic is difficult and there are always exceptions to the rules set for oneself. The following is an attempt to explain why I discuss the people, ideas and events I do and why I might not be discussing your favorite contactee (if, in fact, you have such a thing).

Although the term "contactee" often connotes the specific 1950s and '60s-era men and women who claimed direct physical (or sometimes psychic) contact with a humanoid extraterrestrial, I am using it in a broader sense, taking the term out of its space age, Cold War home and applying it to a broader timespan. This will, I hope, alleviate the confusion that would arise from using multiple terms to discuss what is, at its heart, the same phenomenon: claims that visitors from other worlds (or planes of existence, or other parts of *our* world) have come to convey important information to specific humans for the good of humanity as a whole.

Another terminology issue that often arises when discussing extraterrestrial contact is what to call the supposed ships that the beings supposedly use to visit Earth. "Flying saucer" is often not descriptive of what a contactee saw, while "UFO" or "unidentified flying object" is more the absence of a definition than a definition in itself. For contactees, the objects in question were never "unidentified." They were from Venus, Mars, or any of a dozen other places. For consistency, I am going to use whatever term a particular contactee used to describe the particular craft or crafts with which they had their experience, thus, terms such as flying saucer, beamship, and aethership will be part of our journey.

While the broader history of the question of UFO sightings, flying saucers, extraterrestrial contact and the like are a part of this story, this is not meant to be an all-encompassing narrative of the phenomenon. While I will present a brief précis of the UFO story and how scholars have viewed it in the first two chapters, the focus of this book is on the stories of contact between humans from Earth and humans (or human-like beings) from elsewhere. Particularly, I will focus on the messages the space brothers (and occasionally space sisters) passed along to humanity through those contacts, and how those stories evolved over the past six decades since the advent of the modern contact phenomenon.

Thus one area, while of importance to the history of extraterrestrial narrative, I will not be discussing in depth: the so-called alien abduction phenomenon. I will, of course, include it my brief trip through UFO/flying saucer history, but while these abductions are a form of "contact," they have little in common with the classic "contactee" narrative. Particularly missing from most abduction experiences is a specific message for humanity—a key component of contactee narrative. The "abduction" phenomenon is an important part of the ongoing cultural story of the anomalous and weird, but it is a distinct genre of extraterrestrial-themed anomaly that is outside the scope of this investigation. Like every rule, however, my self-imposed ban on abductees has exceptions. There are occasions where the relationship between abductor and abductee crosses an odd threshold into the realm of what one might conceivably consider a classic "contact" experience. In that same vein, I will address the themes of biological reproduction which exist in many abduction stories in Chapter 5, as the abduction phenomenon became a cause for concern among contactees in the 1980s and 1990s, as well as Chapter 7, which deals with gender and sexuality in contact narratives.

It is not my purpose to pick apart the illogic and inconsistencies of classic or contemporary contact narratives. There have been many books published, and still on the market today, which debunk the prosaic aspects of contactees' stories. It is not new, nor is it revolutionary, to point out that this or that photograph of a flying saucer is, in reality, a photograph of a hubcap. Our understanding of Cold War culture is not enhanced by pressing home the crucial point that someone who called himself "professor" did not, in fact, have any academic credentials. The importance of these narratives does not rest on whether or not they are true in a literal, physical sense. Rather, the importance of these stories stems from their cultural and historical presence as conduits for reforming ideas. The contactees deserve historians' attention because of their role as aspiring change agents. Despite the paucity of evidence that contactees met with extraterrestrial beings (either physically or psychically), the longevity and resonance of their *messages* are undeniable. The question historians and cultural scholars must ask is not "Did Jane the contactee really ride in a flying saucer?" but rather "Why did Jane the contactee think claiming to ride in a flying saucer was a valid way (let alone the best way) to convey her message of a racially tolerant society?"

It is the latter question this book seeks to address. Beginning in the 1950s and continuing into the 21st century, the trope of positive and beneficial contact with extraterrestrial beings has been a vital aspect of paranormal experience in the western world. It has also provided a lens through which to examine the changing political, social, and spiritual concerns not only of those who claimed contact (or believed their contact stories), but of those they sought to influence through their writings and activities. The contactees represent a slice of cultural life over the past half century that provides a record of hopes and fears from the Cold War to the Global War on Terror and beyond.

Even counting only those who published books, and not considering those who were the subject of magazine articles, who only spoke at local meetings, or who — in the present day — are among the thousands with a website full of their personal extraterrestrial channelings, there were and are far more contactees than one book could competently discuss. In the following chapters I have chosen a relatively small number of contactees which, when taken collectively, give as accurate a picture as is possible of the overall phenomenon. My criteria for selecting specific contactees to discuss in this volume generally fall within two broad categories.

The first criterion is overall significance. Over 1,100 contactee writings are listed in J. Gordon Melton and George M. Eberhart's bibliography, *The Flying Saucer Contactee Movement, 1950–1994*. Few of these contactees, however, said anything that previous contactees had not already said better and to a larger audience. Significant contactees are those who either influenced others or brought something new and lasting to the genre. Thus, I will not discuss every single contactee, but will rather focus on those who were influential or out of the mainstream of the contact genre.

The second criterion is much more prosaic. As I discuss below, many of these contactee tales were published in very small print runs, often paid for by the author him- or herself. Of course, the tales of many contactees were not written down at all. They existed as oral presentations at flying saucer conventions, comments at local group meetings, or telephone calls to late-night radio shows, like that hosted by "Long" John Nebel out of New York City. Occasionally, recordings have survived for scholars of contact culture to scrutinize, but, for the most part, we must acknowledge that there are pieces of the puzzle that are out of our reach. Thus, I have focused my study on those contactee sources that I was able to obtain (and which, more importantly, an interested reader would be able to obtain).

Organization

In general, this book is organized chronologically, devoted broadly to the contactees of the space age (the 1950s and 1960s) and the New Age (the 1970s to the present day). This is partially because I'm prejudiced by my training as a historian to look at things in the order in which they happened. There is, however, a clear development and evolution of the contactee movement and the narratives it created over time from the 1950s to the present day. While, in general, a chronological approach is useful, three specific topics and concepts within the larger story of contactee culture and narratives deserve special attention.

The first is George Adamski. Adamski was the first of the 1950s contactees and was a crucial influence on later contactees. Adamski's writings and teachings which predate his flying saucer activities also provide evidence and examples of the continuity between extraterrestrial contactee narratives and earlier forms of western spiritualism as well as Adamski's own political and social convictions. Exploring Adamski's development, both as a contactee and as the key public figure in the contactee movement, provides important context for the discussion of later contactee writers.

The second area is gender and sexuality. Women were, in general, underrepresented, especially in the contact narratives of the 1950s and 1960s. When women did appear it was usually in connection with a man who was the primary contact between the human and alien realms. Women like Helen and Betty Mitchell or Elizabeth Klarer brought something unique to the stories of extraterrestrial visitation and contact. Sexuality, as well, is fairly understated in the bulk of contactee works, but in some cases (such as that of Antonio Villas Boas and, again, Elizabeth Klarer) it comes to the fore. The narratives involving women, sexuality, and women's sexuality are sparse enough that I feel they deserve examination on their own terms.

The final area of specific consideration is that of religion and spirituality, particularly with regard to the development of more sinister interpretations of extraterrestrial encounters which emerged as early as the 1950s. While some of the significant aspects of contactee culture and narratives, such as political, religious, or social thoughts, theories and ideas flow and develop alongside the general trend of contactee narratives, the emergence of darker, more sinister forms of extraterrestrial contact tales exist along a parallel track. Sometimes these tracks intersect, but largely they are separate. Discussing this aspect of contact culture and narrative provides a greater opportunity to explore the intricacies of this particularly convoluted strand of an already complex phenomenon. One area deserving of special attention is the reaction of some fundamentalist-leaning evangelical Protestants to the concept of both benign and sinister varieties of extraterrestrial contact. While some on the religious right have chosen pornography or abortion as their battles of choice in the culture war, others have decided the space brothers represent the most pressing of enemies.

Examining the mainstream of contactee thought and stories chronologically requires us to make a decision on whether they should be considered within the context of the time the story was published or at the time the alleged contact occurred. For example, Elizabeth Klarer's autobiography *Beyond the Light Barrier* was originally published in 1980 but relates a series of extraterrestrial contacts which began in 1956. Complicating matters is the fact that contactees often discussed their encounters in newsletters and public appearances long before publishing a book for wide public consumption. I've made the decision to leave these works cemented in their published, public context, regardless of when the events described within particular works are claimed to have occurred. Where there are substantive differences from earlier, unpublished accounts, those changes often provide informative evidence of the changing and developing narratives.

A Note on Sources

Much of the contactee writing of the pre–Internet era was privately published with very small print runs. As a consequence, not everything is readily available to the researcher. Fortunately, saucer enthusiasts have created digital copies of many contactee writings which, having slipped into the public domain, are out of copyright, and have posted them to the Internet. While the benefits to the researcher are obvious, there are also some potential pitfalls. The Internet — despite the efforts of Google and the Internet Archive — is often ephemeral. Sources I reference in the following pages may one day disappear. For that reason, I made a conscious effort to stick with — when at all possible — the originally published sources. When I refer to a digital copy of a source, I will indicate the fact in the notes.

1

The Saucers Arrive

The Cold War Context of Flying Saucers

Beginning with Kenneth Arnold's sighting of saucer-shaped craft and the publicity surrounding that sighting (which I will cover in more detail in Chapter 2), huge numbers of people have claimed to have encountered similar phenomena over the past half century. They have authored books and given lectures that number in the thousands. Throughout the past six decades, these writers described countless sightings of anomalous craft. Some reported nothing more than strange glowing lights. Others saw metallic discs in the bright sunshine. The contactees, on whose stories this study focuses, proclaimed to the public that they had met the pilots of the saucers and that the people from space had taken them on fantastic journeys to the planets of our solar system and beyond. The first large wave of flying saucer sightings coincided with the early years of the Cold War, and that conflict had a marked effect on the early years of anomalous craft sightings. The sightings and the stories surrounding them provided a platform for, among other topics, discussions of the uses of atomic energy and other new technologies. Saucer believers and non-believers speculated that the objects might be American or Soviet secret weapons. One contemporary theory was that "disk- and cigar-shaped Flying Saucers" were various governments' ultra-secret means of "decontamination" of the Earth's atmosphere, which the military had contaminated with countless atomic weapons tests.[1] The explanation that gained the most popular acceptance, however, was that the mysterious objects in the sky were highly advanced spacecraft from an alien civilization.

While a relatively small number of people wrote major books on the flying saucer mystery, major magazines such as *Life, Look, Time, and Newsweek* debated the origin of the mysterious objects, and the major authors often found themselves defending their views on national television programs. From 1947 to 1970, the question of the flying saucers was a continual presence in the popular media of the United States. For many in the press, the topic existed on a blurred line between news and entertainment. One day would see a seriously worded piece on U.S. Air Force reactions to the latest sightings. The next day's news would contain a back-page story (complete with photograph) of individuals like Andy Sinatra — the Cosmic Barber — who single-handedly saved United Nations headquarters from being demolished by malevolent space beings using only the power of his mind and a tin-foil hat.[2]

Despite the difficulty of proving flying saucer claims in a rational, scientific way — and the repeated dismissals of any significance to these claims from government, military and scientific institutions, controversy — over saucer sightings and extraterrestrial visitation claims persisted throughout the Cold War and has continued up to the present day. Flying saucer or UFO belief has never, however, existed simply as a monolithic system with a commonly accepted orthodoxy. Believers advanced many different theories about the origin and purpose of the mysterious craft. The adherents of these different strands of belief often attacked each other in print or on the lecture circuit. Did the saucers originate in our solar system or from another? Would the occupants be human in appearance or horrible monsters? Were the aliens (if they were aliens) friendly or belligerent? Some believers held that the answer to the question of extraterrestrial life lay in the hands of scientists. Others believed that the solution would prove more esoteric and spiritual than material and scientific. Despite the differing opinions amongst believers between 1947 and 1970, common threads run through them all.

Belief that the strange lights in the sky were alien spacecraft was not, of course, universal. While the question of the saucers' reality did appear in numerous popular media outlets, the topic had little lasting effect on the majority of Americans. A small core of true believers, however, used the possibility of extraterrestrial visitation to push forward a political and social discourse that challenged many aspects of Cold War America and Western Europe. The years after the Second World War brought many changes to the United States. Enormous technological and economic advancement was balanced with the threat of nuclear war with the Soviet Union. Many Americans lived more affluent lives than ever before. Inflation was down and unemployment was low. With this new economic power came the belief that the government could sustain the country's prosperity by encouraging increased consumer spending. Contrasting with this new-found economic freedom for many Americans were increasing restrictions on the range of political thoughts and opinions that they could express. The threat of Soviet Communist expansion led to incredible scrutiny of Americans' political beliefs with government authorities searching for any hint of leftist sympathies. It was within this context that some believers in the extraterrestrial nature of the flying saucers addressed the need for change in three broad aspects of American society.[3]

The first aspect that believers addressed was that of societal change. The danger of growing materialism and threat of nuclear conflict were the most prevalent of these concerns. All of the major saucer writers, to some degree, expressed hope that the possibility of life on other worlds would encourage Americans to look outside their confined, suburban world and embrace the possibility of— on one level — extraterrestrial visitation and — on another — the possibility of changing American society and culture for the better. Their concerns went beyond that of proving the existence of flying saucers. Rather, many wished to effect lasting, significant change. Saucer believers also expressed concern with what they saw as the increasing secrecy in government, particularly with regard to national security matters. Although accusations of vast, overarching governmental conspiracies would not become the focal point of saucer and UFO belief until the 1980s, writers of the 1950s and 1960s called for governmental openness on the question of flying saucers. Believers of all stripes held that the government knew more than it was saying about the phenomenon. This pointed to a chink in the armor of a united American front during the Cold War and provided for the possibility of criticizing other aspects of governmental policy.

In incredibly varied ways, the most prolific of writers and researchers during the 1940s, 1950s, and 1960s used their outrageous, largely unprovable tales of flying discs to make important statements about the nature of Cold War America. These statements addressed the era's growing emphasis on the virtues of a rampant consumer culture, the dangers of the nuclear arms race and atomic brinksmanship on the part of the U.S. and USSR, and concern over the nation's scientific endeavors being mainly focused on building new and more destructive atomic weapons systems. The manner in which flying saucer believers expressed their dissatisfaction with these fundamental aspects of Cold War America is an important, but little studied, category of Cold War dissent. The number of articles, television programs, and radio specials produced during this time ensured that the question reached most Americans. Far from being "puff-pieces" about an easily dismissed fad, saucer stories questioned fundamental premises underlying Cold War American society. Economic development, material consumption, the arms race, and the growing national security structure all fell under the magnifying glass of saucer believers.

The United States was not the only nation which experienced debate and discussion of the flying saucer issue during the Cold War. Britain, France, Australia, and New Zealand also had their share of sightings, magazines, and saucer investigators. It was saucer aficionados and experiencers from the United States, however, who planted the seeds of saucer contact and belief around the world. Contactees such as George Adamski (see Chapters 2 and 3) had global reach through their writings and personal appearances. This was not, however, *only* an American phenomenon. An Irish writer, Desmond Leslie, was responsible for getting Adamski's story to a wide public. Significantly, some of Adamski's greatest support, lasting decades after his death, was from European followers. George King (see Chapter 4) had his first contact experiences in Britain, and only later (once his story and reputation were established) moved to the center of the contactee world, California. In the later years of the Cold War, significant contactee narratives would come out of Switzerland, France, South Africa, and Canada. While born in the United States, contactee stories are found in every part of the world.

The Scholars' Approach: Cold War Culture and Thought

This study examines the extraterrestrial contactee phenomenon from its beginnings in the 1950s through the present. The advent of the movement during the Cold War, however, merits special attention. The construction of the narratives, themes addressed, and basic vocabulary of contact stories stem from the period of the early Cold War (roughly 1947–1963). While individual details — particularly specific social, cultural, and political concerns — reflect the times in which the particular narratives emerge, they often slot fairly neatly into the categories and types of contactee stories which emerged in the post–World War II years. Thus, it is useful to examine scholars' assessment of the politics and culture of the era which saw the advent of the contactees.

Scholars have examined the Cold War years of the 1940s, 1950s, and 1960s in extraordinary detail. Numerous political changes throughout the world — especially the division of the world's nations into two competing spheres of influence led by the United States and the Soviet Union — prompted wide-reaching changes in American culture and intellectual life. The economic, political, and social changes spawned by the end of the Second World War, however, unsettled the American people. American politics and culture evolved throughout the Cold War. Despite an initial burst of liberal, progressive government action immediately after the Second World War, a conservative retrenchment came amid the growing Cold War with the Soviet Union. As the Cold War wore on, American politics and culture changed. The space race began in the late 1950s, providing a more benign cousin to the arms race. This Cold War world existed on a taut wire: events such as the U-2 espionage incident, the rise of Soviet-controlled regimes in Eastern Europe, and the development of the hydrogen bomb all threatened to turn up the Cold War thermostat, leading to armed conflicts. The manner in which Americans responded to the pressures of the Cold War changed as they came to terms with the new order.

In the aftermath of the Second World War, the people of the western world struggled to understand the meaning of the new age of technology that offered both vast destructive power and the promise of a future that, economically, surpassed that of any nation on Earth. Historian Paul Boyer examines this transition from fighting in a life-and-death struggle between democracy and fascism to a world where the United States was the only superpower. He asks, "How does a people react when the entire basis of its existence is fundamentally altered?" Boyer argues that the discussions and debates over newly emergent nuclear technology were not confined to the intellectual and scientific elite. On the contrary, debate over nuclear power and weapons permeated American culture and discourse. The language of the atomic age began to appear in the nomenclature of everyday items. Children played with "atomic" decoder rings and middle-class Americans came to embrace the concept of the "nuclear" family. Reorganization at high levels of government reflected the realities of this new age. The federal government undertook the greatest reorganization ever of the national defense structure. They created new agencies such as the Central Intelligence Agency and the National Security Agency, acknowledging that the advent of the atomic age had changed the way the government carried out its work of national security and intelligence gathering. In the scientific realm, too, reorganization took place. While many top scientists took work with the government, developing newer and more powerful weapons, other scientists banded together to demand that control of atomic energy and weapons be put under the umbrella of an international regulatory agency. These demands, made at a time of international tension, brought into question the political loyalty of these scientists.[4] It was during these years that the first saucer sighting appeared in the national press. The advent of flying saucer belief possibly provides one answer to Boyer's question. Historians' treatments of Cold War America rarely mention the phenomenon, however. When historians have discussed the question of saucer belief, they often dismiss it as a byproduct of fears and tensions brought on by the threat of nuclear exchange.[5]

On a superficial level, one could apply that explanation to the contactees of the 1950s and 1960s. They often claimed, after all, that concern over escalating nuclear development was the reason saucers began visiting Earth. Such an approach, however, ignores other concerns expressed by contactees, such as issues of social justice, economic equality, and so on. It also ignores the earlier activities and writings of some of the contactees, particularly George Adamski. Although the contactees receive the most play from historians as the epitome of saucer belief during the Cold War, many other forms of the belief existed. Boyer's discussion of American response to the atomic age, although lacking any mention of flying saucers or their proponents, provides a valuable template for analyzing American saucer beliefs from the same era. Throughout the early Cold War years, a common motif was the attempt to predict what technological advancements would come in the future. From the World of Tomorrow at Disneyland and an increasing interest in science fiction in movies and television to the advent of television and artificial satellites, many Americans looked to the future as a technological utopia. Flying saucers possessed futuristic, advanced technology, but at the same time, that technology appeared attainable. Humanity might someday build craft like these. Flying saucer belief—through its utilization of a technological medium for its message—fits well with Boyer's discussion.

A common theme running through the different strands of saucer belief during the Cold War was dissatisfaction with several aspects of American society and government. This connects saucer believers to a different set of Cold War analyses. W.T. Lhamon, Jr., in *Deliberate Speed: The Origins of a Cultural Style in the American 1950s*, examines such diverse aspects of 1950s culture as the writings of Jack Kerouac and Thomas Pynchon, the art of Jackson Pollack, and the music of Little Richard and Thelonious Monk as being of a piece in terms of their effect on the culture of the 1950s. He argues, "They became a set of strategies for cultural action."[6] These artists and writers did not fit the mold of the dominant middle-class white culture. Thus, as outsiders, they were in a position to critique that culture. Some were outsiders by virtue of their race; others chose to withdraw from the dominant culture in order to critique its values. To the selection of artists, novelists, musicians and poets discussed by Lhamon, one could add flying saucer believers. Some believers were outsiders throughout their lives. Others left behind conventional careers to pursue the question of the saucers. Whatever their different backgrounds, from the most outrageous claims of the contactees to the most conservative theories of "scientific" saucer researchers, one detects a desire for a change in priorities, away from the competition and materialism that prevailed in the United States.

Dissent, however close to the surface it might have been, largely remained hidden behind what Alan Brinkley calls an illusion of unity. According to Brinkley, this illusion grew from the tremendous economic success of the United States in the postwar years. This enormous financial power, combined with military strength and ideological fervor in the face of perceived Soviet aggression, provided Americans with a sense of purpose and of superiority that overshadowed social or cultural criticisms. With this superiority, bolstered by the appearance of solidarity on the part of the American people, it appeared that Americans would not only prevail against the Communist threat, but also have the ability to solve social problems at home. Like the artists, musicians and writers addressed by Lhamon, Brinkley points to intellectuals like Archibald Macleish and the sociologist C. Wright Mills as staunch critics of the middle class suburban veneer presented as a unified "America." And just as was the case with Lhamon's discussion, many saucer believers would fit this analysis.[7] While Lhamon and Brinkley do not discuss flying saucer believers, their analytical approach and basic argument apply to the flying saucer phenomenon. While most saucer writers were assuredly non-intellectual, they were outsiders.

Margot A. Henriksen, in *Dr. Strangelove's America: Society and Culture in the Atomic Age*, focuses on "the often quieter and less visible development of the atomic age culture of dissent" which arose in the 1950s rather than the more visible aspects of Cold War culture. Examining such things as films, youth crime and violence, and the bomb shelter craze, she uncovers a schismatic America suffering from juvenile delinquency at the same time that its television programs presented "idealized representations of the forces of law and order," and supporting a government that relied on informers to "name names" before HUAC while celebrating Arthur Miller's play *The Crucible* which "honor[ed] individual conscience against mass hysteria." This depiction of a schizoid America helps explain both the presence of and ambivalence toward saucer believers. For many, their apprehension over the changing world and the threat of nuclear war was mingled with hope that humanity had within itself the means of rising above destruction.[8]

As the 1960s dawned, American thought and culture shifted again and, according to Howard Brick, the result was "an age of contradiction." Intellectuals of the 1960s, recalling the brief flare of optimism that occurred at the end of the Second World War, "approached the coming decade ... as a chance to realize far-reaching goals of social progress." As the 1960s progressed, the New Left asserted itself after the conservatism of the 1950s. The youth and Civil Rights movements protested, sometimes violently, against the policies of a national government that they viewed as existing only to protect the rights of the privileged. With the ascension of Richard Nixon to the presidency in 1968, contradiction reasserted itself, signaling "a conservative trend [while] liberal and radical forces had not yet lost their energy." Despite this final reversion, Brick considers the late 1960s as "the acme of reform ideology in modern America."[9]

One can see parallels between the reform-minded spirit of the 1960s and the actions of saucer believers during the same time. The 1960s saw increased efforts to get the federal government involved in saucer research. The same contradictions discussed by Brick played out in the story of the flying saucers. Government was more open during the 1960s than it was during the 1950s. At the same time, many believers began to present saucer research on more scientific, rational lines. They held out hope that a scientific approach, combined with the cooperation of an activist government, would solve the mystery of the saucers. Organizations like NICAP (National Investigations Committee on Aerial Phenomena) used scientific investigation as well as active lobbying of the federal government to conduct an open, public investigation into the mystery of the flying saucers (see Chapter 2).

While most historians of the Cold War have not discussed flying saucer belief, they have laid extensive groundwork explicating the social, cultural, and political context in which the flying saucer movement existed. They have also chronicled and analyzed the development of similar dissenting voices of the time. The few historians who have undertaken the task of chronicling the development of saucer belief in the United States have generally followed one of two paths. The first is to focus on the political and military aspects of saucer belief. This approach, while admirably analyzing and explicating the role of the military in the question of flying saucer research, tends to minimize smaller fringe groups, especially contactees and their followers. The second path is less analytical than critical. Authors who choose this path argue that saucer belief was a fear-reaction to the changing America of the Cold War years. While this argument is quite tenable, to focus exclusively on this ignores the proactive steps believers took to improve their nation and world.

David M. Jacobs, in *The UFO Controversy in America*, chooses the first path, focusing on the conflict between the political/military infrastructure that sought to monopolize research into unexplained aerial phenomena and the large, national saucer investigation groups (particularly Donald Keyhoe's National Investigations Committee on Aerial Phenomenon), which sought cooperation between government and civil research efforts.[10] Jacobs also extensively documents NICAP's quest for open congressional hearings into the question of the saucers. Jacobs's work is more narrative than analytical, but the topics upon which he concentrates clearly indicate that he considers scientific and political approaches to the saucer question much more worthy of analysis than other types. Jacobs deftly describes the motivations, goals, and results of NICAP's quest for government and scientific validation of their saucer beliefs. By almost ignoring other types of saucer beliefs, however, Jacobs misses the opportunity to explore the ways in which different strands of saucer belief intertwined.

Unlike Jacobs, Curtis Peebles in *Watch the Skies! A Chronicle of the Flying Saucer Myth* and Brenda Denzler in *The Lure of the Edge: Scientific Passions, Religious Beliefs, and the Pursuit of UFOs* both encompass all aspects of saucer belief from political and scientific to religious interpretations of the phenomenon. Unfortunately, while both authors explore the broad spectrum of saucer belief, they come to very narrow conclusions.

Peebles dismisses the convictions of flying saucer believers as "a mirror to the events of postwar America — the paranoia of the 1950s, the social turmoil of the 1960s, the 'me generation' of the 1970s and the nihilism of the 1980s and the early 1990s."[11] Denzler explores the relationship between flying saucer belief, science, and religion, concluding "at every turn science leaves humanity essentially alone in the universe. The saucer movement, however ... suggest[s] that not only are we not alone but we have been and can be and are in contact with alien forms of intelligent life." Saucer belief, for Denzler, is a middle ground between the barrenness of science and the mysticism of religion.[12]

Thus, both Peebles and Denzler remove from saucer believers a great deal of agency. To Peebles, believers are simply the product of their environment, their convictions a reflection of the world around them. For Denzler, saucer belief is an internal coping mechanism, concocted by those unable to deal with either science or religion. Both authors fail to consider the possibility that saucer belief was not a simply reaction to or escape from reality, but that it could be a medium through which its adherents could convey a desire for fundamental change in American society. Cultural theorists have thought more fruitfully about flying saucer belief over the past 20 years. These works focus largely on the conspiracy theory and paranoid aspects of modern belief in extraterrestrial visitation. While it would take until the 1980s and 1990s for conspiratorial thinking to become the overriding focus of flying saucer belief in the United States, there existed in the beliefs of Cold War saucerdom a faint undercurrent of conspiracy and cover-up on the part of the United States government. Thus, some of these researchers' ideas prove useful to an examination of saucer belief during the 1950s and 60s.

Jodi Dean, in her 1998 book *Aliens in America: Conspiracy Cultures from Outerspace to Cyberspace*, examines the presence of "aliens in everyday life." Rather than provide a close examination of flying saucer beliefs, Dean focuses on popular images of aliens, popular presentations of alien abduction, and conspiracy tales that have escaped the flying saucer subculture and have subsequently presented themselves as cultural artifacts in 20th century American society. Dean examines the connections between these "cultural artifacts and social and political life." She does not, however, deal extensively with the 1940s through the 1960s, focusing instead on current cultural expressions of "UFOlogy." In her treatment of flying saucer culture during the Cold War, she does say that "in the 1950s and 1960s ...

[UFOlogy] was doing something; it wasn't just spinning an outlandish conspiracy tale."[13] Rather, it was using the "conspiracy tale" of government efforts to hide the "truth" about flying saucers to challenge military and scientific hegemony. Thus, Dean's analysis of saucer conspiracies grants saucer believers significant agency in their attempts to change the world around them, but leaves developing an analysis of the 1950s and '60s to others.

Peter Knight and Timothy Melley have both explored the nature and meaning of paranoia in postwar America. Melley argues that writers use conspiracy theories to "represent the influence of postwar technologies, social organizations and communications systems on human beings" and that these theories "are symptoms of a more pervasive anxiety about social control."[14] But attempts at social control certainly existed during the 1950s and '60s, enforcing a vision of a unified nation, bound together by a veneer of upper-middle-class consumerism. Saucer believers, particularly the contactees, rebelled against these attempts at control. Peter Knight explains "conspiracy theories have traditionally functioned either to bolster a sense of an 'us' threatened by a sinister 'them,' or to justify the scapegoating of often blameless victims."[15] Saucer believers of all stripes often felt that the escalating Cold War promoted a false dichotomy that would disappear if the saucers proved to be real. The end of the Cold War conflict would strip the governments of the world of their reason for stockpiling weapons and promoting fear of the other side in the conflict. When the conspiracy is focused on keeping secrets (such as the truth behind the flying saucers), those trying to expose the secrets become noble, heroically bringing the truth to a populace that had been misled. Scholars who study conspiracy theory ask the question that I ask of saucer believers in the '50s and '60s: to what extent did these beliefs help their holders cope with a situation they felt was out of control? Like the conspiracy theorists discussed by Melley, Knight, and Dean, flying saucer believers of the 1950s and 1960s used their ideas to explain aspects of their world that were otherwise inexplicable. While writers on contemporary conspiracy theories often insist that their subjects' views result from those individuals' being alienated from mainstream society, I contend that during the early Cold War, saucer believers sought to use the issue of saucers to effect change and initiate discourse from within American society. Scholars would do well to examine the stories of the contactees, not solely as fear reactions, but as active pushback against a world teetering on a dangerous precipice.

Scholars have investigated Cold War–era contactees and contact narratives most thoroughly within the context of religious thought. Christopher Partridge, in summarizing the Theosophical philosophies of Helena Blavatsky, points out that her teachings were "the result of her instruction in an 'ancient wisdom' which was, in turn, the source of the principal spiritual themes and ethical ideals found in the world religions.... More particularly, and important for understanding much UFO religion, is Blavatsky's believe that certain masters dwelt on Venus."[16] As shown in subsequent chapters, George Adamski, George King, and other contactees from the phenomenon's beginnings to the present, would use language and concepts borrowed from Blavatsky's teachings. J. Gordon Melton also explores the spiritual heritage in extraterrestrial contact literature, going back to Emmanuel Swedenborg's 18th century works, tracing a path through H.P. Blavatsky's Theosophical Society and the space adventure fiction of Edgar Rice Burroughs. Melton asserts that contactees "should be approached as participants in an occult religious movement ... they are people who have been swept into a movement because of a direct experience." He argues that "they seek, as a group, religious, not scientific, goals ... in their naiveté, they do not see the lines between their religious quest and the search for information about unidentified flying objects."[17] While Melton rightly highlights the tension between the ephemeral world of contacteeism and nuts-and-bolts UFOlogy's science-based quest for answers about extraterrestrial craft, origins, and visitations, he ignores the social and political messages with which exist in nearly all contactees' material.

Similarly, Robert Ellwood has explored the manner in which new religious belief systems move from their point of origin to other locations around the world. He notes strong similarities between the way 19th-century spiritualist traditions and movements traveled from the United States and Britain to New Zealand and the popularity of contactee George Adamski's visits in the 1960s. One of the key similarities was that "both endeavored to indigenize the new faith to New Zealand by finding parallels in Maori or settler folklore, and both appealed to motifs deeply engrained in the New Zealand experience."[18] Again, Ellwood focuses on the spiritual aspects of contactee narratives and culture — indeed, focusing on *one* contactee, in one place, at one time.

Scholars utilizing this "case-study" method of examining extraterrestrial contact narrative and belief have produced several important works in the early years of the 21st century. Diana Tumminia's *When Prophecy*

Never Fails: Myth and Reality in a Flying-Saucer Group is an ethnographic study which examines the Unarius Group, a contact-based religious group which emerged in the 1950s and grew dramatically during the 1970s and 1980s. Similarly, Susan J. Palmer's *Aliens Adored: Räel's UFO Religion* studies the religious movement founded in the 1970s by extraterrestrial contactee Claude Vorhilon (who renamed himself Räel). Both Tumminia and Palmer, while focusing on specific organizations, movements, and individuals, also to a certain degree position their subjects within the larger context of the extraterrestrial contactee narrative, as well as within the spiritualist traditions with which these groups and thinkers emerged. These two books are thorough studies of the Raelian Movement and the Unarius group in the context of both religious belief systems and the cultural and social context in which these groups arose. Thus, this book will not address the Raelian or Unarius organizations, focusing on lesser-studied people and organizations.

There is no way to deny that contactee beliefs have their roots in occult and Theosophical traditions, but the significance of contactees and their stories does not begin and end with their position as a new variation on occult religion. Just as examining contact narratives solely in light of the Cold War's threat of atomic annihilation limits our understanding of their message and impact, so does focusing exclusively on the spiritual and religious aspects of their stories and activities. However, while the spiritual traditions at the heart of contactee narratives and culture possess a great deal of significance, they are not the focus of this study. Rather, I am focused on the actual stories which contactees spun. While these experiences/storytellers may have — like George King and his Aetherius Society, or the Unarius group — gone on to establish formal religious organizations, the initial tales which they wrote or told tended to also detail their core concerns about politics, society, and culture.

Beyond intellectual histories of the Cold War, scholarly treatments of new religious movements, narrowly focused UFO histories, and the writings of cultural critics on conspiracy theory, historians of science also provide a fertile background for exploring the meaning of saucer belief in Cold War America. Both wild-eyed saucer believers and advocates for the careful, rational study of often-questioned American uses of new scientific knowledge have argued that scientists should focus their advances toward more peaceful ends. Historians in recent years have examined the role of science and scientists in the Cold War, and the absorption of science by the American national defense culture. Boyer's *By the Bomb's Early Light*, Stuart W. Leslie's *The Cold War and American Science: The Military-Industrial-Academic Complex at MIT and Stanford*, and Jessica Wang's *American Scientists in an Age of Anxiety: Scientists, Anticommunism, and the Cold War* provide three different perspectives on the impact science and Cold War politics had upon each other.

Boyer traces what he considers to be a political agenda held by nuclear scientists. He attributes this agenda to the fact that "many scientists concluded after August 6, 1945, that it was their urgent duty to try to shape official policy regarding atomic energy."[19] The most urgent of their requests was the creation of an international authority to control nuclear material and even — in the case of such visionaries as Leo Szilard, Eugene Rabinowich and even Albert Einstein — the creation of a worldwide government that would supplant nation-states, a goal also advocated by some contactees. Thus the goals and aims of some believers arose within a previously established context of political change. The saucer believers did not exist in an ideological vacuum. Rather, they appended UFO beliefs onto political causes in which they believed.

Though Jessica Wang deals with the same time period and many of the same individuals, she does not discuss the push for world government. Rather, Wang approaches the problem of the growing anticommunist feeling in the U.S. from 1945 to 1955 and the ways that those sentiments affected scientists of the era. Wang argues that through their inadequate response to the rabid anticommunism of the time, the American scientific establishment effectively changed the nature of American science. "Domestic anticommunism did more than interfere with individual scientists' lives," Wang argues, "it affected the entire scientific enterprise." Many saucer believers held that, for many different reasons, science had become ideological rather than open-minded. While not referring to the anticommunist movement, saucer researchers in the 1950s and '60s had indeed been co-opted and adhered to a party line rather than form their own opinions about new phenomena.[20]

Stuart Leslie examines the relationship between government and scientific institutions. Leslie argues that the linking of MIT and Stanford to the national defense structure through patronage work and research grants resulted in "academic programs and corporate products so skewed toward the cutting-edge performance of military technology that they had nothing to give to the civilian economy."[21] Many flying saucer believers of the same era shared these feelings. Their desires for alternative scientific advances ranged from medical treatments to American-made flying saucers for exploring the solar system. The examination of the growing governmental influence in science provides valuable insights into the changing nature of the American government during the Cold War and that government's relationship with traditionally civilian areas of society. Saucer believers focused upon these changes in government in their writings, indicating a desire for change. The works of Boyer, Wang, and Leslie aid our understanding of saucer believers by illustrating the incredibly broad array of Americans who resisted — in various ways — the growing militarism of the American government. Contactees were part of this spectrum and, thus, not as far outside the mainstream as it might first appear.

A final category of analysis relating to flying saucer belief in the Cold War is that of science fiction in general and utopian/dystopian fiction in particular. While not ostensibly writers of fiction, flying saucer believers often expressed utopian and dystopian themes in their writings. The contactees, for example, would discuss the wonders of life on Venus and praise the Venusians' technological and spiritual advancement. Following that, as a counterpoint, they would lament that the peoples of Earth were not as advanced. They then often predicted certain atomic destruction if humanity did not change its ways. Analysis of science fiction and utopian/dystopian writing provides useful models for interpreting the writing of flying saucer contactees.

Tom Moylan observes that dystopian narratives are "largely the product of the terrors of the 20th century. A hundred years of ... war ... provided more than enough fertile ground for this fictive underside of the utopian imagination." Dystopia is not, however, merely an "anti-utopia." Rather, a dystopian storyline often "develops around [an] alienated protagonist."[22] Another shared feature of saucer narratives and science fiction more generally is the prevalence of travel narratives.[23] This similarity is especially strong when considering the works of those contactees who claimed to have traveled on flying saucers. Their journeys had a twofold purpose. First, they enabled the experiencers to escape what they saw as a world that was inadequate. Second, the saucer experience gave the believer a medium within which to hide messages promoting society and culture change.

The sensationalist science fiction and fantasy pulp magazines of the 1930s, 1940s, and 1950s also provided a significant portion of the cultural context for reports of flying saucers in general and extraterrestrial contact narratives in particular. For example, Christopher F. Roth, in his essay "Flying Saucerlogy as Anthropology: Race, Extraterrestrials, and the Occult," discusses the connection between late 1940s pulp writer Richard Shaver, whose stories told of ancient lost civilizations (like Atlantis and Lemuria) and races living within the hollow Earth, and the flying saucer contact tales which would emerge by the end of that decade. Shaver is discussed in much more detail in Chapter 2, but his presence in pulps like *Amazing Stories* represent an important stepping stone on the path to the flying saucer era. As Roth explains, "Shaver's stories of extraterrestrials, Atlantis, and Lemuria betray a familiarity with Theosophical ideas."[24] Also significant is the fact that Shaver (aided and abetted by editor/publisher Ray Palmer) asserted that his tales of suspense below the Earth were actually true — not fantasy like all the *other* stories in the pulp magazines. This blurring of fact (the assertion of Shaver that his stories were true) and fiction (those stories appearing in fiction magazines and presented — initially — as fiction) will be a defining characteristic of contact tales through this history of the phenomenon.

Conspiracy theory, science, and science fiction all appear, on the surface, to be natural cognates of the UFO and flying saucer phenomena. The study of those who not only professed belief in flying saucers, but also devoted their lives to evangelizing their views to people around the world, is remarkably interdisciplinary. From the starting point of the flying saucers, one can discuss military policy, the changing organizational structure of the U.S. government, popular culture, the use of media, and myriad other topics. While it is tempting and very easy to get caught up in the entertaining and often humorous accounts of the believers, one must always bear in mind that these writers were doing much more than telling readers in America, the United Kingdom, France, or South Africa about the spacemen. They talked and wrote about the space beings as a way to talk about their fellow Earth men and women. They pointed out the wonders of Venus to point out the deficiencies of Earth. In doing this, they revealed much about the Cold War's impact on government, society, and science.

While flying saucer belief during the Cold War comprised differing and often contradictory theories, flying saucer believers of all varieties consistently sought to bring about lasting change in American society, culture, politics and science. The contactees wrote tales of travels and conversations with otherworldly beings who had humanity's best interests at heart. Their messages, if adhered to, had the potential to transform Earth into a peaceful paradise. Other saucer believers and researchers claimed no contact with the machines or their operators. These individuals and the organizations they formed simply wanted "the truth" about the strange devices in the sky. Many saucer researchers and enthusiasts, convinced that the United States government knew more than it was telling about the strange lights and vehicles in the sky, pushed for open hearings and the release of classified documents. For the American people (and humanity as a whole) to know this truth, the government would have to lower the walls of secrecy they had built since the advent of the Cold War. All these groups and individuals, regardless of their views on the saucers, had serious messages for the governments and citizens of the United States and other nations.

While public interest and enthusiast activism on the subject of flying saucers as well as the phenomenon of extraterrestrials extended far past the era of the early Cold War, it was this period which established the patterns and ideas upon which the movement would build over the subsequent decades. Science, technology, religion, and connections to the science fiction tales which permeate popular culture would all appear well into the 21st century.

2

A Brief History
of Flying Saucers

Flying Saucers and the Dawn of the Cold War:
1947–1970

While the story of flying saucer belief (and its attendant personalities, theories, and organizations) is complex, a brief history of the UFO/flying saucer phenomenon is a useful starting point and will provide important context for understanding the world in which the contactees operated. Throughout the 1940s, '50s, and '60s believers and skeptics alike carried on the flying saucer debate in very public forums. In addition to coverage from flying saucer clubs, local newsletters, and pulp magazines devoted to the question, many mainstream publications such as *Time*, *Life*, and *Look* also gave extensive coverage to the topic. A brief overview of the major turning points in the flying saucer phenomenon in Cold War America provides useful insights into the ways in which various saucer beliefs and debates changed over time. Between 1947 and 1970, flying saucer beliefs were diverse: no single explanation existed for what the saucers were, where they came from, and what their purpose was. The people involved in saucer research during this time went to great lengths to promulgate their various views of what was happening in the skies above the United States. In doing so, they often sought to spread their beliefs about aspects of America which they felt needed reform or improvement.

The differences between strands of saucer belief and the ways in which these beliefs developed demonstrate that as the 1950s and 1960s wore on, saucer believers refined their arguments into forms that would have the most impact on the public. These developments would culminate in a major scientific investigation into the validity of saucer claims which was funded by the U.S. government. Ironically, this would lead to the twilight of the first phase of the flying saucer movement in the United States. The investigations and debates of the saucer believers did not, however, occur in a vacuum. The actions of the American military establishment, particularly the Air Force, served to fuel speculation about the nature of the saucer phenomenon thus feeding the saucer believers' views and giving them longevity.

PRELUDE TO THE SAUCERS: RICHARD SHAVER AND THE HOLLOW EARTH

The flying saucer phenomenon — and the tales of contact which proceeded from it — emerged in a specific cultural context. Throughout the first half of the 20th century, science fiction tales of visitors from other worlds (and of humans traveling to other planets) had filled the pages of pulp magazines like *Amazing Stories*. One pulp writer who survived to become a part of flying saucer lore — if not an actual flying saucer writer — was Richard Shaver. His tales of the "Hollow Earth," deros and teros, and — yes — flying saucers were a significant precursor to the era of the contactees.

Richard Sharpe Shaver was born in 1907. Moving to Detroit after graduating high school, he became a student at the Wicker School of Art, working as a nude model to earn money. In the 1930s, Shaver took a job at the Ford auto body plant in Highland Park, Michigan, and held this job for several years.[1] Shaver's move into "hidden history" and the mysteries of the Hollow Earth began with a 1943 letter to *Amazing Stories* magazine in which he explained that he had discovered "the phonetic key to all languages" called Mantong.[2] This was a system through which the 26 letters of the alphabet not only represented sounds but thoughts and ideas. These thoughts and ideas were consistent throughout different ancient languages. Shaver opined that the existence of this language was evidence for the existence of lost lands such as Atlantis. He explained it in this way: "A great number of our English words have come down intact [such] as romantic — ro man tic —'science of man life patterning by control.' Trocadero — t ro see a dero —"good one see a bad one"— applied now to theatre.[3]

Amazing Stories editor Ray Palmer added a comment to the letter, asking readers to contribute any information about this language they might have. Despite *Amazing Stories* being a science fiction magazine, many readers wrote in claiming that following Shaver's instructions of how to use the language to understand concepts had worked. Palmer asked Shaver to contribute more material to the magazine. Shaver responded with a 10,000–word piece entitled "A Warning to Future Man." Palmer rewrote it, turning it into a 31,000–word novella, and published it in the March 1945 issue of *Amazing Stories* as "I Remember Lemuria!"[4]

Although "I Remember Lemuria!" was fiction, Shaver makes it clear in an introduction to the story that he had to present it "in the guise of fiction." Shaver claims that he is the modern incarnation of a being named Mutan Mion who, thousands of years ago, lived in ancient Lemuria. He asserts that his story is, in fact, true: "What I tell you is not fiction! How can I impress that on you as forcibly as I feel it must be impressed?... I can only hope that when I have told the story of Mutan Mion as I remember it you will believe."[5] In ancient Lemuria lived a race of people known as the Titans. While these Titans had a civilization that was far in advance of our own technologically, their society had a terrible enemy. These were the deros — short for "Detrimental Energy Robots." In a footnote to Mutan Mion's story, Shaver explains these deros: "Every thought movement is concluded with the decision to kill. They will instantly kill or torture anyone whom they contact unless they are extremely familiar with them and fear them ... to a dero all new things are enemy.[6] Shaver claimed that over time, the Titans left the Earth (though they visit from time to time). The deros now live in caves, terrorizing the human population and kept in check only by the heroic teros, another underground race.

When "I Remember Lemuria!" was published in the March 1945 issue of *Amazing Stories*, it sparked a tremendous response from readers. One letter that typified many of the more fantastic responses was from an alleged Air Force captain who claimed that he and a companion fought a machine-gun battle with deros. Other Second World War veterans reported encounters with the deros on Iwo Jima and Guadalcanal.[7] Editor Ray Palmer, knowing a good thing when he saw it, encouraged more material from Shaver and contributed significant parts to the underground saga himself.

As the stories of the underworld poured out of the pages of *Amazing Stories*, the tales became more extensive in their connection to other fringe topics such as spiritualism, "hidden history," and — after 1947 — reports of flying saucers. The stories of deros and teros became a type of unified field theory for explaining the strange and unexplainable. What differentiates the Shaver stories from the rest of what appeared in *Amazing Stories* magazine is that they purported to be true. This riled some of the readers of what was supposed to be a science fiction magazine, and in 1948, William Ziff, the publisher, ordered an end to the Shaver stories. According to a May 21, 1951, story in *Life* magazine, he based his decision on the number of complaints of the hardcore SF fan readership.

Palmer resigned from *Amazing Stories* and began many magazines of his own — including *Fate*, which is still published today — devoted to true accounts of the strange and unusual. As the Shaver Mystery, as it became known, developed, it began to expanded to address issues of what the deros might be doing through their powers and technology of mind control. This mind control, dubbed "tamper" by Shaver, could affect anyone at any time and accounted for odd, unexplainable ideas and even, perhaps, political events and war. Shaver claimed that the deros used their mind control rays on him from time to time. Richard Toronto, editor of the fanzine *Shavertron*, explained "tamper" this way in a spring 2008 editorial:

> Tamper! You haven't heard much about that lately, have you?... well, other than in U.S. elections and especially not since Richard Shaver went to his reward in 1975. Tamper was a key issue in the Shaver Mystery, and explained, at least to Shaver, why the Mystery was nipped in the bud. It also explained why Shaver was blacklisted from *Amazing Stories* magazine; why he couldn't sell the timber on his Wisconsin farm; why he was the patsy of a porno publishing ring and why there is neverending war, poverty and famine.[8]

Tamper, by definition, is to "interfere with something or make unauthorized alterations." In Shaver's world, tamper is caused by deros using the fabled telaug, a thought-augmentation device that can put thoughts in people's minds while making them think it's their own idea. Thus, for Shaver, the deros represented a source of evil that could be used to explain a number of unfortunate incidents that could not be easily understood.

Shaver and Palmer's work tied into a number of concerns extant from the 1940s through the 1970s (both men worked on theories and stories about the possibility of hollow Earth civilizations until their deaths in 1975). For example, the original Shaver stories of the late 1940s discuss the fact that the Titans and teros were aware of the dangers of atomic weaponry and radiation. Likewise, the early days of the flying saucer phenomenon were fraught with confusion over just what these things in the sky were, with many people concerned they represented Soviet superweapons. By placing these crises at the feet of the deros, Shaver's readers who believed in the stories he told found comfort. This transfer of fears and hopes to nonhuman entities (both benign and malevolent) would be a hallmark of various flying saucer belief systems from the late 1940s onward.

THE MYSTERY BEGINS: 1947

Most UFO researchers, if pressed for an actual start-date for flying saucer fanaticism in the United States, will point to June 24, 1947. On this day, Idaho businessman Kenneth Arnold was flying a private plane from Chehalis to Yakima, Washington. Arnold claimed, as he flew toward Mount Rainier, that he saw "a chain of nine peculiar looking aircraft flying from north to south at approximately 9,500 feet elevation and going, seemingly, in a definite direction of about 170 degrees." Since the local FBI office was closed, Arnold reported his sighting instead to the *East Oregonian* newspaper. The story found its way to the Associated Press news wire. Within days, the story of the strange objects that "flew like a saucer would if you skipped it across the water" flashed across headlines throughout the United States.[9] Though some had claimed to see unexplained aerial phenomena before this date, June 24, 1947, marked the beginning of the United States' popular reaction to and interaction with those who made claims of encountering these phenomena.

The remainder of the summer of 1947 carried with it a number of further "flying disk" claims from witnesses such as police officers, harbor patrolmen, and airline pilots. Subsequent to the first few instances of unexplained activity, the Army Air Force (AAF) issued a statement denying that any of their current projects were responsible for sightings and that the sightings that had been reported did not warrant investigation. This attitude would quickly change. In July of 1947, several AAF pilots allegedly chased unidentifiable disk-shaped aircraft and proved unable to match their speed or maneuverability. The experiences of these pilots caused concern in the upper echelons of the AAF.

At the Technical Intelligence Division of Air Materiel Command, headquartered at Wright-Patterson Field in Dayton, Ohio, opinion was split as to the origins of the strange craft. One leading theory was that the craft were extraterrestrial, piloted by beings from another planet. The second theory was that they were experimental craft developed by the Soviet Union and secretly being tested in the United States. Since the U.S. Navy had also been developing a disk-shaped aircraft (the XF5U-1), this explanation seemed the most plausible, and by the end of 1947, it had become the prevailing opinion of the AAF.[10]

By the end of the summer of 1947, the Pentagon had reorganized the AAF into the independent U.S. Air Force. Along with this change came the institution of Project Sign. Sign was a permanent flying saucer investigation program with orders to "collect, collate, evaluate, and distribute to interested government agencies and contractors all information concerning sightings and phenomena in the atmosphere which can be construed to be of concern to the national security."[11] With Sign in place, the USAF took official, concerted action on the question of flying saucers.

Throughout 1948, saucer sightings continued. The most spectacular event occurred in January of that year. On the 7th, Thomas F. Mantell, Jr., a captain in the Kentucky Air National Guard's 165th Fighter Squadron, was flying from Marietta, Georgia, to Standiford Air Force Base in Kentucky. As Mantell and his three wingmen approached Standiford in their F-51D fighters, they spotted an immense metallic object that did not resemble any aircraft with which they were familiar. The four fighters pursued the object, but as they approached 25,000 feet, all of them broke off except Mantell. Mantell continued pursuing the object until he ran out of oxygen. His fighter went into a sharp dive and crashed on a farm in Franklin, Kentucky. Although Air Force officials found no evidence that the crash was anything more than an accident, the *Louisville Courier* dramatized the story with the headline "F-51 and Capt. Mantell Destroyed Chasing Flying Saucer."[12]

The sensationalist headlines introduced the idea that saucers might not only be interacting with humanity but also might prove dangerous. It also indicated to the public that the American military had an interest in discovering the identity of the visitors. After the Mantell incident, Sign personnel began to view saucers as an extraterrestrial phenomenon and issued an "Estimate of the Situation" which concluded that the flying saucers were real and that they came from outer space. USAF Chief of Staff Hoyt S. Vandenberg rejected this estimate. He did not think that the evidence gathered by the Air Force justified such a radical explanation.[13] This verdict somewhat deflated the members of Sign, who felt they no longer had any real incentive to rigorously investigate saucer reports. Vandenberg ordered the USAF saucer project to shift to a more scientific basis, with an emphasis on explaining sightings in terms that could be easily conveyed to the public.

According to J. Allen Hynek, scientific advisor to Project Sign, the Air Force now "entered upon a long period of unfortunate, amateurish public relations. The issuance of propaganda and public relations handouts, which were often ill-considered and contradictory, ushered in an era of confusion from 1950–1970." Hynek would remain the Air Force's advisor on UFO matters from 1947 through 1969. He summed up what he saw as the Air Force's flawed handling of the saucer situation with one question: "If there was nothing whatever to the UFO phenomenon other than mis-perceptions, hoaxes, etc., why continue a UFO program?"[14]

The USAF changed the name of Project Sign to Project Grudge on February 11, 1949. They gave no reason for the name change. One expla-nation was that the name "Sign" had been compromised in some way, which necessitated the name change for security reasons.[15] The changeover to the new name was so subtle that USAF officials did not see a need to inform even their scientific advisor. Hynek stated that "code names were not supposed to have any special significance," but he also reported, "The change to Project Grudge signaled the adoption of the strict brush-off atti-tude to the UFO problem. Now the public relations statements on specific UFO cases bore little resemblance to the facts of the case."[16] The Air Force dismissed complex cases with simple explanations. For example, multiple lights, moving at high speed in different directions, were explained away as being a sighting of the planet Venus.[17] This growing disparity between the sightings reported to the USAF and their subsequent explanations of those sightings led to the creation and growth of civilian saucer research organizations.

These changes encompassed both the way that saucer believers pre-sented their views and the ways in which American society and government accepted these views. Three major developments occurred: increased gov-ernment scrutiny; increased reports of UFO sightings which often got attention in the popular press; and the advent of a group of UFO experi-encers known as contactees. These years also began to see a splintering of saucer belief into different factions. Each of these factions had different explanations for sightings and wildly divergent interpretations of their meaning. By the end of the 1960s, flying saucer belief had grown in both scale and complexity.

Government response to the saucer question escalated during the 1950s and 1960s. One manifestation of this was the changeover, in the summer of 1951, of Project Grudge to Project Blue Book. Blue Book would be the primary means by which the government and military dealt with the saucer phenomenon until 1969. Although faced with a similar mission as Sign and

Grudge, the USAF wanted Blue Book to provide more solid explanations of saucer sightings and events. They wanted the solution to the flying saucer question to be mundane and attributable to natural phenomena.

A prime example of this occurred in 1966. Two sheriff's deputies in eastern Ohio spotted a strange object in the night sky. They pursued it over 60 miles into western Pennsylvania. Other witnesses in Pennsylvania also saw the object. When the witnesses reported their sighting to the Air Force, they received a perfunctory five-minute telephone interview. The commander of Blue Book at the time, Major Hector Quintanilla, dismissed the sighting as being a particularly bright satellite. The witnesses, believing that the Air Force was not taking their claims seriously, contacted their members of Congress. The Congressmen put pressure on Quintanilla to come up with a more convincing explanation. This time, Quintanilla traveled to Ravenna, Ohio, to interview the witnesses in person. The final explanation arrived at by the Air Force was that the witnesses had seen and pursued the planet Venus, even though the witnesses clearly stated that they saw Venus in addition to the mysterious object.[18]

The Blue Book reports and explanations gained credibility with the press and the public largely due to the efforts of Dr. J. Allen Hynek, Blue Book's scientific advisor. His calm, soft-spoken appearances on radio and television programs lent an air of rational assurance to the Air Force explanations of sightings.[19] He seemed to acknowledge that a genuine mystery or important discovery might lie at the heart of the sightings. Unfortunately, due to the volume of cases and the USAF's pressure to provide an explanation, Hynek was never able to investigate sightings deeply enough to know for sure if anything might be behind them.[20]

Increased sightings, especially in 1952, led to increased government scrutiny of the mystery. The summer of that year saw Blue Book personnel inundated with sightings from all over the country, including a so-called "saucer-fly-over" of Washington, D.C., which radar operators were powerless to explain. As mysterious lights flashed in the night over the Pentagon, White House, and Capitol Hill, the Air Force scrambled fighters to intercept. By the time the planes were airborne, the lights had disappeared from the skies and the radar screens.[21] This incident convinced many in the government that whatever was going on, it was vital to determine whether or not there existed a threat to national security. By early 1953, one of the newest governmental creations of the Cold War would try its hand at understanding the situation.

On January 14–17, 1953, the Central Intelligence Agency convened the "Scientific Panel on Unidentified Flying Objects." Chaired by physicist E.P. Robertson of the California Institute of Technology, the panel concluded, much like the Air Force, that there existed no evidence that "these phenomena constitute a direct physical threat to national security." While no "physical threat" existed, the panel acknowledged "that the continued emphasis on the reporting of these phenomena does, in these parlous [*sic*] times result in a threat to the orderly functioning of the protective organs of the body politic." The panel suggested that the media be used to "strip the Unidentified Flying Objects of the ... aura of mystery they have unfortunately acquired."[22]

The findings of the Robertson Panel, though initially classified and not reported to the public, were significant for two reasons. First, they helped establish that the government saw flying saucers as a threat — not because they were invading craft from outer space, but because the public's perception of them could derail the government efforts to convince Americans that the Soviet Union was greatest threat imaginable. Second, and more far-reaching, was the effect that the Robertson findings had on flying saucer believers when its existence was eventually leaked to the public. To many saucer believers, the report confirmed that the government did, despite its previous public statements, have a strong interest in flying saucers. What was even more shocking was that the agency involved was not the Air Force, but the CIA: a new, secretive creation of the Cold War. Knowledge of the scrutiny given to the question of flying saucers by the military and intelligence organs of the U.S. government fueled believers' desire for governmental disclosure of any UFO information they might have had and reinforced the notion that the government was being unduly secretive about the topic.

Discussion of flying saucers was not confined to private researchers and government committees. Prominent national media outlets also posited theories and presented the views of the Air Force to the public. The prevailing approach that the national media took was to minimize and marginalize fringe views, preferring instead to focus on Air Force responses to saucer reports and on more plausible sightings. As saucers became more of a mainstream topic, however, some media outlets called into question the honesty and thoroughness of Air Force investigations. A useful point of comparison is the treatment given the saucer question by *Life* magazine at two key points in the saucer story. These two stories not only demonstrate the attention that the national press paid to saucer sightings but also illustrate the degree to which the focus of coverage changed between 1947 and 1952.

The first is a short article in the July 21, 1947, issue of *Life*, shortly after Kenneth Arnold's initial saucer sighting. The article recaps the Arnold sighting, and mentions a few others that happened during that first "UFO wave." The article then segues into various theories of the saucers' origins. For example, "San Franciscan Ole J. Sneide, explained that the saucers were sent out by 'The Great Master' who left earth in disks after the fall of the Roman Empire and now resides on the dark side of the Moon." Another explanation came from Boris Artzybasheff, who opined that "obviously the residents of the planet Neptune, having attained a civilization far in advance of what is now enjoyed on earth, are shelling the universe with crockery saucers."[23]

While the 1947 article was less than a page long and largely dismissive of saucer sightings and their proponents, *Life*'s April 7, 1952, article titled "Have We Visitors from Space?" took the subject much more seriously. The focus of this article was the Air Force's new initiative to investigate saucer sightings.[24] Whereas the earlier article was distinctly tongue-in-cheek, this article had a darker tone. Contributing to this tone was the relation of Captain Mantell's fighter crash while pursuing a perceived flying saucer, and other frightening encounters with saucers that either resulted — or easily could have resulted — in loss of life. The *Life* reporter also criticizes previous Air Force investigations into the phenomenon: "These occurrences, jarring though they must have been to the participants, left the official calm of the Air Force unruffled. The operations set up to investigate the saucers ... seemed to have been fashioned more as a sedative to public controversy than as a serious inquiry into the facts."[25] In the 1952 article, *Life*'s writer acknowledged that a mystery existed, that it was possibly threatening, and that the government had not taken the proactive role that the mystery demanded.

Major broadcasting systems ABC and CBS also looked at the new flying saucer phenomenon in the late 1940s. ABC broadcast *Search for the Flying Saucers* on July 10, 1947, only weeks after Kenneth Arnold's initial Mount Rainier sighting. This 15-minute program focused on the many saucer sightings that witnesses reported in the weeks following Arnold's encounter. Witnesses presented serious theories as well as humorous ones. Calling flying saucers "the biggest whosit, whatsit story of the year," narrator Walter Klernon admitted that there were, at the time, no solutions as to the origins or meaning of the saucers. They had, however, "taken our minds off of taxes, toil, and trouble for a little while, and that's not bad."[26] Two years later, in May of 1949, CBS presented *Case for the Flying Saucer*, a 30-minute program hosted by respected broadcaster Edward R. Murrow. Unlike the 1947 program, this show's tone was decidedly less whimsical. Murrow asserted, "Sane and reliable people have been involved in this flying saucer business." This was not a show about crackpots or lunatics, but people to whom the audience could relate. When discussing possible origins of the saucers, the show placed a good deal of emphasis on the theory that the craft were creations of the U.S. government, generally top-secret aircraft or new types of guided missiles.[27] Like the articles in *Life*, these radio programs illustrate the presence flying saucers had in the late 1940s and the shift in the way the media handled them. Subsequent to their first appearances, journalists treated the subject lightly. Later articles and broadcasts treated the subject much more seriously, focusing on the reliability of the witnesses rather than the more outrageous tales. In the 1950s, however, some saucer stories would appear which were too spectacular to ignore.

In 1953, within a few months of the Robertson Panel voicing its desire to demystify the flying saucer question and amidst increased popular press coverage of the phenomenon, some enthusiasts added a new level to saucer belief. Called contactees, they told stories centered on physical and psychic encounters with the occupants of the saucers. These stories not only introduced elements of mysticism to saucer research but also lodged concrete complaints about contemporary social and political problems. The stories of the contactees polarized saucer belief into those who accepted these tales with blind faith and those who still searched for a rational, scientific solution to the question of the saucers. Flying saucer discourse, which many had considered based — however loosely — on apolitical, conventional science, would soon change drastically. Unlike many turning points in history, one individual carried almost total responsibility.

The child of Polish immigrants, George Adamski became one of the most influential and controversial figures in flying saucer lore. Born in 1891, he traveled the United States doing odd jobs and educating himself in a number of philosophical systems, including the teachings of the Theosophical Society of Madame Helena Blavatsky. He settled in California sometime in the 1920s and founded the Royal Academy of Tibet. The

Academy served as a soapbox for Adamski's teachings on the Cosmic Law and his interpretations of various Theosophical and mystical themes. According to some cynics, its main purpose was to manufacture and sell "sacramental" wine during the Prohibition years.[28]

Adamski's headquarters was Palomar Gardens, a four-stool hamburger stand, where he worked as a handyman. By the end of the 1930s, Adamski's fame as a teacher had spread and he regularly held courses on the Cosmic (sometimes called the Universal) Law. This was Adamski's somewhat vague term for a system of beliefs centered on principles of love for one's fellow people, humility, and a rejection of materialism.

Like many others in the United States, Adamski became interested in the question of extraterrestrial life after Kenneth Arnold's 1947 sighting. The Air Force and others approached the phenomenon from a scientific perspective, asking questions like "what are the saucers?" or "where do they come from?" Adamski was more interested in finding out what the visitors were trying to communicate to humanity. Just as he used the vocabulary of mysticism to spread the message of his Cosmic Law in the 1930s and '40s, in the 1950s Adamski used the phenomenon of flying saucers to convey the same message. Adamski had an interest in astronomy, fed by the proximity of the Palomar Observatory to Palomar Gardens. He purchased several telescopes and began taking photographs through them. In time, he would claim that he was photographing flying saucers through the telescopes, laying the groundwork for the saucer myth through which he would promulgate the Cosmic Law. A turning point in Adamski's career came in 1949 when he wrote *Pioneers of Space*, a science fiction novel in which American astronauts travel to many of the planets in the solar system, interacting with humanoid space aliens and learning of their ways and philosophies. Adamski based these alien philosophies on his own Cosmic Law, using the medium of science fiction to convey his ideas. *Pioneers of Space* was a commercial flop, but in 1953 Adamski struck upon a plan to spread his philosophy and make a name for himself at the same time.

In early 1953 Adamski contacted British writer Desmond Leslie, who was close to publishing a book on the saucer question. Adamski conveyed to Leslie an experience that allegedly occurred on November 20, 1952. On that day, Adamski and several friends drove to Desert Center, California. Adamski told his friends that he had a feeling he would be able to get some very good pictures of flying saucers. The group saw several strange craft in the sky from their car. Adamski had them stop the car. He said that they should wait for him and he jogged off into the distance. After a while, he returned, saying that a flying saucer had landed. Adamski claimed that he met with the sole occupant of the saucer — a young man with flowing blond hair who was completely human in appearance. Through a combination of sign language and telepathy, Adamski determined that the saucer pilot hailed from Venus and that his saucer was only a scout ship dispatched from the mother ship, which remained high in orbit. Adamski further learned that the Venusians had grave concerns about the continued atomic testing which endangered the entire solar system. After his meeting with the Venusian, Adamski took some plaster casts of the alien's footprints, which revealed strange, undecipherable hieroglyphs. Several of Adamski's friends swore affidavits that they not only saw what appeared to be a spaceship but that they also saw Adamski speaking with someone.[29]

Leslie thought the story had merit and convinced his publisher to add Adamski's account to the end of his own forthcoming book, *Flying Saucers Have Landed*. Leslie's book was a dry recitation of unexplained sightings and objects throughout history from Biblical times to the present. Adamski's unique tale of his encounter livened up the volume and almost immediately overshadowed Leslie's own work. Soon, Adamski became one of the most controversial and discussed figures in flying saucer circles.

In this way, Adamski created a new genre of flying saucer belief. The contactees were unlike others who had been studying the saucer question in that they offered no proof, no evidence for their claims. One either believed the contactees or one did not. They offered nothing except their stories. Once Adamski's story hit the presses, others came forward with their own tales of extraterrestrial visitors. Some, such as that of British ornithologist Cedric Allingham, resembled nothing more than a retelling of Adamski's story with Mars as the visitor's planet of origin rather than Venus. Other contactees, such as George Hunt Williamson, claimed that extraterrestrials communicated through psychic channeling and automatic writing rather than through face-to-face contact. The contactee movement split saucer belief. Individual researchers and organizations which were searching for physical proof of the saucers' existence and extraterrestrial origins found their efforts undermined by these upstarts who had no convincing proof and who, through their outrageous stories, threatened to discredit all of saucer research.

Despite the lack of proof offered, the contactees enjoyed enormous popularity. And many people took their encounters as fact. Adamski would author two books on his own which built on the contact experience in *Flying Saucers Have Landed*. His 1955 book *Inside the Spaceships* dealt extensively with the beliefs and lifestyles of the various races of the solar system. Like *Pioneers of Space*, this book mirrored the philosophical beliefs that Adamski had promoted since the 1930s. After *Inside the Spaceships* was published, Adamski became the object of an extensive investigation and debunking. This would have an effect on the way in which Adamski would convey his message in the future.

Key to the debunking of Adamski was James W. Moseley, one of the most enduring figures in American saucer research. Born in 1931, Moseley was the son of a U.S. Army general and a wealthy steamship line heiress. After dropping out of Princeton and, almost simultaneously, inheriting a large amount of money, Moseley found himself free to indulge his two great interests: pre–Columbian antiquities and the burgeoning mystery of flying saucers. He began his investigation of the phenomenon in 1953, taking a months-long trek across the United States, interviewing every saucer researcher he could find. His interviews crossed the boundaries of different beliefs, and he interviewed strait-laced scientific investigators as well as the king of the contactees, George Adamski.

Upon returning to his home in Fort Lee, New Jersey, Moseley formed an organization called S.A.U.C.E.R.S. (Saucers and Unexplained Celestial Events Research Society) and began publishing a flying saucer magazine called *Nexus* (later changed to *Saucer News*). From the very beginning, Moseley's approach was unique among saucer investigators. In the first issue, he explained the position of S.A.U.C.E.R.S:

> We feel that flying saucers exist and are probably interplanetary, and we also feel that we are as serious-minded about the subject as anybody. However, we cannot persue [*sic*] our interest in saucers with a continued deadpan expression, and for that reason NEXUS is particularly slanted for those who, like us, can get a laugh out of a rather serious subject.[30]

This is not to say that Moseley did not take the subject of saucers seriously, only that he openly acknowledged the humorous nature of some aspects of it, particularly some of the personalities involved. According to Moseley, "Saucer fans of all stripes needed a journal where they could read the latest sighting reports and insider dope, trumpet their views to their associates, and enjoy a chuckle or two."[31] *Nexus* filled that need. For the first 15 years of its existence, *Nexus* and its successor *Saucer News* had a paid subscription of around 2,500, higher during times of increased saucer activity.[32] Unlike newsstand magazines which touched on the saucer mystery, such as *Fate* and *True*, Moseley aimed his subscription-only publications at an audience which already had their minds made up — one way or the other — about the nature of the saucers. Thus, the *Nexus/Saucer News* publication carried very little in the way of material that tried to persuade readers to think in one way or another about the saucers. Rather, their goal was to bridge the gap between the different strands of saucer belief in the 1950s and 1960s.

Moseley's most lasting contribution to the field of saucer research was an investigation that exposed many of George Adamski's claims as outright fabrications. Moseley's first impressions about Adamski were almost charitable. In his journal, recording his experiences interviewing Adamski, Moseley wrote:

> There is a very, very small possibility that Adamski's account is a deliberate and unscrupulous hoax; there is a much greater chance that it was a psychological or so-called "psychic" experience, in which case there are two possibilities: (1) This represents a normal operation of the mind, an operation that we do not understand; (2) Adamski is crazy. There is also a good chance that Adamski may in all good faith be lying in order to expound doctrines and ideas that he sincerely feels to be true.[33]

Moseley continued to feel that Adamski was sincere about his underlying message, if not his experiences. By 1954, however, testimony from Adamski's witnesses in which they claimed to be lying and careful analysis of Adamski's saucer photographs provided abundant proof for Moseley's exposé.

Not all flying saucer enthusiasts were convinced that Adamski was lying. John Lade, writing in Great Britain's *Flying Saucer Review* in 1956, argued that the skepticism regarding Adamski's claims was due to the attitude of the English being too "conservative and traditional." Lade claims, "In other countries, other attitudes prevail: in Norway I have met normal businessmen who are personally interested and convinced of the present reality of interplanetary travel — as is natural among a race of explorers."[34] Despite the title of Lade's article, he presents a "reasoned" support more of the concept of life on other planets than of Adamski's particular story. He does, however, assert that Adamski's story should not be dismissed solely on the basis of skepticism of extraterrestrial life.

While Adamski shrugged off the efforts to debunk his claims, seemingly unaffected by the exposé, his works after 1955 had a defensive quality that not only attempted to prove his claims but also detracted from his philosophical message. His third and final book exemplified this shift in tone away from the philosophical meanderings of *Inside the Spaceships*. In *Flying Saucers Farewell* (1960) Adamski spent a great deal of time explaining the ways in which current scientific knowledge supported his claims about the space visitors, their technology, and the possibility for life on Venus, Mars, and Saturn. Though Adamski claimed not to be troubled by Moseley's exposé, his panicky and often illogical "proofs" told a different story.

One piece of proof Adamski used was a 1957 letter from one R.E. Straith of the State Department Cultural Exchange Committee. The letter indicated that, unofficially, the State Department felt that the Air Force secrecy was misguided and, "while certainly the Department cannot publicly confirm your experiences, it can, I believe, with propriety, encourage your work and your communication of what you sincerely believe should be told to our American public."[35] Adamski paraded the letter as proof that the government not only knew the saucers existed but that they endorsed *his* vision of what the saucers meant and his message from the space people.

Unfortunately for Adamski, the Straith Letter sprung from the minds of James Moseley and his friend and fellow saucer researcher Gray Barker. Barker had received from a friend several dozen samples of letterhead from various government departments. One weekend at Barker's home in Clarksburg, West Virginia, he and Moseley drafted the hoax letter to Adamski, simply to see if he would tout it as proof of his claims. When he did, saucer researchers almost universally condemned the letter as a hoax. Some, through careful analysis of the typestyle used, even correctly identified Barker as the source. Adamski and his followers, however, continued to hold up the letter as validation of their beliefs. More than just a prank on a gullible saucer believer, the Straith Letter hoax reveals important truths about the nature of saucer belief in the late 1950s. At the time, Project Blue Book was in full swing, and groups such as the National Investigations Committee on Aerial Phenomena (NICAP) pushed the government for open, public investigations into the saucer question. In perpetrating the hoax, Moseley and Barker were able to take advantage of the credibility which government involvement lent to saucer research. Likewise, the letter gave Adamski's claims of his theories' importance considerable weight. Gray Barker would occupy a prominent role not as an investigator but, rather, as a publisher and promoter of flying saucer personalities, particularly contactees. He would also be one of the key progenitors of the "Men in Black" narrative (see Chapter 6).

While some saucer researchers revered Adamski, others loathed him and all others who would claim physical or psychic contact with the visitors. The flying saucer field suffered several major schisms in a very short time. Those researchers who believed they were taking a careful, scientific approach to the saucer question despised the popular ridicule brought down upon the field by the outlandish stories of the contactees. In the same way, these serious researchers were put off by the gossip and hoaxes of James Moseley and Gray Barker. Thus, by the mid–1950s, saucer research had a tripartite structure. On the left wing lay the contactees, with their wild claims of conversations with the aliens. In the center were figures like Moseley and Barker, freely criticizing and satirizing believers of all stripes, while maintaining fairly open minds. National saucer organizations, searching for solid, physical proof which would reveal the origins and intentions of the saucers, occupied the right wing.

The national saucer organizations, those with the least sensational, most scientific approach, rose to prominence in the late 1950s and 1960s. Clara L. John and T. Townsend Brown founded the National Investigations Committee on Aerial Phenomena (NICAP) in August of 1956. The group's stated goal was to "direct a united scientific investigation of aerial phenomena."[36] From its very beginning, NICAP aimed to be as serious as possible about the saucer question. Its board of directors included retired generals and admirals, physicists, and freelance saucer writer Donald Keyhoe. Born in 1897, Keyhoe served as a Marine Corps pilot until an injury forced his retirement in 1923. In 1927, while working as chief of information for the U.S. Department of Commerce, he was the official government envoy accompanying Charles Lindbergh on his nationwide tour following his historic transatlantic flight. During the 1930s and '40s, after leaving the Commerce Department, he became a freelance aviation writer. Keyhoe's first foray into the realm of the saucers was an article in the January 1950 issue of *True* magazine titled, "The Flying Saucers Are Real!" Within a year, Keyhoe expanded this article into a 1953 book, *Flying Saucers from Outer Space.* This in-depth book firmly established Keyhoe as an authority on flying saucers.[37] In this early work, Keyhoe's focus was on sighting reports and hypothesizing on the reason for saucer visits, rather than on the government cover-up theories he would later develop. Unlike many saucer writers, Keyhoe had a great deal of experience in both the military and the federal government. He emphasized his experience, knowledge and connections by using his full title of "Major Donald E. Keyhoe, USMC, Ret." on his books.

This provided Keyhoe's writings an insider-like credibility that many other flying saucer researchers and writers did not have.

By early 1956, Keyhoe had taken control of NICAP and drastically changed its focus. No longer would the organization concentrate only on individual saucer sightings. Rather, NICAP also began pressuring Congress to hold open, televised hearings on the saucer problem and, in doing so, force the USAF to release secret documents about the saucers, which Keyhoe was convinced existed.[38]

NICAP's new goal of ending the saucer cover-up led to rifts between it and other saucer organizations, particularly Corel Lorenzen's Aerial Phenomenon Research Organization (APRO). The key difference between these two organizations was that APRO, while engaging in serious, scientific investigation of saucers, did not believe that there was a government cover-up nor that an organization like NICAP should spend its time encouraging their members to lobby their Congressional representatives for government involvement in the saucer issue. Rather, believers would find the truth about the saucers from careful investigation and observation of the phenomenon. Keyhoe also alienated the contactee branch of saucer belief by refusing to even report their stories in NICAP publications. This further widened the dichotomy between "serious" and "frivolous" UFO research.

The end result of these rifts and arguments between saucer research factions was that, due to the public nature of its work, NICAP became synonymous with "serious" saucer research in the 1950s and '60s. This marginalized other, smaller organizations which limited their efforts to reporting saucer sightings and trying to solve the mystery on their own, without Congressional help. Thus, when a Congressional inquiry did eventually materialize, NICAP would find its fortunes tied to the outcome.

That inquiry would take place in 1967, fulfilling NICAP's efforts and reflecting the fact that — at least in the eyes of the public — the saucer question was too big for the government to ignore. Congress commissioned the Condon Committee, a group of scientists under the direction of Edward U. Condon, to determine whether or not the issue of flying saucers deserved further government study and expense. Throughout 1967, the committee investigated saucer sightings, and after numerous internal personnel shakeups, delivered a verdict. The committee determined that the vast majority of sightings were of explainable objects. They recommended that the government spend no more time investigating the mystery.[39]

The effects of the Condon Report were immediate. The USAF decided to disband Project Blue Book in March of 1969, with the final shutdown to come in December. In the year following the release of the report, sightings reported to the USAF fell to 146, the lowest number since 1947.[40] Saucer believers attempted to rebound from the overwhelming negative effects of the report. They argued that the committee had never been objective to begin with, and that the committee's report admitted that they could not explain over ⅓ of the sightings addressed. Despite these arguments, many in America took the Condon Report as the final word on the existence of flying saucers. Saucer research, of course, did not disappear after the release of the Condon Report. The nature of the research, however, did change in some ways. NICAP experienced the biggest changes. Being tied in the public mind most closely to the Condon Committee, NICAP saw its membership (which had a mid-'60s peak of 12,000) fall to 7,800 by mid-1969.[41]

The only groups not really affected by the report were the contactee enclaves — which throughout the 1970s increasingly became more cult-like and isolated — and the centrist saucer buffs like Gray Barker and James Moseley. In a letter to *Saucer News*[42] readers, Barker admitted that the was "not greatly disappointed ... in that I never expected too much from it anyhow." He explained that the "complexities of the UFO mystery far transcend the scope of a half-million-dollar project."[43] Moseley was less sanguine. In a 1969 issue of *Saucer News*, Moseley expressed what he thought to be the most troubling aspect of the Condon Report:

> We were worried and sad. What if Condon were RIGHT! What if he could convince US! What if there WERE no saucers! What would we talk about? What would we do with all that leisure time if we stopped slaving at our saucer research on weekends?... Probably we would be reduced to having cookouts, perusing the *Reader's Digest*, showing up at Rotary Club, and Making Money.[44]

If, as the Condon Report asserted, flying saucers were not worth the government's time and expense to investigate, what further relevance would flying saucer researchers have? For groups such as NICAP, the Condon Report led to a reinvention and simplification of the organization's goals: investigation rather than lobbying. For Moseley, there must have been some question in his mind of whether or not saucer researchers had wasted the past two decades tilting at windmills the government now said didn't exist. With the reduced number of sightings and depressed subscription rates, Moseley suspended publication of *Saucer News* for about six years, from 1970 to 1976, and concentrated on his pre–Columbian antique business and real estate ventures.[45] The saucer field, however, would rise again in the mid–1970s and Moseley would be back on board, providing his unique brand of independent commentary, needling believers and skeptics alike.

Kenneth Arnold's 1947 saucer sighting and the 1969 Condon Committee report served as bookends to the incredibly varied, prolific, and outspoken Cold War subculture of flying saucer belief. The many ups, downs and turning points in the saucer story during these years, as well as the personalities that brought these about, show that saucer research was not a dogmatic monolith. Like religion and politics, saucer research comprised a number of different beliefs. These schisms often led to bitter rivalries between groups with similar goals and incredible eruptions of animosity when groups with different views or goals crossed paths. The contactees and serious scientific organizations both made statements, often expressing dissatisfaction with the way in which government related to the people of the United States during these years. Whether it was George Adamski proclaiming humanity will never get to where it needs to be unless it abandoned war and materialism or Donald Keyhoe asserting that government had a responsibility to investigate saucers, UFO believers had important messages for the political and social hierarchy of the day.

FLYING SAUCERS AFTER THE CONDON REPORT WATERSHED: FROM THE '70S TO THE 21ST CENTURY

Despite the cold water thrown on the UFO question by the Condon Report, people's investigation into the phenomenon did not end. NICAP and APRO continued on into the 1970s and 1980s before declining and being eclipsed by the Mutual UFO Network (MUFON), an international organization which, like NICAP and APRO, has focused largely on scientific explanation and investigation of UFO sightings. Contactee claims and narratives continued to emerge. Contactee-led organizations and events which emerged during the 1950s and 1960s continued to plug along, often only folding when the original, founding contactee died. Throughout the latter part of the 20th century, psychically channeled communications from beings such as Ashtar filled more and more books, speaking to the believers while abandoning nearly all semblance of providing evidence or proof.

Much rarer during this period are the physical contactees of years previous, although some stories still persisted, such as the claims of Swiss farmer Billy Meier.

Another significant development during the 1970s was the growth of small, dedicated societies of believers which some described as flying saucer cults. Figures such as Räel and the organization known as Unarius emerged (or, if already present, began to thrive) during this period. The "Bo and Peep" group, in particular, led by Marshall Applewhite and Bonnie Nettles would attract the attention of paranormal writer and investigator Jacques Vallee. The Applewhite/Nettles group would later gain notoriety as the impetus behind the Heaven's Gate mass suicide in the spring of 1997. The emergence of devoted groups of UFO and flying saucer believers coincided with the emergence of writers like Vallee and John Keel who brought a more journalistic, intellectually diverse approach to the documentation and investigation of paranormal claims and claimants. Jacques Vallee and John Keel shifted their focus from stories of being on the possible craft in the sky to the people behind the sightings and contact claims. Often, Vallee and Keel attributed such claims to non-extraterrestrial phenomena. Not that Keel and Vallee were dedicated to undermining the claims of flying saucer witnesses. On the contrary, they often promulgated ideas that were even stranger than that of alien-piloted flying saucers. Ideas about time travel, parallel universes, and interdimensional beings often populated their writings, stretching the notions of what "aliens" might be. But while the contactee phenomenon persisted through the 1970s and 1980s, the major shift in thinking was that theories of extraterrestrial visitation shifted to a much darker vision. This trend toward a more sinister view of the visitors and the way such visitors shaped the world manifested through two main ideas: the alien abduction narrative, and the increasing prevalence (since the late 1980s) of political conspiracy theory penetrating UFO and flying saucer mythology.

The alleged alien abduction phenomenon emerged in the 1960s with the experiences of Betty and Barney Hill, who — while under hypnosis — claimed to have been taken aboard a spaceship. They were subjected to medical experimentation by creatures who had skin with a gray pallor, small bodies and large heads with black eyes. These beings, which would become known as "Grays" in the parlance of UFO, indicated that they came from a distant star system. The Hills' story was made public through John G. Fuller's book *The Interrupted Journey* in 1966 and was dramatized in a television movie broadcast in 1975.

At the time, and well into the 1980s, many UFO researchers (especially those associated with the older, more established organizations like NICAP and APRO) considered the notion of abductions like those claimed by Betty and Barney Hill to be outliers — interesting stories, but rare. By the 1980s, researchers like University of Wyoming psychologist R. Leo Sprinkle, artist Budd Hopkins, and Harvard psychologist John Mack began to aggressively pursue interviews with paranormal experiencers under hypnotic regression.

These researchers perceived similarities between these accounts which led them to assert that abductions by alien creatures, similar to the experiences of the Hills, were far more common than researchers had previously assumed. The 1987 publication of *Communion*, novelist Whitley Strieber's account of his own alleged abduction experiences, brought the core story of humans being taken against their will for experimentation to a wider public. Reading the books about the abduction phenomenon being published by the turn of the century, one might assume it was rare to *not* be abducted by aliens. In 1999's *The Abduction Enigma: The Truth Behind the Mass Alien Abductions of the Late Twentieth Century*, Kevin Randle, Russ Estes, and William Cone wrote:

> The phenomenon of alien abduction is real. There are, literally, thousands of people who are suffering from the effects of alien abduction and who do not understand what has happened to them.... Research by both social scientists and abduction investigators suggest that between three million and six million Americans have been abducted. Support groups and abduction researchers can be found easily throughout the country. Abduction is so common, that many of the support groups are organized around specific aspects such as those who believe they were abducted by reptilian aliens, those who believe they were impregnated by aliens, and those who believe they are victims of an extremely long-term, longitudinal study of their family histories.[46]

This brief summary is typical of how proponents presented the abduction phenomenon: vague numbers, a sense of menace and a veneer of scholarship. The presence of credentialed academics brought credibility to the question of alien abductions. One of the academics who has had the longest tenure in the alien abduction field is David Jacobs.

David Jacobs, a retired associate professor of history at Temple University, has been one of the main exponents of the abduction research community since the 1990s. However, he did not enter the abduction field until late 1980s, culminating in his books *Secret Life* (1992) and *The Threat: Revealing the Secret Alien Agenda* (1998). Jacobs, like other abduction researchers, used hypnosis to explore and reveal the experiences of alleged abductees. Jacobs, in *The Threat*, differentiates between those whose abduction experiences were negative and those which were positive — relating those as the descendants, in a way, of contactees. Jacobs asserts that his research led him to believe that the "aliens" were a force for evil. He concludes that "integration into human society is the aliens' ultimate goal" which will be carried out through four methods: abduction, breeding, hybridization, and integration. There are strong reproductive and sexual overtones to the aliens' actions as they "collect human sperm and eggs, genetically alter the fertilized embryo, incubate fetuses in human hosts, and make humans mentally and physically interact with the offspring." Jacobs's portrayal of the abducting aliens is in line with the darkest aspects of the UFO conspiracy theories which emerged in the 1980s.[47]

Running parallel to the alien abduction was a strain of political conspiracy theory which attempted to explain the reasons for the supposed abduction while, at the same time, tying together the story of the flying saucers with the political history of the United States in the postwar era. A key component of this meme was the allegation that a spacecraft had crashed in 1947 in New Mexico and was taken to Roswell Army Air Field. Indeed, in July of 1947, the Roswell base reported that they had recovered a crashed flying saucer. The announcement from the base's public information officer, 1st Lieutenant William Haut, was fairly unambiguous: "The many rumors regarding the flying disc became a reality yesterday when the Intelligence office of the 509th Bomb Group ... was fortunate enough to gain possession of a disc.... The flying object landed on a ranch near Roswell.... Action was immediately taken and the disc was picked up at the rancher's home ... and subsequently loaned ... to higher headquarters." Within hours the USAAF retracted this story and — for a time — the issue was laid to rest. As Don Berliner and Stanton Friedman wrote in their book *Crash at Corona: The Definitive Study of the Roswell Incident*, "For a few hours on July 8, 1947, the lid was off and it was possible to take a peek inside the mystery. The lid was then slammed back down so firmly and so authoritatively that nearly everyone soon forgot it had ever been off."[48]

In the late 1970s, a string of eyewitnesses came forward to assert that there *had* been an alien craft and, more shockingly, the Army Air Force had recovered the bodies of the craft's crew. Numerous authors published books during the 1980s and 1990s — reaching a high water mark in 1997, the alleged incident's fiftieth anniversary. Though organizations such as

NICAP had alleged for decades that the Air Force was engaged in a cover-up of the facts concerning flying saucers, the accusations surrounding the Roswell Incident went much further, implicating a secret cabal within the government of keeping the truth not only from the American people but also from elected officials. The Roswell conspiracy theory tied into other conspiracy theories which abounded during the late 20th century.

Pilot John Lear and writer William Cooper were two of the key exponents of the political conspiracy narrative. In 1987, Lear published a statement on several UFO-oriented computer networks. This statement became one of the foundational documents of the darker, more conspiracy-oriented UFO world of the late 20th century. The notions Lear presented would be the source of television shows like *The X-Files* and *Dark Skies* and were referenced in movies like *Independence Day.*

At the heart of John Lear's revelations is the idea that the U.S. government is colluding with alien forces. Lear claims:

> In its effort to protect democracy, our government sold us to the aliens. The "horrible truth" was known by only a very few persons: They were indeed ugly little creatures, shaped like praying mantises and who were more advanced than us by perhaps a billion years.... President **Truman** quickly put a lid on the secret and turned the screws so tight that the general public still thinks that flying saucers are a joke [emphasis in original].

The abductions, Lear claimed, were part of this Faustian bargain made between the Grays and shadowy elements of the U.S. government (often referred to as MJ-12): "The 'deal' was that in exchange for 'technology' that they would provide to us, we agreed to 'ignore' the abductions that were going on and suppress information on the cattle mutilations. The EBE's assured MJ-12 that the abductions (usually lasting about 2 hours) were merely the ongoing monitoring of developing civilizations." In fact, Lear explains that the aliens suffer from a genetic condition which requires them to process parts of human bodies for nourishment. The aliens, then, are vampires, literally sucking the life out of humanity.[49]

William Cooper, a writer and lecturer on conspiracy and paranormal topics, spoke at the 1989 Mutual UFO Network conference on "The Origin, Identity, and Purpose of MJ-12," tying the alien abduction theories of John Lear in with right-wing anti-government rhetoric in a mélange of paranoia:

> Many people are abducted and are sentenced to live with psychological and physical damage for the rest of their lives.... In the documents that I read, 1 in

40 humans had been implanted with devices, the purpose of which I have never discovered. The Government believes that the aliens are building an army of implanted humans who can be activated and turned upon us at will.... The Government will then suspend the Constitution and declare martial law. The secret alien army of implanted humans and all dissidents ... will be rounded up and placed in the one-mile-square concentration camps which already exist.... Anyone who resists will be taken or killed.... When these events have transpired, the SECRET GOVERNMENT and/or ALIEN takeover will be complete. Your freedom will never be returned and you will live in slavery for the remainder of your life. You had better wake up and you had better do it now![50]

Figures like John Lear and William Cooper wove a new strand into the fabric of alleged human-alien interactions.

Conspiracy theories used a wide variety of evidence during the 1980s to support their claims. One piece of evidence of a governmental cover-up was a 1977 television program called *Science Report: Alternative 3*. Produced by Anglia Television for the United Kingdom, *Alternative 3* was only broadcast once. The plan was for the broadcast to occur on April 1. Delays, however, meant that the show was shown later on a day that was not known for practical jokes.

Alternative 3 was a pseudo-documentary which asserted that there was in place an elaborate plan to move the elites of western society to secret bases underground and — eventually — Mars and the moon, which were much more habitable than NASA space probes indicated. Despite the outlandish and baseless accusations made in the broadcast and subsequent novelization, conspiracy theorists and researchers maintain that *Alternative 3* had been essentially true: the "elites" were planning to leave the bulk of humanity behind to suffer some catastrophe while they escaped to safety. As late as 2010, the 33rd anniversary of the broadcast, an anonymously edited and introduced edition of Leslie Watkins's book based on the broadcast asserted that the book's many editions and fair amount of success were no accident of publishing: "Miracles *do* happen, or concerted disinformation campaigns are sanctioned regularly by establishment stalwarts." For the anonymous introducer, the fact that *Alternative 3* even exists is evidence that the goals of its creators were suspect: "*Alternative 3* is a bona-fide diversion, as is the original Anglia Television hoax. Its aims are suspect as it has been permitted a life that better books have been denied; it has assumed an undeserved aura, especially as so many calculated deceptions lurk in the details.... The heavy employment of misinformation should be dealt with expeditiously." The writer goes on to explain that this 2010 version of the book has been "edited of overt disinformation."[51] *Alternative 3*, it seems, will never die. It is "a haphazardly-contrived and opportunistic disinformation exercise with one primary objective: misdirection." We will see references to it in contactee and channeling claims in the late 20th century.

In the 1950s and 1960s (and, as we will see, continuing into the present), contactees saw the visitors from other worlds as helpful or, at worst, benign. Researchers of the 1980s and 1990s who focused on abduction reports generally viewed the visitors (the "Grays") as more sinister — these visitors' experiments caused physical and psychological trauma to their subjects. The experiments, however, were shrouded in the notion of science. Some abduction researchers and commentators defined the relationship between abductors and abductees as being similar to that between scientists and lab animals. The scientist working on a cure for cancer used the animals and it might cause those animals great pain. However, the scientist does not have any particular animosity toward the lab animals. The Grays, some asserted, were so far advanced that they couldn't comprehend the terror they caused.

In contrast, Lear, Cooper and other conspiracy theorists projected distinctly human attributes and goals onto the Grays. By presenting these marauding, torturing aliens as acting in collusion with traitorous government insiders, Lear and Cooper succeeded in presenting the American government as alien and, indeed, alienated from the common people of the United States. This political paranoia was not confined to the United States. Cooper's warnings of a tyrannical world government fed into already existing fears of regionalism, globalism, and a world that was changing in the wake of the Cold War.

Despite the overall darkening of the flying saucer–oriented culture in the late 20th century, contactees and the notion of benevolent, friendly contact between Earthlings and their space brothers and sisters did not totally disappear. Channelers such as Tuella (See Chapter 5) and writers like Gerard Aartsen and Benjamin Creme (See Chapter 3) continued to keep the ideas and stories of the space brothers alive and also provide new perspectives on stories — such as George Adamski's — long considered discredited. The optimism of the contactees also combined with the conspiratorial thinking which came into vogue during the 1980s and 1990s in a movement called Exopolitics (see Chapter 5). In the narrative world of

Exopolitics supporters, friendly, helpful extraterrestrial beings stand ready to help humanity to the next level of their spiritual development — along with technological marvels like free energy, cures for diseases, and other delights. The only thing standing in the way of the golden age for humanity are shadowy government forces around the world and their controllers in multinational corporations which would find themselves suddenly irrelevant in the new order.

The history of flying saucer culture and belief is asymmetrical. The 1950s and 1960s era — up until the release of the Condon Report — often saw the question of what flying saucers might be addressed in popular media outlets as well as niche publications. Flying saucer interest was also a broad church during this period with scientific-minded investigators and wild-eyed contactees existing side-by-side at meetings held in places like Giant Rock. After the jarring dividing line of the Condon Committee's dismissal of the phenomenon as largely prosaic, flying saucers (and even more so, the contactees) moved closer to the fringe of society, fading from the mainstream. The resurgence in the 1990s, fueled by the rise of conspiracy-focused computer bulletin boards and the nascent Internet, focused largely on the darker paranoid fantasies rather than the optimistic visions of the contactees. This paranoid darkness was also reflected in popular television events like *The X-Files* and Fox's *Alien Autopsy: Fact or Fiction*.

There were also nonfictional outlets for paranormal topics. During the 1990s, one of the main outlets for allegedly factual information about flying saucers, alien visitors, and any other paranormal trends was *Coast to Coast AM*, an overnight radio call-in show hosted by Art Bell. Much like the Long John Nebel radio show of the 1950s and 1960s, *Coast to Coast* was a clearinghouse for abduction stories, rumors about Area 51 (including a memorable show on September 11, 1997, when Bell designated a special hotline for Area 51 employees to call the show and tell their secrets), government cover-ups and the like. Art Bell, the show, and contactee claims burst on the public scene in the winter and spring of 1997. As the Hale-Bopp comet became visible in the skies above Earth, some authors and investigators claimed there existed evidence of a massive spacecraft following the comet, coming to make contact with humanity. The group known as Heaven's Gate believed this to be true, and there is testimony connecting the claims of a spacecraft to the group's mass suicide in March of that year.

A hardcore group of believers continues to investigate claims of flying saucer sightings and examine declassified government records for evidence of the cover-up they so earnestly believe to exist. The contactees — maintaining a chain of activity which stretches back to the 1950s — continue (largely through psychically channeled messages) to spread a gospel of intergalactic peace and love.

3

The Dawn of Contact

George Adamski

While George Adamski may have been the first modern flying saucer contactee, the concept of human beings coming into contact with wiser, more advanced beings (human or nonhuman) had existed for a very, very long time. Over the centuries, spiritualist thinkers throughout the western world have discussed the reality of contact between humans and beings from other realms. As early as 1758, Swedish scientist and spiritualist Emmanuel Swedenborg published a book titled *Concerning Earths in the Solar World, Which Are Called Planets; and Concerning Earths in the Starry Heaven; and Concerning Their Inhabitants; and Likewise Concerning the Spirits and Angels There from Things Seen and Heard.* Swedenborg's book describes what he asserts to be a literal, physical trip thorough the solar system. Others, particularly those mediums who claimed to "channel" the words of beings from other planets or who existed in ethereal realms, conveyed messages from Mars, the Astral Plane, or other places. Another example is *A Dweller on Two Planets or The Dividing of the Way*, an 1886 tome psychically transmitted from "Phylos the Thibetan" to Frederick S. Oliver. This book discussed then-standard spiritualist topics such as the history and fate of Atlantis, reincarnation, and the means by which people can learn the details of their past lives.

Thus, while technologically based tales of contact with extraterrestrial intelligences in flying saucers began during the Cold War, the concept of humans interacting with extraterrestrial beings — whether they hailed from other planets or other planes of reality — was not unheard of at the time. What was, however, different, was the tight connection to tangible concerns and fears of the time, as well as the contact phenomenon's role as an aspect of the larger mystery of flying saucers.

© Adamski Foundation

George Adamski, ca. 1953 (permission granted by 2012 © G.A.F. International/ AdamskiFoundation.com).

The most strident of contactees' calls for reform during the Cold War addressed American society and culture. Many prominent saucer writers asserted that militarism, materialism, and spiritual emptiness all characterized American culture of the 1950s and '60s. Although calls for changes in America came from different areas of the saucer spectrum, the contactees remained prominent and outspoken in their warnings of doom if America did not abandon its path of military buildup and mistrust of other nations. The contactees also placed a burden on individual Americans to be more understanding and tolerant of each other, and to rely less on material gain for happiness. As the 1950s wore on, prominent writers on the flying saucer mystery would downplay contactees' beliefs and teachings, focusing instead on the unbelievable nature of their stories. This dichotomy not only emphasized the conflict within the saucer community but also helped undermine the contactees' efforts to influence society.

George Adamski, the prototypical flying saucer contactee, claimed his first encounter in 1952, and published the account in 1953. However, the historical narrative of his contact stories and their connection with broader trends in American history and culture stretch back much further. Adamski's stories and ideas would inform claims of contact for decades afterward. Adamski's claims and arguments have their roots not in the Cold War world, but in the world of a generation before — a world of looming fascism and war.

I discussed George Adamski's early life in Chapter 2, including the foundation of the Royal Order of Tibet in the 1930s and the broad outline of his career, including the exposés which discredited him in the eyes of many "scientific" flying saucer researchers as well as the public. In this chapter, we will examine Adamski's writings in more detail — particularly the writings he composed prior to his alleged flying saucer sightings and his contact with extraterrestrial beings described in *Flying Saucers Have Landed*. George Adamski rarely spoke of the Royal Order after he attained recognition as an extraterrestrial contactee. In his first published work, he described himself simply as a "philosopher, student, teacher, Saucer researcher," making no mention of a specific organization.[1] By not explicitly acknowledging his past as head of the Royal Order (aside from his label of "philosopher"), Adamski was able to portray himself as a saucer researcher who was spreading the space visitors' messages rather than his own. Adamski had several students who listened to him lecture on Eastern philosophies and the Cosmic Law — his somewhat vague term for a system of beliefs centered on principles of love for one's fellow people, humility, and a rejection of materialism. One of these students was Alice Wells, who owned the hamburger stand that would serve as Adamski's base of operations once his contactee fame took hold.[2] Adamski's activities during these pre-contact days were not confined to bootlegging wine and informal philosophizing. He authored a number of pamphlets and a science fiction novel, which addressed many of the themes he would later incorporate into his contactee writings. Two writings in particular, both from 1937, highlight the philosophical views that would resurface in his later flying saucer books.

"The Kingdom of Heaven on Earth" conveyed both Adamski's frustration with the condition of humanity and his solution for Earth's problems. Adamski claimed that the "kingdom of heaven" was a condition that would one day occur on Earth and that it was not someplace people went when they died. The creation of this paradise depended upon the degree to which humanity would embrace peace, cooperation and liberty. "Such is the heavenly state," he said, "peace and brotherhood of man, which is something that must be evolved gradually out of chaos." In 1937, he observed, "Freedom is becoming an unknown quantity in life and peace is little understood." Adamski cautioned against relying upon governments or organized religion to solve the world's problems. "Looking to the outer things for heaven is vain," he said, and "seeking peace or joy from the effective world is useless. If there is to be peace among nations there must first be peace in the hearts of the individuals making up those nations." He used Jesus as an example who tried to achieve these standards: "He did not discriminate between races, colors, creeds, or theories.... His law was not hate, but love."[3] In the late 1930s, it might have seemed to Adamski that humanity might never bring about heaven on earth. Hitler and Mussolini had seized power in Europe, racial oppression was rampant in the United States, and the Great Depression continued. To Adamski, the oppression of dictatorial governments and the hostility of political and religious discrimination prevented humanity from reaching its potential and unnecessarily delayed this kingdom of heaven.

Adamski took this idea of equality and looking within for answers and brought them down to a more personal level in "Satan, Man of the Hour," also written in 1937. In this story, five men (a "great captain of industry," an Army officer, a "well-known" minister, a scientist, and a bookkeeper) talk among themselves about who — in terms of power and influence — is the "man of the hour." A stranger enters and declares that Satan is, in fact, the man of the hour. The men laugh, explaining that Satan is merely a "picturesque figure of a somewhat ancient mythology," no longer applicable to any modern discussions. The stranger smiles and informs the men that he refers not to the traditional representation of the Devil, but rather "the power of selfishness and greed which Satan represents." The five men-of-the-world each protest in turn. The minister, the scientist, and the others all explain that their particular contributions would make the world a better place. The stranger argues against them all and offers them a way out: abandon their self-centered religions and systems of commerce and instead rely upon the Cosmic Law, which "asks nothing of man except a perfect balance in all phases of life." The five men refuse the offer and leave. The stranger stands alone, hearing the mocking laugh of Satan all around him.[4] For Adamski, no one — not even ministers or others seen as wholesome — were free from the taint of selfishness in American society.

These two pamphlets establish Adamski's concerns about several aspects of American society long before he started to tell tales of flying saucers. By pointing out current events such as the rise of militarism and highlighting the dangers of material greed, Adamski demonstrated to readers that he had his finger on the pulse of current happenings such as the growth of fascism and the economic depression. A link between militarism and materialistic greed had long been established in the American public's mind. The isolationism of the United States from the world stage in the 1920s and '30s (exemplified by the country's rejection of the Versailles Treaty with its idealist League of Nations) was due in large part to perceptions that U.S. involvement in the First World War was attributable (at least in part) to the machinations of the "merchants of death"—the munitions industry. This was certainly one of the findings of the Nye Commission in 1936. This committee of the U.S. Congress asserted there was a causal link between the munitions industry's lust for higher profits, the devastation of the First World War, and the failure of peace efforts around the world.[5]

Acknowledgment of this connection was not confined to the halls of Congress. Retired Marine Corps Major General Smedley Butler's book *War Is a Racket* (1935) argued that one of the main goals of United States foreign and military policy was to enrich corporations: "I spent 33 years and four months in active military service and during that period I spent most of my time as a high class muscle man for Big Business, for Wall Street and the bankers. In short, I was a racketeer, a gangster for capitalism.... Looking back on it, I might have given Al Capone a few hints. The best he could do was to operate his racket in three districts. I operated on three continents."[6] From angry polemics by military officers to children's comic books, Americans during the 1930s were not unfamiliar with the notion that financial considerations were the key factor driving military policy. The first *Superman* comic book, published in June 1938, featured the Man of Steel confounding the efforts of Greer, an arms manufacturer, and Senator Barrows to embroil the U.S. in a European war to increase profits from weapons sales.[7] Americans were familiar with the dangers of greed and its implications for provoking deadly conflict.

Of course, during the late 1930s, fear of war was hardly the only issue affecting the American people. The Great Depression continued apace, and unemployment—which had begun a slow decline after 1933—was beginning to rise again. Alternatives to traditional American political and economic thought abounded. The American Communist Party reached a membership peak of 75,000 by 1938.[8] On the opposite end of the political spectrum were the pro–Nazi views of the German-American Bund and militaristic groups like William Dudley Pelley's Silvershirts. Racial divisions were illustrated by incidents such as the 1935 case of the Scottsboro boys—a group of young African American men convicted of raping two young white women. The case, which became news around the world, seemed to highlight the deficits of the justice system in the United States and, indeed, of the basic workability of an egalitarian society. Adamski, in "The Kingdom of Heaven on Earth," wrote: "Can you bring forth that kingdom of heaven within yourself while you are condemning another, discriminating between the yellow, white, black, or red race?"[9]

It must have seemed that the United States was at a crossroads in its history. In his writings of the 1930s, George Adamski addressed concerns that Americans had at the time, and provided the intellectual and philosophical basis for change. Crucially, in both "The Kingdom of Heaven on Earth" and "Satan, Man of the Hour," Adamski pins the hopes of humanity on individuals rather than governments or institutions: "Heaven will be brought upon the earth not through creeds and doctrines or various forms of government but through individual evolvement. When each individual making up the whole race becomes conscious of the heaven within himself, the world will reflect that heaven."[10] Here, Adamski urges change in a resolutely nonpolitical way — a rarity at a time of increasing political polarization. As the 1940s dawned, Adamski had set himself up, on the local scene at least, as a spiritual leader whose ideals could — even if only marginally — have a positive effect on the nation and the world.

Adamski's public profile was lower during the Second World War, though he did continue his work with his Royal Order of Tibet and, with some disciples, purchased some land and a hamburger stand near Mount Palomar. His interests turned to astronomy and science fiction. While the philosophical views expressed in his writings would remain consistent, the next steps in Adamski's public life seem to indicate that he was casting about for ways to spread his message of love, peace, and cooperation to more people than he could speak to at his Royal Order of Tibet meetings.

The first of these was a 1946 pamphlet titled "The Possibility of Life on Other Planets."[11] Here, Adamski outlined his reasons for believing that life on other worlds not only existed, but that the odds were very good that extraterrestrial life was similar to life on Earth. More significantly, he identified belief in extraterrestrial life with forward thinking and social improvement. The aliens could teach us, according to Adamski, "the logical theory of interplanetary education and evolvement." The next step in humanity's development was to make contact with extraterrestrial beings. Adamski's pamphlets, however, did not reach an audience much beyond his Royal Order of Tibet meetings. He sold his pamphlets through the mail and at Palomar Gardens, but that could not have reached enough people to truly spread his message.

After the first saucer sightings in 1947, it would be two years before Adamski issued another public writing. This was a science fiction novel titled *Pioneers of Space: A Trip to the Moon, Mars, and Venus*, and it was Adamski's first nationally published work. Though Adamski never claimed that the novel held literal truth, his foreword made it clear that he saw *Pioneers of Space* as more than escapist fantasy. He stated, "Man upon earth is progressive ... [and] could be taken as a good measuring stick of the vast universe within which he lives. Even though he makes many mistakes which are against himself, we still see nothing but steady progress."[12] While his 1937 essays told readers how they could make the world a better place, the message here was a reassurance that humanity would indeed be able to achieve goals of peace, love, and selflessness. The human characters in this novel had not yet reached that kingdom of heaven on Earth, and journeyed to other planets to observe societies who had. Adamski ended his foreword by saying that he was "endeavoring to reasonably speculate" about what scientific advances might be just around the corner. He encouraged readers to establish community roundtables for discussion using *Pioneers of Space* as their textbook, and he invited readers to write him with any questions they might have. Clearly, Adamski meant for the novel's vision of humanity's technological advancement and contact with enlightened, advanced alien civilizations to resonate among readers at a level deeper than that of a mere work of fantasy.

Pioneers of Space reads less like a science fiction novel than it does a travelogue. The rocket ship crew travels to the moon (where they meet the Moonalites), Mars, and Venus. While on each planet, they question the natives about their lifestyles, culture and beliefs. All three civilizations are humanoid Caucasians, worship a nameless supreme intelligence, and obey the strictures of the Cosmic Law.[13] Members of all three civilizations explain that they once lived as the Earth people, caring more for material possessions and power than they did for love and cooperation. They explain Earth's condition as that of a small child, still learning its way in the world. Certain ancient Earth civilizations, such as those of the Triterions, Lemurians, and Atlanteans, came close to reaching that higher level of consciousness and spiritual harmony. Unfortunately, they were not sufficiently advanced to avoid destruction by the greedy, warmongering elements of their societies. Since their fall, "destruction of the Earth by the hand of civilization has been taking place."[14] For modern human civilization to escape that destruction, society must imitate their space-dwelling brothers and sisters.

Earth, however, may never achieve that higher level, for atomic blasts had thrown off the planet's "balance." The extraterrestrials warn that humans should exercise care when performing future experiments. If such weapons were used in a war, the effects on humanity would be devastating. Such a war was probable because of peoples' greed and selfishness; such qualities led to conflict, and with the advent of atomic weapons, conflict would be much more devastating than in previous years. The space people had avoided such a devastating conflict by overcoming materialism and greed — by observing the principles of the Cosmic Law propounded by Adamski in his pamphlets of the 1930s. In *Pioneers of Space*, Adamski showed these principles being used by civilizations that, on the surface, were not too different from humanity. They had the same physiology, the same language, and had overcome the same problems with which Earth, at the time, was struggling.[15]

If someone were looking for a gripping and cutting-edge science fiction novel, *Pioneers of Space* would disappoint him. The novel contains

George Adamski and his telescope (date unknown). Adamski used this telescope, at his home on the slopes of Mount Palomar, to photograph the craft of the Venusians and other visitors (permission granted by 2012 © G.A.F. International/ AdamskiFoundation.com).

no real plot. Instead it presents a series of set pieces, each discussing a different alien culture, most of which are basically identical. Adamski's development of the characters who make these travels is not much better. The four members of the crew are indistinguishable from each other, and serve only as vehicles to ask the Moonalites, Martians, and Venusians questions. Not surprisingly, the navigator, whose name is "George," always seems to ask the most insightful questions. Eventually, the rocket ship returns to earth after its journey. The story's narrator reports, "The government has requested us to give a world-wide broadcast in the next few days and tell the world what we have actually seen and done. This will be done."[16] The astronauts need to tell the world about the enlightened civilizations they met and of the lessons that those people taught them. Just as Adamski tried to do with his earlier pamphlets, the people in *Pioneers of Space* knew that, in order for humanity to evolve to a more enlightened level, the lessons had to be spread to reach as many people as possible.

Placed in the context of Adamski's earlier urgings that the people of Earth obey the cosmic law, *Pioneers of Space* functions within the genre of the utopian science fiction novel, albeit a poorly written one. *Pioneers of Space* doesn't tell a story. Rather, Adamski used the popular and recognized

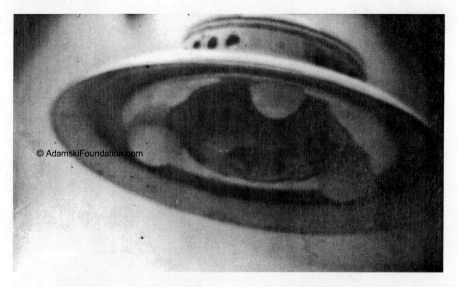

The classic George Adamski flying saucer picture. The high level of detail in the photograph was like an open invitation to those seeking to prove Adamski's photographs to be fraudulent (permission granted by 2012 © G.A.F. International/ AdamskiFoundation.com).

medium of science fiction to convey his view of what the Earth could and should become. By taking themes of pamphlets like "Satan, Man of the Hour" and "The Kingdom of Heaven on Earth" and placing them in a fictional, narrative context, Adamski tried to reach a larger audience than he could with pamphlets and lectures. In 1949, the possibilities of flying saucers and travel to other worlds were not foreign to the American people. A story based around such familiar and popular elements was more likely to make an impact on the reader than Adamski's pamphlets of the 1930s. Moreover, by the late 1940s, groups existed which opposed continued testing of atomic weapons, just as did the Moonalites and other aliens. These groups, composed mainly of scientists, received a good deal of recognition in the early years of the Cold War. Thus, just as in the 1930s, Adamski's goals and concerns were not foreign to readers. Adamski simply placed them in a context that was more accessible to many readers.

In November 1952, however, Adamski moved on from writing science fiction and embarked on a career as a flying saucer contactee. Since 1949, in the wake of the Kenneth Arnold sighting and subsequent flying saucer appearances, he had been lecturing to local groups about the possible origins and intentions of these strange craft. His supposed expertise on the subject stemmed from a number of photographs he claimed to have taken with the help of several telescopes. Then, in 1953, Adamski published his account of meeting a saucer pilot in the California desert. British writer Desmond Leslie's *Flying Saucers Have Landed* was an extensive survey of mysterious aircraft throughout human history. Drawing heavily from ancient myths, Leslie contended that otherworldly beings had been visiting Earth from antiquity and that most major religions supported the idea of extraterrestrial life. Adamski's story made up the last fifth of the book and expanded upon the story he had told his friends the previous November.

Like his earlier pamphlets and *Pioneers of Space*, in *Flying Saucers Have Landed* Adamski used a narrative story to convey to the reader the lesson that humanity needs to ascend to a higher spiritual plane. He began by explaining his idea of the solar system as being akin to a classroom, with Earth stuck in the cosmic equivalent of kindergarten. He went on to describe his meeting with the man from Venus. Like the aliens in *Pioneers from Space*, the man looked "like any other man," except for his ski suit–like clothing and long hair reaching to his shoulders. Through a combination of hand signals and mental telepathy, the Venusian conveyed that his people were concerned over the danger that nuclear warfare represented, not just to humanity, but to the other peoples of the solar system as well. Adamski was not surprised that the Venusian had concerns. He was, however, surprised that "on his face there was not a trace of resentment or judgment. His expression was one of understanding and great compassion; as one would have toward a much loved child who had erred through ignorance and lack of understanding." The Venusian's attitude indicates that he felt humanity could grow beyond its warlike state. Adamski characterized the Venusian as nonjudgmental, caring, and compassionate so the reader would look on the visitors as teachers, rather than prosecutors. They came here to save us, not to destroy us.[17]

Adamski also learned that the craft was merely a scout ship and that the mother ship remained high in orbit above the Earth. Both were driven by magnetic power. After these technical details were out of the way, Adamski asked the Venusian if he believed in God. The Venusian did, but

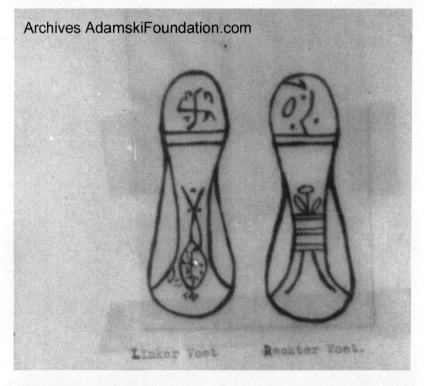

Linker Voet   Reenter Voet

The footprints allegedly left by Orthon the Venusian during Adamski's initial contact experience in Desert Center, California, in 1952 (permission granted by 2012 © G.A.F. International/AdamskiFoundation.com).

George Adamski poses with a portrait of space brother Orthon (permission granted by 2012 © G.A.F. International/AdamskiFoundation.com).

convinced Adamski that "we on Earth really know very little about this Creator. In other words, our understanding is shallow. Theirs is much broader, and they adhere to the laws of the Creator instead of laws of materialism as Earth men do.... He conveyed the thought to me that there they live according to the Will of the Creator, not by their own personal will as we do here on Earth." Adamski closed their conversation by asking why the saucers didn't simply land on the White House lawn or other similarly visible places. The Venusian replied that his people feared the response they would receive from a humanity that was full of fear and so ready to fight rather than understand.[18]

Despite the brevity of Adamski's initial contact story, the thematic similarities to his earlier works are clear. The aliens obey the Cosmic Law, the will of the Creator. They are concerned about humanity's atomic experimentation, and fear the danger to the entire solar system. Despite the lack of concrete evidence for Adamski's account, this contact story served the same purpose as did *Pioneers of Space*. Adamski took popular subject of flying saucers and used it to convey the same message of spiritual renewal and social cooperation that he had pushed since the 1930s. This message, however, existed in a different context. By the early 1950s, Adamski's work and writings focused more on international peace and cooperation than he did in the 1930s. In 1953, the superpowers teetered on the brink of nuclear annihilation. Those desperate times led Adamski to give his space visitor a more direct and forceful message: stop the atomic testing.

Reaction to Adamski's story was immediate. *Flying Saucers Have Landed* went through 11 printings in its first two years of publication. Despite this popularity, the nascent flying saucer research community found itself split over Adamski's experience. Although he had many supporters among saucer researchers, he also had vociferous critics. The most outspoken was James Moseley. While Moseley was critical of Adamski's story, he also sensed that there was a deeper agenda to Adamski's work. On his initial saucer investigation trek across the U.S., Moseley visited Adamski at his café/headquarters in California. He came away from the meeting with the impression that Adamski was "a very kind, intelligent, and sincere man."[19] Moseley doubted that his story was true, but had no conclusive evidence that would disprove it. Over the next two years, however, Moseley would interview those who witnessed Adamski's encounter, and by early 1955 he felt that he had enough ammunition to ground Adamski's saucer tales.

In what he would later call his "only major contribution to the field as a Serious UFOlogist,"[20] Moseley wrote a stunning, damaging exposé on the Adamski encounter for the January 1955 issue of *Nexus*. He began by demonstrating that the saucer in Adamski's photographs could be easily replicated with a Chrysler hubcap, a coffee can, and three ping-pong balls. He went on to explain that, through interviews with several of Adamski's witnesses, it was clear that none of them actually witnessed the things they had claimed. Moseley learned that all of Adamski's witnesses were already saucer believers (a point not mentioned in the book) and that none of their stories agreed with each other.[21]

Another damning piece of evidence was the story of Jerrold Baker, an amateur photographer and saucer researcher. Baker claimed that Adamski attached Baker's name to several the saucer photographs that Adamski took, making it appear that many different people were taking these fantastic pictures. Baker objected to this, but Adamski induced him to stay quiet, saying, "With people knowing that you are interested in flying saucers ... you could do yourself a lot of good." Adamski went on to advise Baker to use what Moseley asserted were the fraudulent photos for evening lectures, which people would pay good money to hear. Moseley concluded that, at the very least, substantial parts of Adamski's story had been fabricated and that "Adamski's narrative contains enough flaws to place in very serious doubt both his veracity and sincerity."

While Moseley's investigation called into question, if not outright shattered, the probability that Adamski's story was literal truth, he went on to discuss Adamski and his convictions on a personal level, aside from any saucer visitation claims. Moseley said, "I have been convinced that he is a kindly man who would do harm to no one. If he has written a fraudulent book, I believe that he did so, not so much for his own personal profit, but to put across, in dramatic form, philosophical principles in which he sincerely believes."[22] Moseley, despite his criticism of Adamski's story, drew a sharp distinction between Adamski's outlandish claims and the message he was attempting to convey. Moseley was the only saucer writer of the time who went to the trouble of making this distinction. Although he thought Adamski a rogue, he recognized that Adamski held his beliefs very strongly and sincerely.

Moseley's exposé and the doubts of other saucer researchers did not call into question or take issue with the philosophical foundations of Adamski's writings, but with the saucer stories through which he conveyed them. Nevertheless, Adamski reacted defensively. He responded to Moseley's accusations in the spring 1955 issue of *The Saucerian Bulletin*, edited by Moseley's friend Gray Barker. In the rebuttal, titled "Time Will Tell," Adamski declared that "the truth needs neither exposure nor defense. Time itself proves all truth." Adamski asserted that he would never tell a lie about meeting with the space people because "the Brothers, who themselves are honest, would never stand for deceit of any kind. Should I ever indulge in a single act of falseness I would there by [*sic*] forfeit the privilege of ever again meeting them and learning from them."[23] Adamski did not present any further "proof" that his tales were true. Just as many of Adamski's desires for the people of Earth were spiritual rather than material, it follows that acceptance of his stories and experiences rely more on faith than on journalistic standards of evidence. Adamski's second contact-related book would depend on more of that faith to gain the acceptance of saucer readers.

Adamski's next book, *Inside the Spaceships*, appeared in 1955, shortly after the firestorm of criticism erupted over *Flying Saucers Have Landed*. The new book described Adamski's adventures aboard the saucers of the Venusians and Saturnians. This book owes much of its structure and ideas to *Pioneers of Space* in that it consists of a series of set pieces that serve to explicate alien beliefs and culture rather than form a cohesive narrative.

While Adamski spends much of the book describing otherworldly customs, food, and furniture, he also describes conversations with the Great Master, an elderly-appearing man, not described as being from any particular planet. The Master is "a greatly evolved being" and "in his present body" over 1000 years old. Conversations with the Master echo the themes that had been Adamski's hallmark since the 1930s. Primary among these themes is that the Earth was at the lowest stage of development of all the planets in the solar system. Because of this lack of development, the space beings do not wish for humans to possess the technology to travel to the stars. The Great Master explains to Adamski, they "would gladly give you this knowledge which has served us so well, except that you have not yet learned to live with one another in peace and brotherhood." Because of this, it is probable that humanity would seek to use this technology to subjugate other worlds in the solar system. But things did not have to be this way. The Master further explained to Adamski, "Understanding of the universal [cosmic] laws both uplifts and restricts. As it is now with us, so it could be on your Earth. Lifted up by your knowledge, this same understanding would make it impossible for you to move against your brothers." Throughout this book — and all of Adamski's writing — there exists a parallel between admonition and hope. For every chiding comment about violence and materialism, there is a reassurance that humanity can improve itself and rise to the next level of spiritual evolution. This idea dates back to "The Kingdom of Heaven on Earth" and is carried through to Adamski's analogy of the solar system as a school with progressively higher grades through which humanity must progress.[24]

In addition to including the character of the Great Master and explicit references to other Theosophical and spiritualist ideas than those found in Adamski's initial contact story, *Inside the Spaceships* was a logical extension of the Adamski belief system. All the conversations with the master are along the same lines: humanity must learn to obey the Universal Law and preserve peace around the world. The book contains only two photographs of alleged spaceships and two drawings by Adamski, rather than the more numerous photos that appeared in the first book. Adamski lists no witnesses, no friends who could corroborate his story. Even more than *Flying Saucers Have Landed*, this book requires the reader to believe Adamski's story on complete faith. Adamski's point, however, is not to convince the reader that he literally flew on a flying saucer. Rather, his ideas about peace and cooperation take center stage.

Adamski's third and final contactee book, published in 1960, was *Flying Saucers Farewell* (published in paperback as *Behind the Flying Saucer Mystery*). This book represented a departure from Adamski's formula of imparting wisdom and lessons on the Cosmic Law couched in terms of flying saucer adventures. *Flying Saucers Farewell* consisted of three distinct parts — two original and the third being a reprint of his earlier pamphlet "Satan, Man of the Hour." In the first part, Adamski responds to criticisms of his saucer tales. Utilizing formulas of "cosmic mathematics" and ill-explained theories of gravity propulsion, Adamski attempts to prove that the technologies he discussed in his previous books were more science fact than science fiction.[25] He mixes this with reiterations of messages from the Great Master from *Inside the Spaceships*, providing more lessons and teachings on the Universal Law and further instructions that would help humanity move up the ladder of spiritual evolution.

Another aspect of Adamski's attempts to convince readers of the saucers' existence is a reliance on ancient myths and religious texts to demonstrate that visits by the space people did not just begin in the 1940s. Adamski devotes an entire chapter to looking back to the Bible and other ancient writings. He points out different lights, stars, and other aerial phenomena and explains that they were actually ancient space ships. He also pulls verses from the New Testament and explains how the holy writings of Christianity and Judaism were completely compatible with the Cosmic Law. Adamski wanted to show readers that the principles he promoted were not necessarily that far off from what they might already believe. In this way, he demystified his teachings and attempted to gain access to an even larger audience than saucer believers: members of mainstream American Christian and Jewish communities.[26]

While it is easy to consider the modern flying saucer contactee movement begun by Adamski to be an overwhelmingly American phenomenon, his appeal was worldwide and, as detailed in subsequent chapters, inspired imitators around the globe. It is in this context that the second part of *Flying Saucers Farewell* is particularly significant. This part of the book discusses some of the UFO lectures Adamski gave in countries such as Australia, New Zealand, England, the Netherlands, Italy, and India between 1955 and 1960. In all these nations he met with loyal followers who hung on his every word, along with detractors, hecklers and — as Adamski portrays it — dark forces bent on stifling his message. His proudest moment, however, and one that he would crow about until his dying day, was a private meeting at the invitation of Queen Juliana of the Netherlands to discuss flying saucers. This invitation led Adamski to believe that she "[had] the welfare of her people at heart. Therefore she [had] an open mind that permits her to look at all facets of life, not bowing to the dictates of the few."[27]

Adamski's visit to New Zealand in January of 1959, in particular, highlights the man's appeal outside the United States, as well as the controversy engendered by his claims. Robert S. Ellwood has studied this visit in the context of the history of spiritualism in New Zealand, providing valuable insight into the different factions of flying saucer enthusiasm in the country. During the 1950s, the differences between the factions — the Australasian Adamski Flying Saucer Group and a rival group called Civilian Saucer Investigation (CSI) — were defined by their acceptance or rejection of Adamski's contact claims. During the mid–1950s, Adamski began an extensive correspondence with the former group, including specially recorded audio tapes. Adamski's popularity increased as his books entered the New Zealand market. This popularity pulled members away from the less contactee-oriented Civilian Saucer Investigation, leading to some animosity between the organizations. In 1959, at the behest of his New Zealand fans, Adamski finally visited in person.[28]

New Zealand news outlets provided numerous editorials about the Adamski visit which were, for the most part, skeptical of Adamski's particular claims but fairly open to the general prospect of life on other worlds. As Ellwood summarizes, "Adamski's reception was decidedly mixed. His films of spaceships were declared 'unconvincing,' and he sometimes met frank laughter and only moderate applause." Despite the ridicule and incredulity of the audiences, attendance at his lectures was generally good. Unfortunately, in the years after Adamski's visit, the inconsistencies in his stories, and the various saucer magazine articles alleging fraud in Adamski's photographs, took a toll on New Zealand's Adamski fan clubs. Despite the disillusioning effect of the exposés, Phyllis Dickeson, who was responsible for the damaging critique of Adamski's photographs, had a clear vision of Adamski's importance at the time. In a 1988 letter to Robert Ellwood, she wrote, "The War had highlighted man's inhumanity to man. Suddenly the F/S [flying saucer] furor spread from the United States to the rest of the world. The George Adamski crusade hit New Zealand." Adamski's tales of a peaceful solar system with helpful space brothers "sounded wonderful to say the least. (How gullible we were.)."[29] Dickeson's characterization of Adamski's New Zealand adventure as a "crusade" is an interesting one. Adamski did, through his writings and presentations, attempt to convert readers and listeners to a new way of life, although it was never as well organized or codified as later flying saucer/contactee-based religious movements.

While his meeting with the Queen proved successful and he met with support from most audiences, other troubles seemed to dog Adamski's every step. In New Zealand, problems with his visa delayed the start of his lectures. In England, he faced a similar problem when he was prohibited from lecturing due to his lack of a work permit. The greatest problem occurred in Zurich, where Adamski was laughed off the stage. Adamski termed this disturbance "our first warning of organized resistance." It was at this point in the narrative that Adamski began to tie together all the misfortunes that occurred on his lecture tour. He interpreted these occurrences not as the unfortunate coincidences that plague many travelers, but as a concerted effort to stifle his message and destroy his mission. To Adamski's mind, the only reason for this would be the core of his message: that rampant materialism and greed were the root of violence and destruction. For humanity to survive and thrive it must abandon those things. But there existed some who did not want to rise above greed and materialism or were too deeply entrenched in their selfish ways to welcome these revelations. To Adamski's mind, it was logical to assume that he should hold these people responsible for his troubles. Adamski called these people the "Silence Group."[30]

The "Silence Group" was a term first used and popularized by NICAP

Chief Donald Keyhoe in the early 1950s. As described in Chapter 2, NICAP eschewed the more lurid claims of contact spread of Adamski and others. Keyhoe used it to describe those elements of the U.S. government that wanted to keep secret the reality of flying saucer visitation from the public. In Adamski's flying saucer universe, the focus of the Silence Group was different. Their conspiracy was worldwide and centered in Zurich: "What happened to the money-changers Christ drove out of the temple? It seems as though they have gathered over the centuries in Zurich.... The invisible reins of financial influence extend from Zurich to puppet organizations in every nation."[31] Given Adamski's identification of materialism and greed as among humanity's greatest enemies, it made sense that the international cabal seeking to stifle him was financial in nature. In Adamski's worldview, the denizens of high finance would have had the most to lose if people adopted Adamski's philosophy on a large scale. This was the first time Adamski used a conspiracy theory to explain resistance to his ideas. He twisted the conspiracy in a typically Adamskian way, however, placing the blame at the feet of commerce and abstract greed rather than framing the conspiracy in a political context. His focus remained on improving the social and spiritual conditions of the United States and the rest of the world through application of the Cosmic Law. Thus, even considering this shift to a more paranoid style of narrative, Adamski remained centered on that Cosmic Law and the improvement of humanity. By presenting elaborate proofs of the physical reality of interplanetary craft and hints of worldly conspiracies, *Flying Saucers Farewell* echoed those UFO writings which dealt less and less with the message of the space beings and more on proving the existence of the saucers to skeptical readers.

While, superficially, Adamski's proofs and claims of international cabals seem forced and unlikely, they served the same purpose as his initial flying saucer stories. The original tale of meeting the Venusian in the desert encapsulated Adamski's longstanding views on needed changes in society. In the same way, the new stories of scientific validation and multinational conspiracy might have convinced the reader that Adamski's ideas were worthy of cover-up. Adamski's introduction of an international conspiracy was not surprising, given what other saucer writers of the time promulgated. When Adamski introduced the conspiracy angle to his story, he echoed the views of his contemporaries. Donald Keyhoe of NICAP — a group dedicated to investigating the "nuts-and-bolts" nature of the flying saucers — had claimed since the early 1950s that there existed a cover-up at the highest levels of government regarding the origins and mission of the saucers. In 1955, Gray Barker wrote *They Knew Too Much About Flying Saucers*, which introduced the concept of the "Men in Black"—mysterious men who visited saucer witnesses and threatened them with harm if they shared their encounters (see Chapter 6). Thus, the framework for a saucer-oriented conspiracy was not Adamski's invention at all. Rather, as he did with saucers, Adamski co-opted an existing mythology and used it to further shore up his message of peace, love, and cooperation.

Although *Flying Saucers Farewell* was the last saucer book that Adamski published, he continued to write and lecture until his death in 1965. Throughout his later years, Adamski's approach focused increasingly on spreading his philosophical message rather than proving the space visitors' reality (although he never abandoned the core tenet of his physical visitations with extraterrestrials). In 1961, he published a series of lessons called *Cosmic Philosophy*, a distillation of his thoughts about the Cosmic Law, a topic Adamski had been teaching since the 1930s in the old Royal Order of Tibet.

Adamski's *Cosmic Philosophy* is notable for not spending a great deal of time discussing the space visitors Adamski encountered. The language and tone of the lessons are much more akin to writings like "The Kingdom of Heaven on Earth" than to *Inside the Spaceships*. Adamski states, "Cosmic philosophy embraces the Universe conceived as an orderly and harmonious system complete in itself." Its principles act as "stepping stones" in the students' "quest for knowledge," providing a way for them to find the "individual expression of their own divinity." This brief, 87-page booklet blends Christian ethics with eastern mysticism, asserting the relativity of truth and the importance of, every day, having "thoughts that remind me of my Cosmic Unity with All Life."[32]

In this first "definition" section, Adamski explicitly discusses beings from other planets, asserting that "our neighbors on the sister planets of our solar system came to the realization a long time ago that every minutest particle the Cosmos is inter-related with every other particle.... They shared a theory with all who were interested and gradually theories grew into facts as they explored further and further and unified all life." This discussion of the space visitors is consistent with Adamski's earlier saucer-themed writings in that he situates the extraterrestrials in a position that is superior to Earthlings not just in technology but, especially, in matters of philosophy and outlook.[33] Near the end of the booklet, the space brothers make a return in a tangential way. In the lesson "Past Civilizations," Adamski discusses the fate of the lost continent of Lemuria — destroyed due to their inequality and "unbalanced conditions." In what appears to be a last-minute addition to this lesson, Adamski states of Lemuria, "The [space] Brothers have told me that they have records that have been kept on their planet regarding the civilizations of the earth, and that these accounts of Lemuria ... are correct."[34]

The space brothers make one more appearance in the last lesson in the book, "The Parable of the Apple Tree." The parable is told by Firkon, one of the Venusian space brothers whom Adamski had met before. Firkon explains that the apple tree is an illustration of reincarnation — the apple tree produces fruit, the seeds of which, in turn, produce more apples. Firkon provides Adamski with the story of Christ at his crucifixion telling the thief on the cross next to him that "today" he would be in Heaven as proof of "immediate rebirth." Additionally, Firkon provides a more con-crete example for Adamski: "Tomorrow you will be privileged to meet the one that you have known as your earthly wife. She is now a young woman living on Venus. She will not recognize you as her husband, but rather as a Cosmic brother. Neither will she wish to be reminded of her life upon earth, for her present life is free from the bondage of self and self interest." The next day, Adamski wrote, this very thing happened and served as "proof positive that we never die."[35]

Reading *Cosmic Philosophy*, one gets the impression that Adamski took his philosophical writings from the 1930s and 1940s and updated them with flying saucer material in order to market the work to a new, space-age audience. His concluding lesson addresses this context, saying, "We are in the Space Age and many of man's egotistical opinions will have to go to make room for our place as a member of the interplanetary family." He reiterates that the space brothers are practical people who live in har-mony with the universe: "they ... will teach nothing that is mysterious or fanatical nor will they deal in emotionalism." Tying in specifically with his earlier writings, Adamski asserts that "if there is to be heaven it must be established upon earth." Writing in the early 1960s, after the public refutations of his saucer stories, Adamski seems to be dialing back the literal truth of his encounters. Firkon the Venusian is present, as he was earlier, but he's not in a saucer. Firkon sits with Adamski on Earth, sharing knowledge and ideas. The space brothers have come down to our level.[36]

In the years between *Flying Saucers Farewell* and his 1965 death,

Adamski's audience was increasingly restricted to those who had accepted his stories and teachings rather than crossing the lines to include more general saucer enthusiasts. These followers were organized into what Adamski called the "Get Acquainted Program." This international network of Adamski followers was the brainchild of the space brothers, who thought it would be an efficient conduit for information on a global scale.[37] One example of the writings Adamski distributed to this group was a 1964 article titled "The Space People," in which he details various differences between the lifeways of the space brothers and sisters from Venus and those humans living on Earth. Much of this article is given over to prosaic descriptions of materials used in building on Venus, as well as to discussions of governance and ethics. For example, Adamski asserts that the other peoples of the solar system "do not need laws such as we have, for their individual code of ethics is so high, that should they transgress the natural, or Universal law, they know it and make the necessary amends to right the wrong they have done." In order to enhance the ethical situation, there is no monetary system on planets other than Earth.

As a way of merging it his philosophical teaching with the flying saucer tales that had brought him international fame, Adamski also met with saucer believers in small groups. People's impressions of Adamski in this setting are significant because at these small groups, Adamski would respond to spontaneous questions from those present. On April 1, 1965, Adamski met with several followers at the home of Mr. and Mrs. Ovila Larochelle in Woonsocket, Rhode Island. One of those present was Lionel Renaud. Renaud found that Adamski's stories held more than tales of saucers. Rather, "the telling of a better way of life can be told in diverse ways, or inter-related to things that are new or strange, but that does not detract from the true facts, and the true facts lie in the goodness of the words spoken and the sincerity of the man himself." Whether or not Adamski's stories came from star visitors or elsewhere, Renaud concluded, "They should be adhered to and practiced by all. The world is in dire need of constructive practices, and has been for too long." Renaud believed Adamski's contact stories to be, at most, "of a nature practicable."[38] Despite this half-hearted acceptance of the saucer aspect of Adamski's story, Renaud recognized the sincerity and importance of their philosophical messages — the same messages that had remained constant since the 1930s.

It was Adamski's philosophies, rather than his specific claims of contact and space travel, that many of his followers remembered about him after his death. A good measuring stick for saucer contact believers' views of Adamski and the significance of his career is the March 1966 issue of *Probe* magazine. Published a few months after Adamski's death, this issue consisted of readers' remembrances of Adamski and some reprints of his writings. Editor Joseph Ferriere, in "George Adamski's Appeal to the Future Leaders," said:

> George Adamski was a man with a purpose. He, most of all, realized that if ever we are to straighten out the mess we have created on this planet, we must take the youngsters into our confidence and impress upon them not only the need to work towards the goal of making this earth a better place in which to live, but also to guide their steps toward the achievement of that goal.

Ferriere went on to describe a lecture Adamski gave to a group of elementary school children in Boston. The theme of this lecture was the "the importance of learning about ourselves ... so that we may then know how to coordinate our senses, thereby achieving a harmonious relationship with nature and the universe."[39] Ferriere makes no mention in this article about Adamski's saucer beliefs, only that his philosophies, if passed on to the younger generation, would have a positive impact on their lives, and on humanity as a whole.

Adamski's Followers and Legacy

Despite the skepticism and doubts surrounding Adamski's claims and the changing nature of saucer enthusiasm toward science-tinged, nuts-and-bolts explanations and away from classic contactee narratives, his stories continued to draw interest from a devoted band of followers. One of the earliest and most persistent examples of Adamski's enduring presence in the contactee field (if not in UFO/flying saucer research as a whole) began with the obituary co-written by *Flying Saucers Have Landed* collaborator Desmond Leslie and longtime associate Alice K. Wells. In her opening comments of the obituary, Wells claims that Adamski was a "member of the Interplanetary Council" which monitors the solar system. Adamski's earthly body died, but his eternal soul is still at work, assisting the space brothers. Leslie confirms that Adamski certainly thought that he had a soul which originated on another, more advanced, planet. He also tells of a detail which, while unverifiable, resonated with Adamski's admirers. Leslie claims that Adamski had shown him a bizarre birthmark. Located where most peoples' navels are located, this was "a huge solar disk with deeply cut rays extending out about six inches all around it, from waist to groin." Leslie surmises that this indicated that Adamski was a "Child of the Sun" and "doesn't believe by any means that we have seen the last of him. If he is reborn on another planet he has promised to come back and contact us when possible."[40]

These observations and predictions would serve as a launchpad for Adamski's recurring appearances in contactee lore over the next several decades. As the first contactee of the modern flying saucer era, George Adamski served as a touchstone for other contactees of his time and afterward. Exposé pieces which damaged Adamski's credibility in the 1950s and 1960s may have put him off limits as a go-to source for "legitimate" UFO information, but by the 1960s, the contactee genre as a whole was largely out of vogue. As discussed in the following chapter, the contactee scene was fragmented between those who claimed physical contact with visitors from other planets, much like Adamski, and those who claimed some manner of psychic contact, presented through channeling, automatic writing or other means. With Adamski's death, the field fractured further.

One strand of contactee thought that has persisted since Adamski's 1965 death is the notion that Adamski himself was, somehow, more than simply a man who spoke to people from Venus. Indeed, the notion arises that Adamski was perhaps more than a man. The quotation from Alice Wells above hints at such an idea: that Adamski continued to assist the space people, freed from his physical body.

The 21st century has seen resurgence in George Adamski's popularity among some in the paranormal community. Colin Bennett, Gerard Aartsen, and Benjamin Creme have each written books which focus on Adamski's life and work and, in doing so, have reframed Adamski as possessing supernatural abilities and significance. These works have transferred Adamski from the collection of elder statesmen of contact to a position within the pantheon of extraterrestrials. Their writings, building on the suggestions and suppositions of Leslie, Wells, and Buckle, place Adamski alongside Orthon, Firkon, and Ramu.

In 2001, Colin Bennett published *Looking for Orthon: The Story of George Adamski, the First Flying Saucer Contactee, and How He Changed the World*. In it, Bennett claims, "*Flying Saucers Have Landed* is a masterpiece. It is a story of about [*sic*] our perception of history, the nature of technological power, and just who or what exactly governs the forces of modern belief." Bennett weaves Adamski into the fabric of the counter-culture of the 1950s and '60s, a witness to and instigator of fundamental change, regardless of what the true nature of his paranormal experiences might have been.

Bennett, perhaps, goes a bit far in giving Adamski credit for the cultural development of the postwar United States. One example puts Adamski at the center of televised science fiction and sets him up as a fundamentally American artiste:

> When we look at Adamski, we look at a part of the very inside of the American mind, pregnant with experimental structures, machines, and ideas, all interwoven with the mysteries of Jayne Mansfield, Marilyn Monroe, and the assassinations. No other mind on the planet is like this. If we laugh at that, we might bear in mind that *Star Trek*, Uncle Sam's national flagship, would not have been possible without taking on something of Adamski's original vision. This alone puts him on the level of Fritz Lang and the creators of the Flash Gordon films.... In Adamski's mind is the source of American triumph and dread.

Along with this credit for *Star Trek*, Bennett provides corroborating evidence of Adamski's initial Desert Center contact, mainly in the form of quotations from the U.S. Air Force's Project Blue Book saucer sighting reports, identifying strange objects in the sky in proximity to Adamski's position at the time of contact: "That this 'unidentified object' was in the same area on the same day as the Adamski sighting suggests it might well have been there ... when the Adamski party made their historic sighting. Many juries have convicted on lesser circumstantial conjunctions of time and space." For Bennett, "Adamski created a permanent pandimensional masterwork." His pictures, writings and speeches comprised an "artist's portfolio" of weirdness. Bennett's *Looking for Orthon* exists in a space between straightforward apologia for Adamski's contact claims and a broader exploration of Adamski's role in American and Western esoteric thought in the second half of the 20th century.

Dutch writer and educator Gerard Aartsen's 2010 book *George Adamski: A Herald for the Space Brothers* blends a brief biography of Adamski with a précis of the views Adamski presented in his major writings, as well as reprints of two very rare Adamski pamphlets from the 1960s Aartsen continues the evaluation of Adamski and his views that began with Bennett's work, claiming that his biographical sketch of the prototypical contactee is "a monograph about the scope and significance of Adamski's work, which is reappraised here in light of the spiritual realities of life with the emergence into full public view of our Elder Brothers — the Masters of Wisdom of the Spiritual Hierarchy, headed by the world Teacher — and the Space Brothers from our neighbouring planets, at the dawn of the new cosmic cycle of Aquarius." Thus, Aartsen is not coming at the question of Adamski's significance from the point of view of a historian or scientist. Aartsen, as was Adamski, is more attuned to the esoteric teaching of H.P. Blavatsky and other Theosophists.[41]

In addition to being an educator, Aartsen is "a student of the Ageless Wisdom" and an associate of Share International, Inc. Share International is, according to its website, "a worldwide network of individuals and groups whose purpose is to make known the fact that Maitreya — the World Teacher for the coming age — and his group, the Masters of Wisdom, are now among us, emerging into the public arena — gradually, so as not to infringe human free will."[42] The prime mover behind Share International is Benjamin Creme, a British artist, writer, and esotericist who studied under the teachings of H.P. Blavatsky and Alice Bailey. In 1972, Creme "began a period of arduous training under his Master's direction to prepare him for his coming task: announcing to a skeptical world the emergence of the World Teacher, awaited by people of every religion under his various names — the Christ, Messiah, Imam Mahdi, Krishna, Maitreya Buddha. Creme's constant contact with a Master of Wisdom gives him access to up-to-date information on Maitreya's emergence, plus the total conviction needed to present this story."[43] Creme himself wrote a book in 2010, *The Gathering of the Forces of Light: The UFOs and their Spiritual Mission*, which also connects George Adamski's activities, claims, and teachings to the larger themes of Theosophy. Both Creme and Aartsen recount stories which — in their view — provide evidence that George Adamski himself was one of these intergalactic spiritual masters rather than a mere mortal who happened upon some friendly space brothers in the desert.

The key story behind Adamski's position as something more than a mere contactee is recounted in Eileen Buckles's *The Scoriton Incident: Did Adamski Return?* According to Buckles's account, in 1965 Ernest Arthur Bryant, of Devon in Great Britain, encountered three jump-suit clad figures and their flying saucer. One of the men identified himself as "Yamski" and spoke in an American accent with slight Eastern European inflections. This alleged meeting took on the same day — April 23, 1965 — on which Adamski died. Yamski lamented that Adamski's early co-author

Desmond Leslie had — apparently — changed his views on the nature of extraterrestrials over the years.

The meme of Adamski's continued existence — in some form — resurfaced in the 1980s in *Angels in Starships* by Italian flying saucer researcher Giorgio Dibitonto, first published in Italian in April 1983. Dibitonto recounted a 1980 incident in which he met Firkon, Ramu, and Orthon, three of the space brothers encountered by George Adamski in the 1950s. Along with them were several other space brothers and sisters, including one who seemed familiar: "Then another man was introduced to us, who impressed us immediately with his kindliness and amiability. He smiled like one who had much to say, but would not speak. 'His name is George,' said Raphael, nodding in my direction, 'the same as yours. This, our brother, lived for a while on Earth, where he chose to come on an assignment. Now he has returned to us.'"[44] Dibitonto's experiences tie his story into Adamski's and reinforce the notion that Adamski ascended to a higher spiritual/dimensional level upon his death. The later contactees, while they did model many aspects of their narratives upon Adamski's, did not experience this kind of continued existence after their deaths.

Although George Adamski was far from the only contactee, his significance lies in both the fact that he was the first modern flying saucer contactee and that his activities, claims, and beliefs were a continuing factor within some realms of the flying saucer community, even after his death. The contactees examined in the following chapters all, to a certain degree, owe aspects of their stories to Adamski's pioneering example.

4

Contactees in the Space Age
George Adamski's Legacy in
the 1950s and 1960s

If George Adamski had been the only contactee to emerge during the 1950s, his impact would have been much less significant. One of the most important aspects of Adamski's place in the development of the extraterrestrial contact narrative was his influence on other believers. Other contactees, no matter what their similarities to or differences from Adamski and his adventures, all owe a great deal to his example. Despite some other contactees' claims that their contacts took place before his, none of them told anyone about these contacts until after Adamski's story had hit the streets. Most of these contactees' stories were explicitly patterned on Adamski's initial contact in *Flying Saucers Have Landed* and his subsequent conversations with the space brothers in *Inside the Spaceships* and later writings. Often, they had a twist such as a different role for women, psychic contact, or some other noticeable difference from Adamski. One key similarity between Adamski and later contactees — from the 1950s to the present — has been their shared focus on deficiencies of contemporary human civilizations and the superiority of extraterrestrial civilizations. This superiority is not only technological, but spiritual and moral as well. While different contactees emphasized different aspects of extraterrestrial civilization, the contention that the space brothers and sisters are far more advanced than humanity remains consistent.

In the narratives produced during what we might call the "Adamski Era" of contactees, the threat of nuclear annihilation is a near-constant presence. This has led some critics to assert that the contactee stories of the time are merely a fearful reaction to the existential horrors of the early Cold War era. These writings, to be sure, often do react to the crises of the time, but despite the fears and forebodings of the atomic age, the stories and beliefs of contactees in the 1950s and 1960s exhibit a peculiar optimism. There is a sense in the writings of George Adamski, George Van Tassel, George King, and others, that humanity is standing at a fork in the road. One way leads to destruction (physical, moral, spiritual). The other leads to humanity's graduation from the cosmic kindergarten, taking its place among its space brothers and sisters. Earth, like Venus and Saturn, would be ruled by a planetary council, or report to the Council of Seven Lights, or some other more perfect union. The space people, contactees argued, had once been like us — warlike, childish, selfish — but were no longer so. Contactee writings of the Space Age were not expressions of reactionary fatalism. There was hope. There was a future.

This essential optimism in the shadow of looming war and desolation was not unique to the world of the contactees, nor should it be particularly surprising. The 1950s were a time of tremendous economic and cultural development. The United States emerged from the Second World War as the sole superpower (for a few years) and, despite the threat of Soviet expansion, largely looked toward a bright future. The U.S.–Soviet space race was an expression of east-west competition which was essentially forward-looking in its perspective. Even in the war-torn nations of Western Europe there was a wave of music, art, and commerce that came out of the 1950s and persisted into the 1960s.

Lawrence R. Samuel, in his book *Future: A Recent History*, discusses the explosion of science fiction media in popular culture as illustrating the tensions between humanity's (especially Americans') hope for the future and the fears of what that future might actually contain. For every glorious vision of humanity taking to the stars (such as *Rocketship XM* or *Missile to the Moon*), there was a countering vision of the dangers of war, both nuclear and conventional (such as *Invasion USA* or *Panic in Year Zero!*). The world hung in the balance, between a pushbutton future of technological convenience or a desolate forecast of technology-based destruction.[1]

George Adamski and subsequent contactees also viewed the future with this dichotomy of fear and fascination. We can interpret the extraterrestrial civilizations presented by contactees as visions of a potential human future. If humanity, however, failed to follow the teachings of their space brothers, then the future would be much less pleasant. Even when a contactee's narrative does not prescribe specific remedies or courses of action for humanity to follow, it provides a positive way forward by implication and example.

Contactees such as George Hunt Williamson claimed that their contacts with the space people took place purely on the psychic level; hence no one could expect them to have any proof of their claims. Others, such as Truman Bethurum and Howard Menger, claimed to have experienced physical contacts, like Adamski. Still others, George Van Tassel for example, claimed both physical and psychic contact events. Whether the contacts were physical or psychic, contactees often shared with followers philosophical messages similar to Adamski's. Even when the messages were dissimilar the structure and presentation of the narratives owed much to Adamski's work. These writers connected their experiences to the worlds of science, the esoteric, archaeology, and history. Despite the differences between them, all of these contactees took cues from the original Adamski contact described in *Flying Saucers Have Landed* (indeed, George Hunt Williamson had been one of the witnesses to this original encounter).

Another similarity between George Adamski and later contactees of the 1950s and 1960s is the presence of Theosophical beliefs and philosophies. There is some debate among scholars about the precise concentration and significance of Theosophical ideas in the writings and ideas of various contactees. Christopher F. Roth, for example, sees a spectrum of Theosophical philosophy in contactee writings with some more solidly connected with Theosophy than others:

> Contactees as overtly Theosophist as, for instance, George King or Eduard "Billy" Meier decades later are the exception rather than the rule. For the most part, occultism has been an oblique influence, as was the case with Adamski, and Williamson, who segregated, even hid, their Theosophical doctrines from their more UFO-oriented readership. Adamski's narratives and theories unite quasi Theosophy, anthropology, and a new model for the relationships between experiences and investigation and between humans and extraterrestrials.[2]

This is not to say that all contactees exhibited explicit — or implicit — Theosophical leanings. Some contactees kept their focus on social, political, or technical issues. One of the contactees who avoided the spiritualist bent of his peers, as well as being one of the earliest on the scene, was Truman Bethurum.

Truman Bethurum

Truman Bethurum is widely acknowledged as the second contactee, after Adamski. Bethurum himself, however, asserted he was the first one, to his knowledge, to have actual contact with space people. George Adamski's tales of saucer contact illustrate the connections between flying saucer interest and Theosophy. Bethurum's story doesn't veer into spiritual areas. It does, however, provide a mirror (however warped) to a man's life in the 1950s, demonstrating how he views marriage, gender, politics, and the Cold War.

Bethurum's adventure begins prosaically, as he accepts road construction work in Mormon Mesa, California. On the night of July 27, 1952, he wanders out to a distant hill, about a mile from the worksite. There, he falls asleep, waking up an hour later when his truck is "surrounded by about eight or ten small sized men."[3] They are, at first, unable to understand Bethurum's words when he tries to speak to them. However, they learn English within a few minutes and invite Truman to enter their saucer and meet their captain. As Bethurum says, "Little did I suspect that their captain would turn out to be a woman — and what a woman!"

Unlike George Adamski, who introduced himself simply — yet grandiosely — in *Flying Saucers Have Landed*, Truman Bethurum went to great lengths to establish his credentials as a down-to-earth, hard-working, honest, trustworthy and sane man. He presented the reader with a short biography, including family and childhood details, which establishes that until his contact experience he was a solidly working class man of unremarkable background. Bethurum even presented a vague, but complimentary, reference letter from the treasurer of his union local. He does not present himself as a man of learning, letters, or great insight. He's a simple man with a story to tell. There is a question, however, of whose story this truly is.

One of the critical issues which arises in discussing Bethurum's work is the question of authorship. Often, as in the case of George Adamski, the question of whether or not a particular contactee personally wrote his own books, magazines, newsletters or other materials is shrouded in mystery, accusation, denial and counteraccusation. Contrary to this approach, Truman Bethurum was open (at least in private correspondence) about hiring a ghostwriter to compose *Aboard a Flying Saucer*. In a letter to saucer publisher Gray Barker, dated November 16, 1953 (before the publication of *Aboard a Flying Saucer*), Bethurum discussed his motivations for creating the book: "I found that many people whom I have told of my wonderful friends from space were using my words in their speaking engagements, etc. So, I finally decided to so something myself and have had my experiences written in book form by a fine writer. It is now in the hands of publishers for consideration. I hope it will be published soon, for it will be a revelation."[4] Additionally, in a later letter to Barker, after the book's publication, Bethurum mentions, "I still have my original notes I gave to Miss Tennyson that did my ghosting," and asks Barker, "Please remember, I am not a proffesional [*sic*] writer, I just wrote down the conversation & what happened and a few of my own conclusions."[5] This candid discussion of his book's authorship leads us to the question of the role the "author," in this case Bethurum, played in understanding contactee narratives.

Arguably, the question of whether or not Bethurum — or any other contactee — wrote his stories himself or dictated them to a ghostwriter is immaterial to the substance of the ideas they wished to convey. Contemporary and modern critics of the contactees often saw accusations (or admissions) of ghostwriting as a reflection on the veracity of the contact stories being told. The literal truth or fiction of flying saucer contact claims, however, is secondary to the messages contactees sought to convey through their stories of contact. The same could be said for the literal authorship of these works. The George Adamski Foundation, in its response to claims that Adamski used a ghostwriter, responded:

> During the last two decades prior to his death in April 1965, George Adamski had at least ten such volunteer secretaries in the U.S. alone: Individuals, who via typewriter, shorthand, etc., transposed at George's personal dictation and instruction, his experiences, ideas and works.... A collaborative effort was encouraged in order to review, correct, and prepare materials for final release. Today, what intelligent person would deny or discourage constructive input before finalizing any significant compositions or presentation?... Would this consequently allow editing parties the right to commandeer or claim ownership from Adamski? Or course not!"[6]

For Adamski's supporters — and one could apply this logic to Truman Bethurum's work as well — Adamski's presence in guiding the writing, telling the story, and overseeing the operation was tantamount to literal authorship.

A useful (if slightly anachronistic) way to think about the prominent contactees is in terms of marketing. Adamski, Bethurum, and other contactees often derived income from sources other than their books. In particular, fees from speaking engagements provided a steady source of support between books. In cases where flying saucer authors published through a vanity press, one could consider the books a loss-leader, hopefully bringing — if popular enough — book deals and speaking engagements. Contactees had to very carefully manage their personal brand and many did so with a great deal of savvy. It is not particularly surprising, then, that Truman Bethurum hired a ghostwriter to help him frame his story or George Adamski ran his writing by several colleagues before releasing it into the wild. It was one way to ensure that the best, most intriguing work made it into the public's hands. This would, ideally, ensure expanded attendance at events and future book sales. Both Adamski and Bethurum spoke of their encounters before publishing their books; thus, at some fundamental level they were the originators of the master narratives which later appeared in print.

Adamski had a background as a self-styled philosophical teacher, saucer lecturer, and author. Bethurum had no such background. Thus, Bethurum's ideas, conveyed through his conversations with the space people from the planet Clarion, do not have the same political, philosophical, or spiritual detail as Adamski's. Bethurum spends much more time than Adamski discussing the scientific and technical aspects of life on Clarion. This is a conscious decision on Bethurum's part. In his November 1953 letter to Gray Barker he states (somewhat confusingly), "Medical and other sciences would naturally be first in any consideration other than the religious life that these people have shown me are their inherent qualities." Accordingly, there is a great deal of discussion in *Aboard a Flying Saucer* about the mechanics of space travel, the location of the planet Clarion, and the design and construction of the "scow" in which the Clarionites travel.

Bethurum does, to a small degree, delve into social and political issues in *Aboard a Flying Saucer*. Aura Rhanes, the captain of the ship, gives Bethurum what he calls "a bit of a lecture" about the deficiencies of Earth humanity. "God," she said, "has been liberal in his blessings.... Your peoples could amalgamate and act in unison instead of constantly warring upon each other, and then you'd find your earth worth living upon." Without this "amalgamation" humanity will be burdened with "the nagging horror and fear of bloody death and maimed and crazed young bodies." Things are much better on her home planet of Clarion. The churches on Clarion are "always filled" and "riches and wealth" are "certainly more evenly distributed than on our earth."[7] Apart from the brief reference to full churches, Bethurum does not prescribe the type of spiritual renewal that Adamski recommends.

Much of Bethurum's account of the Clarionites in *Aboard a Flying*

Saucer consists of a dialog with Aura Rhanes. Aura is an anomaly within the realm of Space Age contact stories in that she is not only a woman, she is a woman in a position of authority. Beyond that, her personality is fairly well developed; she stands out from the other space people in a way that many contactees' extraterrestrial friends do not. Bethurum's relationship with Aura Rhanes (as well as its effect on his marriage) is discussed in detail in Chapter 7.

Bethurum's writings did not end with *Aboard a Flying Saucer*. He released one particularly interesting publication in 1958 titled *Facing Reality*, a collection of essays on a variety of topics. One, titled "Fighting Communism with Common Sense," argued that American foreign aid spending—particularly to fund nations which were fighting Communist insurrections—ran the risk of prolonging and enlarging the conflict between Communist powers and the United States. Similarly, he expressed concern that the label "communist" was being applied to any kind of honest dissent. Bethurum goes so far to assert that threats of communist incursion are used as a tactic to distract Americans from other concerns, including economic ones. "If and when full employment is a reality in America— we will find that the 'bugaboo' of Communism will mean no more than the saying: 'If you don't watch out, the bogey man will get you!'"[8] The following essay, "The Sin Parlors of America," details the corruption of state and local governments in the United States and lays much of the blame for America's problems on the Federal Reserve banking system.

Significantly, Aura Rhanes of the Clarionites appears only briefly in this book, arriving to tell Bethurum he needs to build a sanctuary for people to study universal wisdom. Much of *Facing Reality* is given over to political and social proclamations and discussions such as the above. Bethurum—while he did not include political, social, or spiritual topics overtly in his actual contact tales—used his position as an established contactee figure and the audience which it brought him to espouse his political views in a discrete format. Bethurum would not receive the following or recognition of George Adamski or other contactees. His story, however, was an interesting part of the overall body of extraterrestrial contact narratives, as much for what it did not include as for what it did. It did not take a particularly spiritual viewpoint and did not seem to build upon any sort of earlier spiritualist or Theosophical tradition; it did not feature a large cast of space brother characters, focusing instead on the relationship between Bethurum and Aura Rhanes; it did not claim the visitors hailed from the solar system, instead fabricating a new world. Bethurum is an example of contacteeism stepping ever so slightly out of the shadow of the George Adamski desert contact — more nuts and bolts than sweetness and light.

George Hunt Williamson

George Hunt Williamson was one of those who witnessed Adamski's alleged initial 1952 contact. In 1954, he got into the business of writing books about the flying saucers and detailing his contacts with their occupants. Williamson co-wrote his first book, *The Saucers Speak* (1954), with Alfred C. Bailey, another of the Adamski witnesses (although later editions listed Williamson as the sole author). Unlike Adamski's November 1952 desert contact experience, Williamson and Bailey's extraterrestrial contacts were not physical. Rather, the contacts recounted in *The Saucers Speak* came through transmissions received by amateur radio operators. In the preface to the 1954 book, Williamson and Bailey are clear about their intentions:

> These messages constitute a warning to men on the planet of the third orbit or Earth. There isn't any threat of invasion; but as a father warns a child of danger, these people who are wiser than we, are telling us we have already done untold damage to our world through the use of Atomic Energy. Perhaps it would be more accurate to say, the misuse of that energy. The space craft intelligences know exactly what our insane experimentation has done in the past and they know the prevailing conditions on earth at this time.[9]

This is, of course, similar in many ways to the messages conveyed to George Adamski through his own contacts. The dangers of atomic power and the conception of humanity as being at an earlier stage of development, for example, are recurring themes in Adamski's work.

Williamson's earliest contact was with "Nah-9 of the Solar X Group." Nah-9 confirmed that it was Martian saucers that had been seen over California and urged the people of Earth to come together as one and join the union of planets in the solar system. There were restrictions, however, on which Earthlings the space people would assist: "We are friends of those interested, but we are not interested in those of the carnal mind. By that we mean the stupid preservation of self; disregarding the will of the Creative Spirit and His Sons."[10] Williamson described the "Creative Spirit" as being analogous to humanity's conception of God. Nah-9 also revealed that "evil planetary men" of Earth would destroy humanity with the new

George Hunt Williamson (date unknown) speaking at one of George Van Tassel's flying saucer conventions at Giant Rock (courtesy Gray Barker Collection, Clarksburg-Harrison Public Library, Clarksburg, West Virginia).

hydrogen bomb. Other revelations included the fact that the sun is, in fact, cold and that the representative from Uranus disapproved of the Martians' contacting Earth. Again, Williamson's stories had similarities to Adamski's encounters. Both warned of the dangers of new atomic weapons technology and suggested that humanity would find a solution if they became united in purpose, seeking peace and cooperation instead of war.

George Hunt Williamson, however, was more than simply an Adamski clone. His later works, books like *Other Tongues, Other Flesh*, and *Secret Places of the Lion*, delve into far more esoteric areas than flying saucers. They also show off more of Williamson's background. Williamson, like Adamski, was involved with occult and Theosophical beliefs before the saucer phenomenon began. He did not, however, publish or release writings publicly as did Adamski. Rather, he conversed with other occultists and edited *Valor*, the newsletter of a Noblesville, Indiana-based organization called Soulcraft. Soulcraft was founded and run by William Dudley Pelley. Pelley had a long and checkered career, working as a journalist, screenwriter, and award-winning short story writer. In the 1930s, he was the leader of the Silver Legion, an organization which emulated German and Italian Nazi and Fascist ideas, as well as a potpourri of spiritual and racial ideologies drawn from Theosophy and British-Israelism. Williamson also had an interest in anthropology and often pretended to academic credentials he did not actually possess.[11] These interests in anthropology and spiritualism would play an increasingly large role in the writings he aimed at the contactee and flying saucer readership.

One early example of this was a speech Williamson gave to an audience in Detroit on June 21, 1954. In this speech, he positioned his extraterrestrial contacts in the context of the ethnographic studies he had been undertaking among the Ojibwe (Chippewa) people of Minnesota. Williamson saw a distinct connection between the legends of Native American tribes and the contacts Adamski and others had experienced:

> One of the Chippewa's legends is the account of the "Gin Guin" or the "Earth-rumblers," or the "Wheels-that-rumble-the-earth." The story in essence is this: At various times a rotating wheel or whirling wheel, sometimes surrounded by a cloud, would descend and lightning would sometimes be seen to shoot from it. Then out of it would step a young fair-haired man whom they called "Bococitti," the fair-haired god who comes from the skies. Stories like these are found throughout the United States and in fact almost all primitive people throughout the world seem to have the same kind of legends.[12]

Williamson also relies heavily on New Age and Theosophical concepts in this speech, blending the messages from the space brothers with well-worn concepts such as the ages of Aquarius and Pisces: "In the fall of last year we left the old third density and we are no longer in it. We are in the transitional stage or in the beginning of a new dimension or new density right now. As the change is coming slowly we do not notice it too much. Many people say we are going from Pisces to Aquarius. These space people are here merely to help us, and to usher us into this new dimension — usher us into this New Age."[13]

This is a pattern which Williamson would continue. In later works, especially 1958's *Secret Places of the Lion*, Williamson increasingly emphasizes the significance of the mythic, pseudoarchaeological human past. In the front of this book (right after the request for readers to provide donations which would fund Williamson's next archaeological expedition) is a list of "questions answered by this book," including:

- "Were some of the 'gods' of antiquity really space visitors?"
- "Are there hidden pyramids in North America?"
- "What is the real meaning of the Aztec Calendar Stone?"
- "Did the American Indians guard ancient Lemurian records in Time Capsules?"
- "Who was Joseph Smith in other lifetimes?"[14]

The space brothers, for Williamson, fade into the background of a much wider tapestry of the hidden secrets of human history. This, more than the content of the alleged contacts Williamson experienced, distinguish him from Adamski and other contactees.

James Moseley, in his memoir *Shockingly Close to the Truth! Confessions of a Grave-Robbing Ufologist*, asserts that some degree of animosity existed between Williamson and George Adamski. The reasons for this stem from Williamson's allegations of psychic and radio contact with extraterrestrials as well as his connections with Pelley. According to Moseley, "The former would turn off 'nuts-and-bolts' saucers, and the latter hardly was compatible with the Space Brothers' cosmic sweetness and light message. These differences led 'Professor' Adamski to banish 'Doctor' Williamson."[15] Regardless of the reasons for such a falling out, Williamson did seem to be in some sort of competition with the arch-contactee, Adamski. In *The Saucers Speak* and public lectures like the one in Detroit, Williamson claimed that most of the aliens' messages came to him in the summer of 1952, a few months before Adamski's encounter. Williamson, not content with being a mere witness to Adamski's initial contact, wished to set himself up as pre-eminent among the contactees. Since the basics of his space brothers' messages, in many ways, mirrored Adamski's, this attempt to establish primacy would seem to have been motivated more by personal aggrandizement than anything else — they certainly don't do anything to undermine Adamski's claims.

This aggrandizement continued in Williamson's 1957 *Other Tongues, Other Flesh* and centered on the mysterious footprints left by Orthon the Venusian during the 1952 desert contact. In *Flying Saucers Have Landed*, Adamski printed an image of the footprints and reported that Williamson had taken a plaster cast of the prints in an effort to interpret the meaning of the symbols embedded in Orthon's shoes.[16] Williamson, in *Other Tongues, Other Flesh*, devotes a whole chapter to the footprints, connecting the markings on them to Sanskrit and other ancient languages and symbols. For example, Williamson interprets one of these symbols, a swastika, in this way:

> The swastika symbol evolved from the simple cross symbol, and both are among the most ancient symbols of Earth. The swastika is the Key to Universal Movements. Since Four Great Primary Forces were used in Creation, and are now governing the movements of all bodies throughout the Universe, these forces are working from West to East, and carry all celestial bodies in the direction of West to East. These forces by their actions cause the revolving bodies to continue their force, so that apparently the force comes from the movements of the body.[17]

This discussion of symbolism is not groundbreaking — the various Theosophical movements of the late 19th and early 20th centuries delved into similar topics — but it does allow Williamson to place himself and his work at a level a bit higher than Adamski. Interestingly, Williamson's description of the November 1952 contact barely mentions Adamski at all. At the outset of the chapter on the footprints, Williamson describes it thus: "A man from another world stepped onto the planet Earth on November 20, 1952. My wife and I and our friends witnessed this happening which took place 10.2 miles from Desert Center, California, on the highway toward Parker, Arizona. The full account is given in *Flying Saucers Have Landed* by Leslie and Adamski."[18] While Williamson doesn't claim to have been the subject of the contact, he muddies the waters. An uninformed reader might reasonably assume the encounter happened to a group and Adamski just happened to be the one who wrote the book.

George Hunt Williamson's popularity extended beyond the United States, as evidenced by his contribution of articles on archaeology and anthropology to the British magazine *Flying Saucer Review*. One of these articles, "Project Scroll," detailed Williamson's adventures in Peru exploring what Williamson claimed to be an ancient civilization "that antedated both Atlantis and Lemuria!" As usual, Williamson connected this hidden history of Earth to the visitors from beyond Earth. As he did with his address in Detroit, here he again discussed the prevalence of "sky people" legends in the cultures of indigenous peoples around the world. Additionally, in this particular case, Williamson believe the space people to have a secret base in the ruins of this ancient Peruvian empire.[19]

While Williamson's contact stories shared some thematic similarities with Adamski's, Williamson's reports of his contact experiences (and his explications of other experiences, notably Adamski's) firmly place his version of the contactee narrative within the larger trend of mysticism in the United States. Williamson fits in multiple esoteric categories like few other contactees. Beyond this, his fairly aggressive attempt to position himself as a pioneer in extraterrestrial matters — attempting to soak up as much paranormal, pseudoarchaeological, and spiritualist attention as possible — makes him a fascinating character.

George Van Tassel and Ashtar

George Van Tassel, another California contactee, was also the exponent of the psychic or etheric genre of contact narrative and a key figure in the ongoing development of contactee beliefs from the 1950s until his death in 1978. He wrote several books (including his first, *I Rode a Flying Saucer*) which detail the origins and meaning of the contacts and visitations he and others had.

While Van Tassel's first book is significant for a number of reasons, key among them are the contrasts between this book and Adamski's seminal contact story related in *Flying Saucers Have Landed*. The greatest contrast is that Van Tassel's contacts with space beings were transmitted through multiple long-distance channeled transmissions rather than through a single face-to-face meeting. The second "revised and enlarged" edition of *I Rode a Flying Saucer* is short — 50 pages — and consists of a series of short transmissions from various space beings which Van Tassel claimed to receive between January 1952 and March 1953. The transmissions are often repetitive and, overall, the book has little to say, but this and subsequent works by Van Tassel launched flying saucer contact memes which persist into the

21st century. Chief among these is the figure of "Ashtar," an extraterrestrial who commands a fleet of spacecraft surrounding Earth. Due to the channeled nature of the messages from Ashtar, subsequent contactees will resurrect the figure, providing a continuity that lasts decades.

Van Tassel began his book with an introduction (written in third person) in which he established his credentials within the aerospace industry through his work with Douglas, Howard Hughes, and Lockheed. He then discussed his move to Giant Rock Airport, which he operated at the time of his contact experiences. Van Tassel attributes his contacts to his relocation to the desert locale of Giant Rock: "Four and half years of this natural freedom made it possible for the author to find his true being." Where Adamski was deliberately mysterious in describing himself at the outset of his story in *Flying Saucers Have Landed*—"philosopher, student, teacher, saucer researcher"—Van Tassel not only provides more detail on his background but uses that background to construct a narrative of transition from the urban to the rural, from the man-made to the natural. This narrative mirrors the difference between Van Tassel's contacts (psychic and ethereal) and Adamski's (physical and tangible).[20]

Van Tassel's approach also differed from Adamski's in the way Van Tassel set up his political and social point of view from the title page of the book. A blurb on the title page describes the book as "Radioned [*sic*] to you by Other-World Intelligences in Reaction to Man's Destructive Action." In the introduction, the explication of this viewpoint continues, preparing the reader to be receptive to the messages which follow. Van Tassel argued, "Today man builds the means to destroy.... Realize that you and your loved ones are present victims of continual destructive influences.... listen to that 'inner voice' that will cause you to recognize truth when it appears."[21] While the earlier emphasis on the importance of the natural environment and being open to one's "true being" prepared the reader for the non-tangible medium of the messages, the clear allusions to the threat of global annihilation prepared the reader for the content of the messages.

While the medium of contact between George Van Tassel and the space beings was intangible and etheric, he explains the mechanism of these psychic contacts in a distinctly technological and materialistic manner. "Man," writes Van Tassel, "views television, listens to radio, rides in airplanes and *causes* all these things to operate through, or on, or in an *unseen* medium. He cannot even see his *own* thought, the *unseen* intelligence that *caused* these material things to be manufactured. Yet man goes through his daily life *accepting this unseen intelligence* without question [emphasis in original]."[22] Like radio or television signals, one can tune into the transmissions from space beings.

The 51 transmissions Van Tassel records in *I Rode a Flying Saucer* have a distinctly apocalyptic tone. The brief first transmission, from January 6, 1952, sets up the context of the space visitors: "I am Lutbunn, senior in command first wave, planet patrol, realms of Schare [a space station for flying saucers]. We have your contact 80,000 feet above this place. Your press will have more to report on your so-called flying saucers. We return your contact. Discontinue."[23] Over subsequent messages Lutbunn and her/his colleagues introduced themselves, establishing a backstory of a constellation of saucers and way-stations in Earth's galactic neighborhood who report back to a control group called "The Center."

Once the visitors establish these credentials, the messages begin to convey "prophetic" messages of future saucer sightings, including the 1952 Washington, D.C., flap (see Chapter 2), and increasingly dire warnings about the dangers of humans meddling with atomic weapons. For example, Van Tassel reported an April 19, 1952, transmission in which a being called Kerrull, based on Mars, said, "We are instructed from the center to inform you that due to inaccurate calculations, many of your fellow beings will *suffer prolonged illness* from an experiment.... This folly in the use of atomic power for destruction will rebound upon the users [emphasis in original]."[24] Not all predictions were so dire — on May 9, 1952, Hulda predicted, "Your people shall witness more fireballs."[25] These prediction messages are followed by commentary by Van Tassel in which he confirms that these things did, in fact, happen.

This is familiar territory for students of Adamski's contact narratives. The first 30 pages of *I Rode a Flying Saucer* warn of the dangers of atomic weapons and verify that the strange craft seen in the skies are, indeed, of extraterrestrial origin. The entry for July 18, 1952, however, introduces an extraterrestrial character which will persist in contact narratives (particularly channeled narratives). His name was Ashtar, and he introduced himself as "commandant quadra sector, patrol station Schare, all projections, all waves."[26] Ashtar is the "chief" of the extraterrestrials with whom Van Tassel had been communicating. Ashtar's message is more dire and explicit than the warnings that previous messages had conveyed.

Ashtar discussed the development of nuclear science on Earth, explaining that he and his people "have *not* been concerned with [humans'] explosion of plutonium and U235 [emphasis in original]." The splitting of the hydrogen atom, on the other hand, is of great concern to Ashtar and his people, since hydrogen is a "life-giving element of the Creative Intelligence." Hydrogen, Ashtar argues, is a "living" element, as opposed to uranium or plutonium, which are "inert." The planned destruction of the hydrogen atom indicates a "deliberate determination to *extinguish* humanity and turn [Earth] into a cinder."[27] Ashtar concludes his first transmission by promising to stop any development of hydrogen-based weapons.

For the remainder of the book, Ashtar's words make up a majority of the transmissions, with his subordinates taking a back seat. Besides warnings about the hydrogen bomb, Ashtar accuses Earth officials of suppressing information about the saucers. Van Tassel, in his commentary on this transmission, addresses the withholding of information from the public, arguing that "many officials in governments have appointed themselves as judges to determine what the public should be informed of, 'for their own good,' 'for national security,' or some other reason." This echoes the sentiments of the more conservative saucer investigation groups such as NICAP (see Chapter 2), which believed a "paper curtain" of official secrecy and obfuscation prevented the truth of interplanetary travel from being common, public knowledge. Van Tassel's dismissal of "national security" as a cover-up device indicates more than sympathy with other saucer organizations; it is, like similar concerns in writings of George Adamski, indicative of mistrust and skepticism of the rising Cold War national security state.

In closing *I Rode a Flying Saucer*, Van Tassel asserts "the 'Saucer beings' are here to stay, to direct man back upon the path.... Greet the Saucer beings with thoughts of love and receive them as friends, not with 'jets' and guns and fear."[28] Van Tassel was much more explicit about the role played by those with whom he had contact than were Adamski or Williamson. Also significant is the time spent by Van Tassel in constructing a setting, a cast of characters, and even a language (Earth is "Shan," a flying saucer is a "ventla," and so on), which provides a world into which the willing reader can escape. As we will see, Van Tassel's narrative choice meant that the character of Ashtar and the protective mission of his subordinates would grow, expand, and outlive Van Tassel in a way that other contact narratives do not. His subsequent works would expand further beyond the material realm of the flying saucer and develop in overtly spiritualist directions. Additionally, by the time his second book was published in 1956 after the publication of *I Rode a Flying Saucer*, Van Tassel established the College of Universal Wisdom, an organization for disseminating the wisdom of the space brothers through newsletters and meetings. The book was an opening movement rather than a stand-alone composition. Van Tassel's messages from space would continue for decades.

With a subtitle reading, "A modern proof of the origin of humanity and its retrogression from the original creation of man," Van Tassel's *Into This World and Out Again* speculates on an ancient connection between humans and the space people. Through a dialog between two spacemen, Abon and Bor, Van Tassel states he received the information through "thought communication."[29] Much of the material is a potpourri of notions that were well-worn even by the 1950s. Thus, *Into this World* not only exists in the mainstream of flying saucer contact tales but also crosses into a spiritualist world that stretches back to the 19th century.

Abon and Bor describe the space people as the "Adamic Race,"[30] a term whose use appears prominently in 19th century spiritualist writing and thought. It appeared, for example, in an 1882 book titled *Golden Thoughts in Quiet Moments*. Lily, the pseudonymous author, describes the Adamic race as souls from a planet other than Earth who were forced to reincarnate here to be "pioneers of progress" for the less advanced humans on Earth.[31] This is not too far afield from Van Tassel's vision of the space people's mission as expressed in *I Rode a Flying Saucer*. Additionally, Van Tassel's use of "thought communication" to send and receive messages from beings like Abon and Bor is standard practice in many spiritualist traditions.

Van Tassel's use of the term "Adamic race" evokes another long-standing belief system — British-Israelism. The belief that the Anglo-Saxon "race" directly descends from the 10 Lost Tribes of Israel has its roots in the mid–19th century and reached a peak of interest in the early 20th century. This tradition was part of the constellation of pseudo-scientific racialist thinking that pervaded the turn of the century period and helped prop up institutionalized segregation. On the surface, this connection would seem to indicate overtones of racism in Van Tassel's work. While this is a criticism one could level at many contactees, with their predominance of white, blond, blue-eyed space brothers and sisters, the mere use of the phrase "Adamic race" does not necessarily imply racism. Given the term's long history, it is not surprising that it has been used in a variety of contexts. Since some have accused figures within the contactee movement of various racist ideas (particularly anti–Semitism), it is useful to explore this idea of the Adamic Race which Van Tassel invokes.

One example of the racist aura surrounding the "Adamic race" being actively undermined appears in a 1914 an article titled "The Ark of the Covenant" in *The Flaming Sword*, a magazine "devoted to the promulgation of Koreshan Universology." Koresh was, in actuality, Dr. C.R. Teed, a Florida cult leader whose ideas were based upon the belief that the Earth was a hollow sphere.[32] Koresh/Teed describes the Adamic race as "the Sons of God in the last golden age" and states that they were "of 'one blood,' as will be those of this coming Golden Age, through ethnic infiltration of many nationalities ... all of the tribes, together with the nations of the earth, melted in the crucible of ethnic unity and power."[33] Thus, according to Koresh/Teed, the ancient Adamic race was an amalgamation of all races. Further, the future will belong to a multi-ethnic, multi-national human race. It is possible, therefore, that by invoking the concept of the Adamic race, Van Tassel sought to identify himself with its broader spiritualist traditions rather than its racial connotations. At the very least, use of the term places Van Tassel and his beliefs firmly in the continuum of western spiritualism.

Within the Spiritualist context of *Into This World*, Van Tassel addresses a number of concerns faced by contemporary society that place this book firmly in the contactee tradition of social critique, including of traditional Christianity. Van Tassel asserts that "the churches have become the second richest organization on the Earth. Many individuals are controlled by 'churchianity' through propaganda and money."[34] He softens his critique a bit by allowing that the beliefs, while good, are merely managed poorly, but the identification of corruption and materialism in institutional Christianity is a familiar trope within contact narratives.

Also familiar are explanations of why authorities have kept the "reality" of visitors from beyond Earth from humanity. Donald Keyhoe, through his NICAP organization (see Chapter 2), argued that the Air Force was responsible for the continued secrecy surrounding the flying saucer mystery. Van Tassel confirms that there are those within the government who wish to continue the cover-up. In an afterword to *Into This World and Out Again*, Van Tassel confirms Keyhoe's assertions of cover-up and, going further, states, "It should be evident by now, that those who deny that the spacecraft and space people are in our skies, are agents of the Anti-Christ," and invites readers to "decide which camp they are affiliated with."[35] Van Tassel shifts the conspiratorial overtones from a political to a spiritual perspective, very much in keeping with his overall approach.

While writing his books and running the College of Universal Wisdom, Van Tassel began other projects which would become hallmarks of the early contactee movement. Key to the contact culture of the 1950s and 1960s were annual meetings held on Van Tassel's property at Giant Rock, near Landers, California. These conventions (the largest of which boasted around 11,000 visitors) continued into the early 1970s.[36] Giant Rock served as a gathering point for flying saucer enthusiasts of all stripes and provided a platform for contactees to tell their stories as well as sell books, pamphlets, and magazines. Most of the major contactees and other flying saucer figures of the time spoke at Giant Rock. Most impressive and lasting, though, was the construction of the Integratron. According to James Moseley, the Integratron was "a domed building built with no nails or other metal of any kind." When completed (which it never was), this structure would

George Van Tassel's Integratron and College of Universal Wisdom (courtesy Gray Barker Collection, Clarksburg-Harrison Public Library, Clarksburg, West Virginia).

include "something called a 'bi-polar magnetic detector,' which would create a 'zero time factor.' This and other gadgets would make it possible for people to walk into the Integratron for a few seconds and come out rejuvenated." According to Moseley, Van Tassel claimed he had received over $42,000 in donations from believers and supporters to help build the device.[37]

Van Tassel continued writing on saucer matters into the 1970s; his last book, *When Stars Look Down*, was published in 1976. *When Stars Look Down* was a compilation of writings over a period of 20 years, mostly concerning the interactions between various cosmic scientific forces and their relationship with the reality of space travel and the existence of the space brothers. Van Tassel also remained active in promoting the Ministry and College of Universal Wisdom, an organization devoted to spreading the ideals Van Tassel received from Ashtar and the other space brothers. Weekly meetings of this organization featured channelings from the various extraterrestrial entities with whom Van Tassel was in contact and, over time, others began to channel messages from beings such as Ashtar as well.

Neither the character of Ashtar nor the concept of discussing philosophical, spiritual, social, or political matter with exalted entities from space ended with George Van Tassel. As Van Tassel continued to host channeling sessions from Ashtar and other beings at his Ministry of Universal Wisdom meetings, some thought that there was more that could be done with such contacts from beyond. The editor of *Interplanetary News*, Bill Rose (a.k.a. Robert Short), allegedly thought that Van Tassel could (and should) commercialize the Ashtar communications more effectively. Van Tassel refused, and Rose/Short began a rival organization called Ashtar Command. By 1955, a number of channeled messages from "Ashtar Command" began to appear in newsletters and magazines, and from New Age and flying saucer–oriented book publishers.

One example is *In Days to Come*, a book published in 1957 by Ethel P. Hill, writing as Ashtar. Like Van Tassel and other contactees, Hill's message not only told of aliens from space but also critiqued the present spiritual, political, and social mores of the United States, as well as the larger condition of humanity. New Age Publishers, who released *In Days to Come*, were not particularly humble about their goals in spreading the message of Ashtar/Hill:

> There are many who feel that ASHTAR and his legions are the forerunners of the Second Coming of Christ — no matter how this is understood. Some expect

to see him in the flesh, others believe that the Spirit of Christ will eventually rule the earth, and the spiritually "unfit" will be eliminated. At any rate, many people feel that our so-called culture is nearing its end and that something is about to happen. A change must come both in world affairs and in religion whose doctrines were fashioned not by Jesus but by medieval priests in order to keep the ignorant in spiritual bondage to the Church.[38]

This flavor of grandiosity is not unusual in contactee writing and it is not surprising. As people who had as their goal the reformation of the very foundations of Cold War society, it would have been startling to not encounter a bit of hubris.

In the introduction to *In Days to Come*, Ashtar (speaking through Hill) sets out the major themes about which he will be speaking. It is, in many ways, a contactee "greatest hits" collection, including such topics as nuclear weapons:

A predominance of resolution by the inhabitants themselves must precede our entrance on the scene en masse to use our superior powers in augmenting those possessed by mortals at this time. Yes, I most certainly do refer to the H-bomb (and other highly dangerous explosives). It is one thing to compound and to explode such a hellish contrivance but where is the mortal who has solved the problem of *preventing* its explosion or nullifying its deadly effect? No such person exists on the planet Shan [Earth]! How dare they release a force of such magnitude without the slightest idea how to control it?

Ashtar also refers to the Universal Law, which will force Ashtar and his compatriots to accept only total peace on Earth:

We Space Men, in whatever capacity we may temporarily serve, are irrevocably pledged by the most solemn of oaths to abide by those Universal Laws which alone can preserve life on every level of conscious existence. To accept or condone any variance from these fixed and unchangeable codes governing all honorable behavior, would be to forfeit privileges we have earned through eons of unremitting effort. We will have no part in any form of "synthetic peace!" It must be genuine, unalloyed, incapable of dissimulation.

And, as begun in the Ashtar channelings of George Van Tassel, there is a very proactive, salvation-oriented tone to this, with Ashtar concluding his opening statement by declaring, "WE COME AS YOUR DEFENDERS AND DELIVERERS! WE COME AT THE URGENT REQUEST OF YOUR HEAVENLY FATHER TO RELEASE YOU FROM INSUFFERABLE BONDAGE. MY LOVE AND MY BLESSINGS!"[39]

Once the body of the channeling begins, there is an unusual shift in tone, as Ashtar moves to an affected Elizabethan style of speech matching the increasingly Biblical language of the warnings and promises he is making to the people of Earth. One of the recurring themes in *In Days to Come* is the inevitability of a battle between the forces of good and evil. In Chapter One, Ashtar promises that the victors in this coming conflict will be those who place their trust in God: "I say to thee in all sacred solemnity of pronouncement, THIS THY COUNTRY SHALL BE SAVED AS BY A MIRACLE! I say not it will be a peaceful deliverance but through the unfaltering loyalty of millions who place their faith in thy Master, the Christ of God, this land will be cleansed from the abominations now infesting it."[40] This forecast of an all-consuming conflict which will destroy parts of the Earth and cause the death of many human beings is similar to some eschatological interpretations of Biblical prophecy. Indeed, beginning with the title, there is a strong overtone of prophecy and determinism throughout *In Days to Come* that is not as prominent in earlier contactee narratives. There *will* be a final battle; there *will* be destruction. In the writings of other contactees, such as George Adamski, humanity is presented with a choice, with destruction being the outcome of staying on the current path of greed and warmongering. Here, Ashtar presents the fiery demise of whole swaths of humanity as a foregone conclusion.

Luckily for humanity, Ashtar and his subordinates are in orbit to support those who choose to fight on the side of Light:

> No matter how previous [sic] be the suffering of many mortals in this final phase in the transformation of thy world, all who will stand firm in their defense of the Right (on whatever battlefield they fight) will soon realize that they have rendered a priceless service to their Master and his conquering legions from outer space, now able to traverse the hitherto impenetrable density of earth's auric envelope and bring succor and strength to the Christ Forces in mortal flesh.[41]

Throughout *In Days to Come*, Ashtar's message is that although humanity may, in fact, be doomed through its obsession with harnessing uncontrollable power for the purposes of geopolitical domination, interplanetary forces stand ready to protect the Earth.

Also significant is that *In Days to Come* takes a more global view of the problems facing humanity. Rather than focusing on the United States, Ashtar makes clear that there are many places on Earth that need the space brothers' help: "The combined forces of Space Men ... are united in what we believe to be the only means of handling this grave problem. Naturally, we do not propose to confine our efforts to this country, by any means.

There are others in far greater need of immediate aid, being in many places, suffering hideous injustice and cruelty."[42] Like the messages of space people encountered by previous contactees, the Ashtar narrative developed by Ethel Hill serves as both a warning to humanity and an explanation of how humanity might save itself. Unlike other contactee texts, including George Van Tassel's early contacts, there is no interaction between the space brother and his human contact. This has the effect of making the figure, in this case Ashtar, far more distant, imperious, and impressive. Ashtar is not just a guy in a jumpsuit with a flying saucer — he is a godlike figure.

Ethel Hill would not be the last to channel Ashtar. The supreme commander of space forces would emerge time and again in channeled contactee literature. Often these channeled messages would present prophecy. This, of course, led to the issue of unfulfilled prophecies. Christopher Helland, in "From Extraterrestrials to Ultraterrestrials: The Evolution of the Concept of Ashtar," explains the effect of this on the concepts of "Ashtar" and "Ashtar Command" as a source of authoritative messages: "These failings took an enormous toll on the Ashtar Command movement, principally because there was no central authority to filter the messages or present a clear response to alleviate the confusion and distress caused by the failed prophecy.... Dozens of people were claiming contact with Ashtar (and therefore authority) and presenting conflicting messages."[43] The story of Ashtar Command, the massive fleet stationed around Earth, and the future of humanity would continue into the 1970s and 1980s. With the advent of the Internet and World Wide Web in the 1990s and 21st century, the messages attributed to Ashtar, Hatonn, Soltec and the rest of the cosmic cast would become increasingly diverse and splintered.

George King and the Aetherius Society

The story of George King and his flying saucer organization, the Aetherius Society, is an important example of the extent to which the notion of personal extraterrestrial contact (either psychic or physical) had spread around the world to, in particular, Great Britain, during the 1950s and 1960s. Although the stereotypical contactee is American, the phenomenon was not confined to the United States.

Born in Shropshire, England, in 1919, George King began to study yoga and other eastern mystical traditions as a young man. His contactee experiences began while he was meditating. Like contactees such as George Van Tassel, this initial contact was psychic in nature. King recounted the origins of his connections with the space people in his 1961 book *You Are Responsible!* The cover imagery of *You Are Responsible!* sets out the basic message of King's message. In the background, a mushroom cloud dominates a city as, in the foreground, a silhouetted mob pulls down a three-dimensional cross. King includes on the cover a statement attributed to "A MAN FROM MARS": "These are the Last Days of the Old Order. The New Order for you will be greater Peace, greater Joy. Conditions beyond your wild imaginings! Or, rebirth upon

George King, yoga master, contactee, and founder of the Aetherius Society (courtesy Aetherius Society).

a younger World to relive the terrors of the history you have made upon this Planet. Choose — and Act!" It is a striking cover, with the title in large letters superimposed in red on a yellow and black background. The title and preface from King's Martian messenger strike a sharper note than other contactee writings, placing the onus for change squarely on humanity's shoulders.

His reason for writing the book was to reveal messages from those "Great Teachers" who would provide humanity with a way out of its troubles. Because of the "age of atomic chaos" humanity found itself in, the human race had to "turn the tide ... away from the great cataclysm it is so surely making for itself." One day in May in 1954, George King sat meditating. While doing so, he heard a clear, loud voice command, "Prepare yourself! You are to become the voice of Interplanetary Parliament!" King was not bewildered by the fact that he had received a message through

The striking cover of *You Are Responsible!* Note the lengthy quotation of a Man from Mars, as well as the cross superimposed on a mushroom cloud (courtesy Aetherius Society).

telepathic means ("the Bible records many such happenings"), but he was concerned at the implications that he would be responsible for communicating great changes and opportunities to his fellow human beings.[44]

The message and call to action came from the Master Aetherius, a being from Venus. What does the name Aetherius signify? According to King, humanity is not ready for that information: "This name was chosen because of a deep occult significance which cannot be revealed at this stage. Those who know the underlying reason for the action will appreciate the need for secrecy." This assertion, tautological though it be, is representative of King's positioning of spiritual and esoteric knowledge as being crucial for communication with the space people: "Meditation is the key to the door of ALL knowledge, whether it be the details of the propulsion units of a flying saucer, or why some potatoes have more eyes than others." All people can learn these techniques and enable themselves to "translate the thoughts of a Member of the Interplanetary Parliament and speak to them." King and his Aetherius Society were, of course, a source for information on these techniques and many of their publications were (and still are) devoted to teaching meditation techniques.[45]

You Are Responsible! comprises two parts. Part One introduces Master Aetherius and the connections between yoga and telepathy. It also recounts King's first trip to Venus and a story about sinister beings attacking friendly beings on Mars. Part Two is given over to typical contactee discussion of world events, lifeways of the Venusians and other races, and answers to potential reader questions about the motivations of these particular space brothers.

King's account of his first interplanetary voyage, to Venus, is also his opportunity to explain the efficiency and relative simplicity of using telepathy to travel into space, relative to the dangers and cost of spaceships:

> Interplanetary travel is not a mere futuristic pipe dream: it is a practical possibility to all those who are willing to sacrifice some so-called luxuries of civilization and exert sufficient effort in order to bring it about. Why wait until science has made a lumbering monstrosity driven by pure brute force?... Already you have at your command, a vessel capable of attaining the speed of light, driven by the subtle forces of thought, which will cover the Earth-Mars distance in seconds.

On his maiden voyage (which came only after four failed attempts) George met Patana, a spirit being on Venus, who took him to the "Temple of Solace" from which came the "outpourings of the Supreme Logos of the Planet

Venus." Patana also told him of the Masters of Venus who, originally, hailed from Saturn. From this temple, the masters "relay this Power unto Their students in a degree determined by their readiness to absorb it." Like that of George Adamski, King's initial contact with the extraterrestrials is fairly low-key, making clear few details of their culture.[46]

While a visit to the Temple of Solace is fairly interesting, Part One of *You Are Responsible!* is particularly notable for its fourth chapter, "The Mars Story." This may be the closest a contactee story gets to overtly modeling itself on science fiction. Though it seems like flying saucer and contactee narratives would have strong overtones of science fiction, they often read more like philosophical treatises than straightforward "spaceship stories." George King's "Mars Story" is an interesting exception to this. In fact, anticipating the obvious parallels readers could draw between his claims and such stories, King prefaces his account by saying, "To those readers who would say that the following account is a piece of imaginative science fiction, let me counter at once with the trite rejoinder: 'Truth is stranger than fiction.'... The Master Aetherius says that there is no such thing as pure fiction, because everything must contain an element of truth."[47]

It all begins when King attempts to reach Mars through his usual method of telepathic astral transport. He lands on a body he believes to be one of Mars's moon. Exploring the area, he finds a building and, curious, enters it. He soon realizes his mistake as red lights flood the corridor in which he finds himself. A "dwarf figure" appears out of a black, void-like opening in the wall and begins firing on him with a ray gun. Using the power of his mind, George King is able to pull his essence back to his physical body in London and, after some treatment from "excellent spiritual healers," is soon back to his old self with no lasting negative effects.[48]

King makes his way to Mars (the real one, this time, rather than a dwarf-infested death-zone). He is invited to a meeting of the General Assembly of Mars, which has convened to discuss a great threat to their planet. A strange planetoid composed of intensely dangerous material is headed for Mars. The planetoid proves to be a piloted device when it destroys a crewed Martian spacecraft sent to investigate. As the Martians continue to investigate and converse with King (who, since he has visited the Temple of Solace, has earned the trust of the Martian assembly), they come to the conclusion that King's previous dangerous encounter with the laser-wielding dwarf had taken place on this mysterious "asteroid." The

Martians plan a response, and King convinces them that he should have a spot on the mission since he has already dealt with the enemy. As the planning commences, King is a bit bewildered, lamenting, "This was my first problem in Interplanetary military strategy and it gave me a worse headache than if I had imbibed a quart of whisky and port wine."[49]

King boards (telepathically, of course) a saucer from Venus, with a mixed Venusian and Martian crew. The Venusian ship is capable of traveling faster than light, making it the only logical choice for this particular mission. The ship, King relates, engages in violent combat with the planetoid, destroying it. Although this story is disturbing, King states that the "Great Master" who told him to relate the tale did so because, as humans began to move among the stars, they needed to know about the dangers present in space. The planetoid, King learns, had been created by four "evil dictators" who controlled a world called Garouche, which is located on the far side of the galaxy from Earth and its solar system. The planetoid had been intended to destroy the Earth; 174 Martians died on this mission, saving the Earth. The Earth, King relates, was the target of the Garouche leader's plans because they are a water-dwelling race. Being largely covered with oceans, Earth would have been an ideal base of operations for the dictators of Garouche. Mars and Venus, supported by the great masters who dwell on Saturn, had saved the human race and the planet Earth.[50]

This blending of contactee tale with almost straight-up space opera is rare in extraterrestrial visitation narratives, especially in an age (like the 1950s and 1960s) when fictional, visual accounts of spaceship combat were not as well established. George Adamski's *Pioneers of Space*, for example, while it was a science fiction tale, was a travelogue rather than an action tale. More than most contactee stories, King's "The Mars Story" chapter in *You Are Responsible!* is influenced by the science fiction literature and film of the time. The tale of the dangerous planetoid, blue-beam-firing ray guns, and an interplanetary fleet defending Mars from attack is, perhaps, the closest that contactee narratives of the 1950s came to aping outright the science fiction tropes of the time. It seems a bit odd and more than a little jarring for King to go in this direction, since the rest of the book is, as we will see, stereotypical contactee fare. The best explanation is that the space battles serve as a narrative hook. Readers who had read numerous contactee books and articles since Leslie and Adamski's *Flying Saucers Have Landed* may have thought they knew what to expect. By placing an actual space battle fairly close to the beginning of his book, King may have been seeking to grab readers with something they weren't expecting in such a book. The Martian's statement on the cover certainly gave a strong indication that *You Are Responsible!* is typical contactee fare. The deadly encounter with a lethal planetoid piloted by dangerous enemies of our solar system subverts the reader's expectations before settling back into the relatively familiar environment of interplanetary education and haranguing by those from other worlds.

The second part of *You Are Responsible!* consisted of a series of questions and answers between a narrator (presumably King, but meant to represent questions the average reader might reasonably have) and Master Aetherius. It is in this part of the book where what one might call the standard contactee philosophy emerges. At one point, for example, Master Aetherius tells humanity that it must cease nuclear testing, which, along with humanity's "wrong thought," is responsible for all manner of disasters including weather problems such as hurricanes. The questioner then asks, "Suppose atomic experimentation was stopped, then how do we protect ourselves in case of war?" Master Aetherius responds, "Two sides are needed to fight a war, not only one side — two.... If you people, this moment could have a hundred per cent faith in Truth, Light, and Love, you could easily throw away all your weapons ... you could easily dispense with all your foolish nuclear toothpicks and still be victors of the universe.... If this were not so, then all your Masters were fools and we know they were not." Master Aetherius goes on to detail all the ways in which atomic weapons (especially the hydrogen bomb) will disrupt the Earth and, by extension, the entire interplanetary system.[51]

George King was known for far more than this or that specific contact experience or story. King, like Adamski, lectured internationally. Unlike Adamski, however, King was able to establish an organizational infrastructure that continues to promulgate his spiritual view (and those of the Cosmic Masters). This organization is the Aetherius Society.

Although King and his organization would eventually establish a headquarters in Los Angeles, King began the process of developing the religious movement which would be known as the Aetherius Society in Great Britain after a July 1958 contact between George King and "Master Jesus." The result of this meeting was an event called "Operation Starlight," which had as its goal the "charging" of mountains with "Cosmic Energy" for the good of humanity. Thus, King is an important exception to the rule that the contactee movement was mostly an American phenomenon.

Operation Starlight lasted until 1961, and it was also during this time that King began to formalize the teachings, goals, and aims of the Aetherius Society.[52] John A. Salba, writing in 1999, summarized these teachings from a number of Aetherius Society publications from the early 1960s.

1. to spread the teachings of the Master Aetherius, Jesus, and other Cosmic Masters;

2. to administer spiritual healing;

3. to prepare the way for the coming of the next Master;

4. to organize the Society so as to create favorable conditions for closer contact and ultimately meetings with people from other planets;

5. to tune in and irradiate the Power transmitted during a Holy Time or Spiritual Push, in order to balance all spiritual practices, irrespective of one's beliefs;

6. to form a brotherhood based on the teachings and knowledge of the Cosmic Masters;

7. to spread the spiritual operation known as Operation Starlight throughout the world, as directed by the Space People.[53]

The Aetherius Society (and George King) would leave Britain in 1959, embarking on several worldwide lecture tours before settling in Los Angeles, California. The organization continued to gain adherents at a steady rate and today, according to their website, there are branches and spiritual centers on nearly every continent, from Royal Oak, Michigan, to Nigeria. Throughout their development, the Aetherius Society has emphasized the need for work and dedication to the teachings of Master Aetherius and to spiritual and esoteric disciplines. A prime example of this is the Aetherius Society's response to the events surrounding the Hale-Bopp comet (see Chapter 2).

With the appearance of the Hale-Bopp comet (and the fictitious object said to be following it), the paranormal and flying saucer media went into overdrive covering what such an event might mean for humanity. After the mass suicide of the Heaven's Gate group, the Aetherius society took the opportunity to decry the tragedy and offer an explanation for ways in which their group was significantly different from the cult which claimed the lives of believers in California: "Don't look for a space craft following Hale-Bopp and don't expect the second coming or the end of the world to follow either. The Aetherius Society believes in many things which remain foreign to modern science, however it is important to use all of one's mental resources when looking at new theories, not just imagination and hope." Here, the leaders of the Aetherius society, while acknowledging that their views are outside the mainstream of modern thought, advocate discernment in seeking knowledge. Crucially, they urge seekers not to rely on "imagination and hope"—which, ironically, is what critics often accuse contactees and their followers of doing. The path to enlightenment is not easy and will not simply drop into one's lap: "In these days of rapid technological growth, especially in the west, we see technology advancing faster than spiritual growth. This is creating a very dangerous imbalance. This has of course been noticed and written about by many. The mass suicide in San Diego is just another example of this trend." A seeker must test the information given to him by a source, no matter how much the seeker may want fairy dreams and stories to be true. This is a skeptical, nearly rational (or at least rational-*sounding*) approach to new thought.

Significantly, this statement from the Aetherius Society never makes any outright claim that they are the only path to truth and interstellar enlightenment. Rather, they put the onus on the individual seeking enlightenment to do work of his own to ensure he is on the correct path: "Continue to seek. But when you find a path that looks good, test it with the test of time. Does it follow the concepts as taught by Jesus, Buddha, and Krishna? Are the others in the group, religion, or church helping others or mainly themselves? And if they all wear Nikes, put your hiking boots back on and take a hike."[54]

While the Aetherius Society continues to hold to the teachings of George King, they have continued to issue their warnings and messages while still asserting that the cosmic masters from various planets have been in contact with the leaders of humanity. The warnings for humanity are similar to what King discussed in *You Are Responsible!* but are updated for the concerns which fill today's' headlines:

> Our World is desperately out of balance. A relative handful of wealthy westerners have control of an unprecedented share of the world's resources, while millions if not billions suffer starvation or lack decent living standards.
>
> Our world is accelerating into a world of selfishness and materialistic hedonism causing an increase in violence and terrorism around the world and a rapid depletion of Earth's resources.
>
> The increase in worldwide pollution and violence, the decrease of Earth's resources such as oil and forests combined with the rapid increase in consumerism is propelling us down a dangerous and deadly slope to disaster.[55]

The Aetherius Society, thus, is an organization which, while being founded on a basis of contactee narrative, has continued to evolve into the 21st century. George Adamski's soul may have survived to become one with the ruling council of Venus, but George King's ideas spawned a constellation of adherents, facilities, and organizations. It represents a different kind of life after death, but arguably a more effective one.

Elizabeth Klarer

Elizabeth Klarer's extraterrestrial contact experience took place in 1956 in South Africa. After several sightings of flying saucers, and fueled by reading the experiences of George Adamski, Klarer would meet a man from Venus on the hills surrounding the Drakensberg Mountains. She learned that these Venusians were vegetarian and that the air on Venus has a higher concentration of oxygen than on Earth. There are also, she learned, space people based on the Moon, and they were "kind, civilized, and cultured." Her host, who was not named, had been studying Earth for some time and was concerned that humans suffered. "He was sad to see the mode of existence, precarious, and always with the threat of war. Aggressive, dominating nations would continue to rise to power, nations that are still uncivilised. The power of brute force still was rampant in the world."[56]

The Venusian offered no solutions to Earth's many predicaments and returned Elizabeth Klarer to her family. This story is brief, and told most fully in an issue of *Flying Saucer Review*. Many contactee tales of the 1950s and 1960s were similar to this: short and mostly copying previously told tales by more prominent contactees. Elizabeth Klarer's story, however, did not end with that 1956 magazine article. In the late 1970s, she would write an autobiography which retold her contact experience. This subsequent iteration bore almost no resemblance to the tale she told in 1956. We will return to Elizabeth's story in Chapter 7, and see how, instead of a bland tale of yet another jumpsuited Venusian, she wove a tale of romance, sexuality and fear of an uncertain future.

Howard Menger

Howard Menger's Contact stories began with a 1956 appearance on the "Long" John Nebel *Party Line* show. This overnight radio talk show

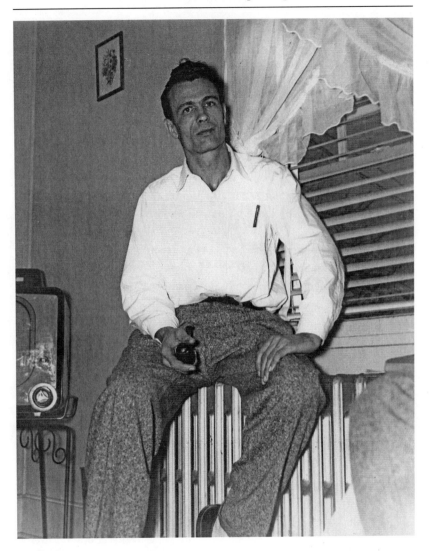

Howard Menger (date unknown), speaking to a gathering of flying saucer believers in his New Jersey home (courtesy Gray Barker Collection, Clarksburg-Harrison Public Library, Clarksburg, West Virginia).

became a template for later paranormal themed shows such as *Coast to Coast AM* and served as a venue for most of the major contactees of the 1950s and 1960s, as well as the more conventional flying saucer figures such as Major Donald Keyhoe and James Moseley.

Menger was a Second World War veteran and sign painter from New

Jersey who, to all appearances, led a normal life until his 1956 radio appearance. Coming on the air with fellow contactee George Van Tassel, Menger recounted a series of encounters with men and women from other planets which began when he was 10 years old. Menger spent the next few years telling his story on Nebel's radio show and at Van Tassel's Giant Rock flying saucer conventions, but did not publish a book until 1959, when Gray Barker's Saucerian Books released *From Outer Space to You*, Menger's one book, in which he detailed his story. This inversion of the usual book-tour-book-tour pattern means that Menger's book is the culmination of his extraterrestrial contact saga rather than an attempt to make a first impression. As such, it presents Menger's story and ideas in a fairly complete manner.

From Outer Space to You begins with Menger's childhood, when he first began to encounter the space brothers and sisters. For a ten-year-old boy, Howard Menger was remarkably perceptive. Recounting his first encounter with a space sister, "the most exquisite woman" he had ever seen, he describes her in terms that certainly seem to be from the perspective of a man older than ten:

> The warm sunlight caught the highlights of her long golden hair as it cascaded around her face and shoulders. The curves of her lovely body were delicately contoured — revealed through the translucent material of clothing which reminded me of the habit of skiers.... Even though very young, the feeling I received was unmistakable. It was a tremendous surge of warmth, love, and physical attraction which emanated from her to me.... She was about my mother's height, slender, lithe, with no exaggeration of voluptuous curves.

As the couple talked, it became clear that Howard Menger was more than a simple 10-year-old New Jersey boy. With words that would resonate throughout Menger's life, the woman told him, "'We are contacting our own.'... She spoke of a great change to take place in this country as well as the world. Wasteful wars, torture and destruction would be brought on by the misunderstandings of people." According to Menger, this encounter took place in 1932, so the events predicted could have presaged World War II. Here, Menger positions himself as having experiences which predated the dawn of the contactee phenomenon and, indeed, the flying saucer craze itself. George Adamski, George King, and others had well-established backgrounds in the mysterious to support their stories, so it is not surprising that Menger should attempt to create one. Much like Truman Bethurum, he is careful to assert that his experiences predate those of other contactees.[57]

Menger's contacts continued as he entered the army in 1942, first during training and then while on detached assignment with the Navy in Hawaii. Once again, he encounters a beautiful space woman and has an instant attraction to her: "She stood about 5' 6," with the dark, wavy hair falling over her shoulders and the tunic floating gracefully around the shapely contour of her body. I stopped in my tracks, staring at her in uncontrolled admiration.... I was filled with awe and humility, but not without a strong physical attraction one finds impossible to allay when in the presence of these women." As we have seen from the story of Truman Bethurum, the presence of beautiful space women was not unheard of. Menger's descriptions of these women move beyond Bethurum's awe-struck crush on Aura Rhanes. Menger's narrative carries a much stronger sexual undertone than Bethurum's (or any other contactees').[58]

As Menger went to battle in the Pacific Theater, fighting in the brutal island-hopping campaigns against the Japanese, his encounters with the space people continued. One contact in particular takes familiar concerns of extraterrestrial contactees and places them in a pre–Cold War context — another example of Menger's effort to establish his space brother credentials in a way that was unique among the contactees of the time. On Okinawa, site of some of the most vicious fighting of the Pacific War, Howard Menger had barely escaped a terrifying encounter with enemy soldiers, three of whom he had killed. Menger was distraught and soon afterward had another contact with a space brother. The space brother assured Howard that the United States would win the war, saving the world from the Germans, "who are far ahead in technical and scientific skills, and —(he paused)— you are yet to learn many things about their developments." The Japanese would soon surrender after their utter destruction by a new, horrifying weapon.[59]

Upon returning to the United States at war's end, Menger returned to New Jersey and picked up his civilian life. The contacts continued and, one day, he once again met the woman he had first encountered when he was a boy in 1932. She told him that the space people would continue to be in contact with him, but he must not reveal anything until the summer of 1957, after which time he should use every available channel of communication to spread the space people's message of enlightenment. Menger also received musical transmissions and ideas from his "friends" which would eventually be released on LP (Slate Records, #211). These regular, though secret, contacts and space-brother-possessed piano sessions continued through 1956.

In October 1956, Menger met George Van Tassel. As a result of their meeting, Menger's story broke a bit earlier than the space people had recommended. Menger made a number of public appearances and also lectured privately in his home. At one of these meetings he met a woman he called "Marla" (in reality Connie Weber); to his shock, he felt an enormous and initially inexplicable pull toward the woman. Menger's conclusion was that they had known each other in previous incarnations. All humans can see into their past lives if they get past the "memory blocks" that exist, Menger asserts: "All of us have past lives. Some have expressed themselves on this planet in other bodies, other locations, but none of us originated on Earth. Thus life is an endless variety of continual growth." It was in a previous life that Menger and Connie supposedly knew each other. Menger related that, in June 1946 — ten years earlier — a space sister had told him that he would meet her sister (from Venus, who had incarnated in the body of a New Jersey woman) and that the sister would "work with" him for the rest of his life. Menger assumed that it would be an older woman who would assist him with his lectures because, as he said, "a younger woman would conflict with my marital state."[60]

Despite this conflict, Connie was a "younger woman." Menger takes some time to explain "natural couples" — of which he and Connie were one, back on Venus in their previous incarnations — couples who are polar opposites and who complement each other in every way throughout time, even beyond death and reincarnation. Menger claimed that on Venus, "Their unions last hundreds of years and sometimes continued for several lifetimes." In contrast, Menger's Earthly marriage to his wife Rose Menger manifested "differences in mental and spiritual makeup" as his contacts grew more frequent. Eventually, the couple divorced and Menger married Connie. They would remain married until Howard's death in 2009.

Marla addressed her romance with Howard in her own book, *My Saturnian Lover*, which predated Menger's *From Outer Space to You* by a year. Writing as "Marla Baxter," she presented a fictionalized version of the romance between her and Menger (named as "Alyn" in the book). This seeming confirmation of the stories that Menger had been telling his audiences for the past couple of years helped to create an atmosphere of easier acceptance for Connie and Howard's stories and ideas. It also contributed to a kind of shared universe between their ideas. Menger's association with George Van Tassel also lent an air of additional truthfulness, as it was a different approach from the every-contactee-for-himself approach that typified the earliest days of the phenomenon. While the earliest contactees avoided actively undermining their fellow experiencers' stories and claims, this was one of the few examples of a "team-up" between contactees. Often, their stories contradicted each other enough to make such cooperation impossible.

Following Menger's discussions of his childhood connections with the space people and his visits to the Moon and other planets is a selection of "Questions and Answers about Flying Saucers." These explanations of various aspects of extraterrestrial lifeways contain the bulk of Menger's philosophizing and didactic use of the space visitors. The space visitors, Menger asserts, come from our own solar system. They come with peaceful intentions: "They say no man can leave his planet with the purpose of conquering or controlling another world. They are not hostile. They come in love and service to the Infinite Father." The space people do not eat meat. They have been visiting Earth for hundreds of thousands of years and the only reason this is not public knowledge is that the vast majority of humanity have ignored the message of the space peoples' chosen contacts. The contactees are those "born with an awareness of truth within themselves, or they are reborns [*sic*] from another planet, in which case their own are contacting them and awakening within them that one small spark of truth so that they 'become the flame of truth.'" What is that message? Why are they coming to Earth? According to Menger, "To try and awaken within us a yearning for higher understanding so we can help ourselves in preventing any further destruction of our planet, which could conceivably have a bad effect in our solar system."[61]

Menger spends some time on the social and political organization of the space people as well. "They do not have authorities or government officials of any kind. They live in peace and harmony and everyone knows what his or her particular talent is so that they work at that particular job — and they love their work.... They live in small communities, built in the forests and close to natural surroundings. They do not denude the land of all trees and shrubs and then build boxes. Their communities are kept small, usually contain no more than a few thousand people. They are spread out and decentralized." While most of the contactees focus on the geopolitical and military implications of the Cold War (and Menger does address this), he also, uniquely, addresses here the urban sprawl and homogenization of American suburbia as well as the struggles of Americans in the workaday world, pining away at jobs they neither loved nor were suited for. In this brief section, Menger echoes books of the time such as *The*

Organization Man and *The Crack in the Picture Window,* which critiqued the stultifying nature of stereotypical American suburban life in the early Cold War era.[62] Menger also devoted about a quarter of *From Outer Space to You* to the subject of nutrition, a trenchant topic in that age of increasingly processed foods and the emergence of the TV dinner.

Unusually for the contactees of the 1950s and 1960s, Menger more or less recanted his story barely a year after *From Outer Space to You* was published. In 1960, he appeared on television with radio host Long John Nebel, on whose show Menger had first publicly told his story. In his 1961 book *The Way Out World,* Nebel describes the live event thus:

> Howard [Menger] said nothing, and un-said most of what he had originally claimed. The show was a disaster. The show was sensational. All depending upon your point of view. Where he had once sworn that he had seen flying saucers, he now felt that he had some vague impression that he might have on some half-remembered occasion possibly viewed some airborne object — maybe.... Where he had formerly stated that he had been to the moon, he now suggested that this had most likely been a mental impression of the other side of his consciousness.... In other words, Howard Menger backed up, and backed up, until he fell into a pit of utter confusion and finally sank forever into the waters of obscurity.[63]

Menger continued to work on free energy devices through the end of his life, but he never again wove the elaborate contactee tales that won him notoriety in the first place.

Buck Nelson

Not all contactees were destined to become icons of the genre, like George Adamski or George King. Buck Nelson's story has often been held up as an example of the more humorous and outlandish extreme of the contactee phenomenon. Nelson was a farmer and rancher in Mountain View, Missouri, and beginning in 1954 he alleged a series of encounters with beings from Mars and Venus. His tale is folksy and colloquial (the effect of being dictated rather than written), somewhat vague, and utterly guileless. Fanny Lowery (who took the longhand dictation which became Nelson's short, self-published booklet) acknowledges that the story is difficult to comprehend but that it becomes easier "if you think of him as a person whose work is similar to that of JOHN the BAPTIST, foretelling the coming of a great teacher."[64]

Nelson's first encounter was on July 30, 1954. It is best told in his own words: "I was listening to my radio at my home at four o'clock in the afternoon when it began to go crazy wild. My dog too set up a barking and my pony outside began to raise all kinds of cain." He saw a flying saucer, which shot him with some sort of ray. Following this encounter, Nelson no longer had a need for eyeglasses and his longtime back pain had disappeared. On subsequent encounters, he met a number of the crew including Little Bucky. Originally from Colorado, Little Bucky had gone to live with the Venusians, where he taught English (which explains how the Venusians were able to communicate with contactees). Along with Little Bucky was another visitor, named Bob Solomon, who was 200 years old, but looked about 19 or so. Finally, Nelson met Big Bo, a 385-pound dog. As the title of his pamphlet implies, Nelson visited the Moon, Mars, and Venus.[65]

As other contactees did, Buck Nelson used his story as a platform for conveying political, cultural, and religious ideas and critiques. In Nelson's book these critiques are brief, dropped into the narrative. He presents few original ideas. Like George Adamski and others, he believes that the world would be a better place without war and asserts that human religion has gone off the rails since the time of the original teachers of those religions. Life on Venus is very unlike ours on Earth. The cars on Venus glide along the street without the need for wheels of any kind. There are "no roads, no police force, no jails, no government buildings and no wars." Taxes on Venus "compare to ours like a nickel compares to a hundred dollars."[66] Nelson also delivers unto humanity the "Twelve Laws of God" to which the Martians and Venusians adhere. These are, basically, a reworded Ten Commandments of the Old Testament combined with some extras. For example, the second Law adds "includes accidents and war" to the familiar "Thou shall [*sic*] not kill."[67]

Another standard contactee complaint, that of nuclear warfare, was the subject of a Christmas address which Little Bucky allegedly delivered to Buck Nelson and tape recorded on December 25, 1955. Little Bucky states: "This world must give up ATOMIC WEAPONS AND WARFARE. The next war, if fought, will be on American soil. America will be destroyed, then civilization all over the world will be destroyed.... We have stood by and seen other planets, one other, destroy itself. Is this world next? We wonder, and watch and wait."[68] During his Christmas visit with Little Bucky, Nelson learns that on Venus, things are just about the opposite of Earth and that — unsurprisingly — the Venusian way is better. Nelson goes on a bit of a tear about things that need to be improved in the United States. He narrows down his focus from the dangers of nuclear war to such topics as truth in advertising: "Advertising, just as anything else, should be truthful. Labels on cans, for instance, should tell the contents first, brand names afterword. Take a can of pork and beans; it should be labeled beans and then pork. Why should a sliver of pork have first place over a whole can of beans?"[69] This may be the most trivial concern ever expressed by a contactee.

Buck Nelson's down-home delivery and straightforward expression set him apart from contactees who were more polished, more attuned to what their public wished to hear. Nelson delivered lectures and appeared on television, all the while wearing his trademark bib overalls, not putting on any airs. Nelson did not assert his credibility through scientific explanations but by invoking the name of George Adamski, claiming that the original contactee accepted his story of Little Bucky, Bob Solomon, and Bo the giant space dog. Like Truman Bethurum, Nelson viewed George Adamski as a standard for truth and credibility.

The ending of this slim volume is strangely abrupt. After noting that Mrs. Lowery, his transcriptionist, has been working fairly diligently, writing his words in longhand, Nelson declares, "This tale is getting longer than the tail on the fireball I photographed in January, 1956 so I HAD BETTER QUIT."[70] The tone of *My Trip to Mars, The Moon, and Venus* is informal and unpretentious. Buck Nelson had no proof for his claims, beyond some very fuzzy photographs that show nothing distinct. Bob Solomon seems a very unlikely name for a Venusian, and the tales of Bo the Giant Space Dog made Nelson's stories more humorous than astounding or moving. Buck Nelson held a series of annual flying saucer conventions at his ranch, advertising for speakers, musicians and the like in ads at the end of his book. Like Andy Sinatra, the Cosmic Barber (see Chapter 2), Buck Nelson often falls into the category of novelty more so than other contactees. Despite the homespun goofiness of Nelson's story, it illustrates that no matter how outlandish the contactee tale, there is a substrate of serious concern.

The Legacy of the Early Contactees

The contactees whose contact experiences came after Adamski possessed similar concerns about the dangers of warfare and atomic weapons and the need for cooperation and understanding among the people of Earth. Few of them, however, gave any indication of holding these views before they published their contact stories. This fact does not diminish the significance of their calls for change, particularly in the areas of social and cultural change such as a desire for a more authentic spirituality and concerns about the economic inequalities of the time. Rather, it bolsters the significance of Adamski: Other saucer believers, seeing that Adamski had found a workable means to evangelize his message of peace and cooperation, decided to do so for themselves. Adamski's writings not only established a template that other contactees used to spread their messages about how humanity needed to change, but also created a mutual forum through which they could agree with Adamski's initial calls for change.

When evaluating the contactees, one cannot disregard the profit motive. In the 1950s and '60s, being a contactee meant that one sold books, was paid for lectures and public appearances, and, like George Van Tassel and George King, had the opportunity to start organizations which would continue to bring in money from members. The contactees' critics have used this profit motive to cast aspersions on the message the contactees spread. Logically, however, a contactee could have made the same money and sold the same number of books without the moral messages about peace and cooperation. Stories about otherworldly visitors and their advanced ships would have intrigued Americans, as evidenced by the number and popularity of science fiction comics, books, and films during the time. The fact that the contactees included these moral and philosophical lessons indicates a degree of sincerity (if not outright truth-telling) on their part.

Another important consideration is that not all contactees were on the same level, either commercially or in terms of their impact on the genre of contact narratives. George Adamski's writings served as a template for other contactees. George Van Tassel not only provided a focal point for contactee and other flying saucer believers with his Giant Rock conventions, but also established the Ashtar myth. No one ever imitated Buck Nelson, and despite his hosting flying saucer gatherings at his farm in Missouri, he is largely a forgotten figure (although Bo the Venusian dog seems to stick in most peoples' heads long after they've forgotten about poor Buck Nelson). Not every contactee was a superstar, but even those who were fleeting and now forgotten provide insight into the effects the contactees had on the world around them.

The international appeal of these contact stories is also important to keep in mind. Although the contactee movement was an American development, key contactees such as George Adamski, George Hunt Williamson and others had followings and readers outside of the United States. George King, also, began his contactee career in Britain before coming to the United States. The British magazine *Flying Saucer Review* was one example of the readiness with which British publications accepted contactee stories during the 1950s. In an uncredited, untitled editorial piece in a 1957 issue of *FSR,* the writer asserted:

> The right course of action for any individual now on Earth is to start applying in his or her daily life the teaching of the Illuminated Ones, who have repeatedly given to us the same message which is now stated to be coming from the space people: "Love ye one another." The message now coming through from all the contacts said to have taken place between those of other worlds and people living on this planet has been fundamentally the same.... Everyone knows that the world today is divided into two armed camps. Nuclear weapons and guided missiles are being tested at an ever-increasing tempo. The space people have pointed out the remedy. It is the same one that was prescribed 2000 years ago. It is up to us to follow that admonition. The alternative is to continue to play with our dangerous nuclear toys and accept the consequences of that pattern.[71]

This was written several years after the exposé which asserted the Earthly nature of Adamski's flying saucer photographs. Despite that blow to the credibility of Adamski — and by extension, other contactees — the editor of *Flying Saucer Review* saw value in the message of these storytellers.

Adamski and the other, subsequent contactees used their stories as a tool in their attempt to change American (and the larger western) society for the better. Though their stories were unbelievable to many and easily disproved — at least on a literal level — they succeeded in reaching many people who might never have heard their messages any other way. The contactees took messages of cooperation and peace, and warnings about the dangers of materialism and militarism, and wove them together with stories that capitalized on a mystery that had captured the public's attention. Tales of flying saucers held the interest of many Americans from their advent in 1947. George Adamski saw this, and adapted his beliefs and messages to the mythology of this new phenomenon. Other contactees, who appeared after Adamski, mimicked not only his style of storytelling but also many of the same messages. The question of whether this mimicry stemmed from agreement with his beliefs or an attempt to glom onto a popular genre was not as significant as the contactees' power to spread messages that challenged the Cold War paradigm of material consumption, military antagonism and the development of cataclysmically destructive weapon systems. The contactees who followed George Adamski challenged the existing order within a context that straddled the worlds of popular culture and esoteric spiritualism, providing something recognizable to vastly diverse audiences. From teenagers who might have started reading flying saucer magazines after viewing films like *This Island Earth* or *The Day the Earth Stood Still* to devotees of Edgar Cayce who sought out other examples of spiritual messages from beyond, contactees were denizens of a remarkably big tent.

5

The New Age

Extraterrestrial Contact
Since the 1970s

As discussed in Chapter 2, the published findings of the Condon Committee in 1968 had a dampening effect on enthusiasm for organized flying saucer investigation. Groups like APRO and NICAP saw declines in their membership and overall public interest in flying saucers began to ebb. Extraterrestrial contact narratives, however, continued to survive and evolve.

Channels and Cults: Contact in the 1970s and 1980s

The inaugural generation of contactees which emerged during the 1950s and 1960s reflected both the fears and the hopes of the Cold War. As this first period of contactee history drew to a close, the political, cultural, and social landscapes were changing. Wars in Southeast Asia and Africa illustrated the folly of a simplistic "us vs. them," good guys and bad guys conception of international affairs. From California to Prague, the children born in the shadow of the atom took to the streets demanding peace, freedom, change. As the 1970s dawned, Earth seemed a less straightforward place and the comfortable old dichotomies no longer seemed adequate for explaining the world. Accordingly, the contactee landscape would shift as well.

As in the 1950s and 1960s, contactees of the 1970s both reflected and sought to influence the world in which they lived. During this decade, however, contactee narratives went in several directions at once. Some contactees, such as Switzerland's Eduard "Billy" Meier, maintained a 1950s–style of story in which the contactee related stories of longstanding physical contact with extraterrestrial beings. Others gathered believers around them in groups that observers described variously as new religions or cults.

One of the key aspects of contactee narratives in the 1970s is their relation to the emergence of the New Age movement in the western world. The New Age movement was a combination of various esoteric and non-western religious and spiritual traditions including Buddhism and transcendental meditation, as well as aspects of Christian gnosticism and Theosophical thought. Evolving out of the various subcultural and countercultural movements of the late 1960s, the teachings of the New Age were similar to the spiritual notions which informed earlier contactee narratives in the 1950s.

While pre-existing Theosophical notions certainly contributed to the origins and development of the earliest contactee narratives, the flying saucer-consuming public was — largely — unaware of the Theosophical roots contained in some aspects of contactee writings. From the 1970s onward, however, the rising popularity of New Age ideas, books, and public figures meant that its connections with contactee stories (and flying saucer/UFO topics in general) became increasingly cemented in the public's collective mind. There had always been tension in the flying saucer research community between those who accepted contactee narratives and those (such as NICAP's Donald Keyhoe and APRO's Coral Lorenzen) who believed contacteeism to be detrimental to the public perception of flying saucers as worthy of institutional scientific investigation. In the wake of the Condon Report's (see Chapter 2) dismissal of the scientific value of saucer investigation, the rift between science and spirituality in the UFO world grew wider.

Those who championed a rational, scientific approach to understand what were increasingly called UFOs (as opposed to the more whimsical and less scientific-sounding "flying saucers") spent less of their time engaged in speculation and more time interviewing witnesses, making careful note of the particulars of each sighting, and cataloging reams of details and documentation. Contactees, in a corresponding move to the extreme, sometimes abandoned all attempts to convince the doubting. Channeled psychic messages and increasingly religious overtones came to dominate contact works in this decade.

Another important development in contacteeism during the 1970s was the emergence of criticism and commentary on contact narratives. Writers within the UFO/flying saucer community such as Jacques Vallee examined the nature of contactee narratives in ways that went beyond the simplistic exposé style of earlier years. Vallee examined the question of anomalous sightings and visitations by alleged extraterrestrial beings within the wider context of folklore, parapsychology, religion, and politics. At the risk of employing overused jargon, the writings of Jacques Valle constitute a metatextual layer that examines not just the paranormal (including contactee accounts), but which also examines belief in the paranormal.

JACQUES VALLEE AND THE "MESSENGERS OF DECEPTION"

By the 1970s, most self-described "serious," scientific-minded flying saucer researchers consistently and emphatically rejected the stories of direct psychic or physical contact with extraterrestrial beings. The UFO mainstream banished contactee stories to the fringes, their channeled messages ill-suited for a world dominated by nuts-and-bolts theories of interplanetary propulsion systems. Not all researchers, however, dismissed the contactees and groups of followers that materialized around them. Jacques Vallee, a French mathematician, computer scientist, and astrophysicist, first began writing about the phenomenon in 1965. After his initial investigations into the possible nature of the people's anomalous sightings, he turned to the connections between UFO/saucer stories and folklore. This pushed Vallee's inquires toward stories of contact with extraterrestrial beings; through them he explored parallels between modern and ancient stories of human/other-than-human contact.

Vallee's writing is a valuable resource to any student of contact culture. Vallee, in his writings on anomalies and contact culture, presented himself as an investigator rather than a detached scholar. Integrating himself with experiencers and their followers, he recorded the stories, beliefs, and motivations of many whose ideas may not have otherwise been preserved. Vallee, however, serves as a secondary rather than a primary source. His work interprets the phenomenon as an outsider rather than as an experiencer himself. Thus, we must be aware, in using Vallee as a source of information, that he has just as much of an agenda in telling the contactees' stories as the contactees have when they tell their own stories. Significantly, Vallee sees potentially sinister overtones in the spread of contact tales and —

especially — the belief systems that grow up around the assertions of contactees.

In his 1979 book *Messengers of Deception: UFO Contacts and Cults*,
Vallee argues, "The main effect of UFOs on their witnesses is a conditioning process.... The social process caused by the belief in the phenomenon
takes the form of new sects, movements, and 'contact' cults. Close observation ... shows they are monitored and in some cases deliberately manip-
ulated by occult groups, government organizations, and extremist political
groups."[1] While Vallee certainly discusses those who personally claim contact with extraterrestrial (or extradimensional, or interdimensional) beings,
he also goes further, interacting and questioning those who have not had
personal experiences but adhere to the political or religious teachings of
those who do. *Messengers of Deception* also provides valuable insight into
the stories of some little-known European contactees of the 20th century,
including those that had no connection with the wider world of extraterrestrial contactees in Europe or elsewhere.

Just as a historian's discussion of the ideas contained in a law, or a
religious text, or a novel is enhanced by testimony from people who were
affected by those texts, Vallee's work in *Messengers of Deception* gives us a
valuable window into the lives of those who encountered and, in some
cases, accepted — with varying degrees of enthusiasm — the teaching of
contactees. One group, concerned with what they called Human Individual
Metamorphosis, or HIM, attracted Vallee's attention in 1975. He attended
a meeting on the campus of Stanford University in San Francisco, California, after seeing a poster that claimed, "Two individuals say they were
sent from the level above human, and will return to that level in a space
ship (UFO) within the next few months. This man and woman will discuss
how the transition from the human level to the next level is accomplished,
and when this may be done."[2] At the meeting, the speaker claimed their
group was not intending to "defend ... or prove what we are going to say."
Rather, their teachings were aimed at those who, supposedly, were — on a
subconscious level — waiting for and willing to receive such information.
The unnamed speaker told of the leaders of their group ("The Two") who
had "come from a different level, a level above the human level, an actual,
physical level out in space." Those at the meeting could also transition to
this next physical level. As evidence, sometime in the subsequent two
months, The Two would die and — after three days — come back to life.[3]

One of the things that, at the outset, distinguish a belief system such

as this from the earlier stories of contactees is the emphasis on the importance of becoming something other than human. As this meeting's speaker
pointed out, "A lot of people are really tired of playing the human game,
and a lot of people have already copped out and left, in their own way,
for different reasons. There are some people who are just tired ... even
though they really love the Earth, and care about things here, feel an urge
... to move to something higher."[4] There is a despair to these words; a sad
realization that humanity and human-ness is a dead-end street. For young
people growing up in the chaos of the late 1960s and coming of age in
post–Vietnam, post–Watergate America, there might have been something
appealing about leaving behind not just America, not just the Earth, but
the essence of one's very biology. The tone is far less optimistic than earlier
contactee tales. The organization led by The Two — Marshall Applewhite
and Bonnie Nettles — became known as Heaven's Gate and would continue
with varying fortunes for two more decades until the 1997 mass suicide of
Applewhite and 38 fellow believers (see Chapter 2).

Vallee saw a connection between the goals and teachings of HIM and
events that had allegedly befallen a Spanish man named Jacques Bordas.
As a child, Bordas was weak and sickly. After an encounter at age 12 with
a group of small, but human, beings who gave him a special "candy," Bordas overcame his sickliness and, indeed, became incredibly hale and fit,
his muscles and tissues changing. The beings who gave strength and health
to Bordas would continue to visit him over the years, their messages taking
on political overtones, telling Bordas that "social structure and religion"
will have to change before humanity can achieve a higher level of evolution.
While the trappings of Bordas's story are similar to many contactee tales,
Bordas did not write books or make public appearances. He only spoke
to Vallee reluctantly and because he had been receiving mysterious phone
calls telling him he was going to undergo another physical transformation.[5]

In the contact tales of Jacques Bordas and HIM, in the contactee
beginnings of Räel's religious movement (see Chapter 2), and in the claims
of George Adamski, George Hunt Williamson, and others, Jacques Vallee
discerned a distinct pattern of agitation for political, social, and religious
change. Vallee came to a number of conclusions in *Messengers of Deception*
that — in his mind — suggested a widespread effort to alter the course of
human society. He saw the contactees' tales as driving a wedge between
scientific institutions and the public, as scientists used the outlandish stories

of the contactees as an excuse to ignore the wider phenomenon. He saw the contactees' claims as undermining "the image of human beings as masters of their own destiny." Most troublingly, he argued, "Contactee philosophies often include belief in higher races and in totalitarian systems that would eliminate democracy."[6] The gamut of New Age beliefs circulating in the Western world during the 1970s, of which the various strands of contactee belief were just one example, was indicative to Vallee of a rejection of science and reason that might have a disastrous effect on humanity. The visitors and their message, and the growing assumption that such visitors would lead humanity in the right direction, was potentially alarming: "They are not necessarily coming from nearby stars. *In terms of the effect on us, it doesn't matter where they come from....* People look up toward the stars in eager expectation. Receiving a visit from outer space sounds almost as comfortable as having a God. Yet we shouldn't rejoice too soon. Perhaps we will get the visitors we deserve."[7]

In writing *Messengers of Deception*, Jacques Vallee made an argument for a rigorous, scientific effort to investigate claims of unidentified flying objects and claims of the paranormal. For the scientific establishment to ignore or ridicule them — as had been happening since the release of the Condon Committee report — invites blind belief and the possibility of manipulation. Vallee saw the contactees and their claims as potential dupes of dark forces bent on shaping the future of humanity and bending it to their will. His view is conspiratorial — the contactees and their followers could be, unwittingly, tools of dark powers. This approach removes a good deal of the political and social agency from the contactees. Vallee, in *Messengers of Deception*, views the contactees as reactive. They are not, however, reacting to feat of nuclear annihilation but, rather, to the machinations of dark forces.

BILLY MEIER

One of the most enduring contactee figures to come out of the 1970s is Eduard "Billy" Meier of Switzerland. Perhaps no other contactee since George Adamski has been the subject of so much attention, particularly efforts to debunk his claims. Much of this scrutiny has come from other UFO researchers. Certainly Meier has had more written about him than any other contactee. This is mostly because of his hundreds of photographs of alleged flying saucers. The philosophical teachings related through his contact experiences have received less attention than the photographs. The content of these messages, however, is significant in that they place Meier firmly in the same category as earlier contactees, demonstrating continuity between the American contactees of the 1950s and a Swiss farmer in the 1970s.

Meier's contact claims began in the mid–1970s when he released his photographs and established an organization centered around his contact experiences and teachings, the Freie Interessengemeinschaft für Grenz- und Geisteswissen-schaften und Ufologiestudien (in English, "Free Community of Interests for the Fringe and Spiritual Sciences and UFOlogical Studies"), or FIGU. Meier began reaching a wide audience in the United States during the 1980s and 1990s when flying saucer researcher and publisher Wendelle Stevens published over 1000 pages of translations of Meier's "contact notes" compiled from his experiences in the mid to late 1970s.

Stevens's release of these contact notes, published in four volumes between 1988 and 1995, is more troublesome in terms of provenance than contact accounts originally composed in English. First, of course, is the issue of translation. Stevens reported that he rejected translator after translator because they kept inserting their own philosophy into the translation. He settled on a "transliterated" version of the text which is awkward to read, but — Stevens argues — is devoid of any sort of philosophical or religious slant.[8] Despite this laudable goal of presenting Meier's views as faithfully as possible, Stevens demonstrated a heavy hand in the editing process, stating that he had "purged these notes of defamatory and slandrous [sic] statements about personalities, of unnecessary redundancy, and of harsh comments on our religious and political systems."[9] This expurgation is, presumably, one of the reasons why Meier requested that Stevens cease publishing and selling his unauthorized editions of Meier's contact notes. Stevens refused to stop, arguing that the public good was served through the release of Meier's contact tales. This editing of religious and political information, however, does illustrate the emphasis placed on contact tales by those deeply invested in stories of extraterrestrial visitation. The emphasis in Stevens's edition (expressed through his annotations) is in the "space alien" aspects of Meier's story. Where Meier's contacts hail from, their ships, possible corroborating evidence — from Wendelle Stevens's point of view, these are the most important things one could gain from the contact notes. Meier's views on religion and politics are side issues which one can safely ignore. Despite what might be missing from Stevens's English translations of the Meier contact notes, the Stevens version is significant because it was the format through which English-speaking saucer enthusiasts and researchers first experienced Meier's ideas and messages.

The Billy Meier story is a several-decades-long epic. The epic comprises hundreds of photographs, thousands of pages of text, hours of documentary film footage and interviews, and numerous "representatives" (some official, some not) conveying Meier's views beyond Switzerland. For the past 10 years, Meier and his advocates have had a significant presence on the Internet as well. Those who would claim to have their own experiences with the beings from the Pleiades would also appropriate Meier's ideas, themes and characters. Despite the overall massiveness of the ongoing Meier saga, both his treatment of other contactees and his discussion of human religious beliefs provides an important point of comparison between Meier and other contactees, allowing us to understand his story in the wider context of extraterrestrial contact narratives rather than getting bogged down in the thousands of individual claims and details in the four decades of Meier material. One particularly significant aspect of Meier's universe of contact claims is that they have continued consistently since the 1970s. His followers have developed an elaborate collection of Meier's material (and Meier-inspired speculation) on the Internet that they regularly update. Thus, researchers have a fairly extensive record of how Meier's ideas have developed over the years and how different followers have reacted to the messages. The Meier contacts are an ongoing saga, and subsequent contacts serve to interpret current events. Translations from the original German, as usual, represent a difficulty for researchers, as there are shades of meaning that can be lost through the process.

Meier claimed he first experienced an extraterrestrial encounter at the age of five, in 1942. Throughout his life he had experiences with human-like beings hailing from near the Pleiades as well as the "DAL universe," a realm existing parallel to our own. In January 1975, Meier had his first encounter with the Pleiadian woman Semjase, with whom he would have the most contact. Semjase would later be immortalized as the namesake of Meier's and FIGU's headquarters, the Semjase Silver Star Center. Details of Meier's contacts are often disseminated to a small group of enthusiasts in Sweden — despite the efforts of figures within the UFO research community to debunk his photographs and claims of extraterrestrial contact. Like Stevens, however, these attempts to discredit Meier focus heavily on the "space alien" aspects of his story rather than on exploring his philosophical and religious ideas.

At the outset of the contact notes compiled by Wendelle Stevens, we learn that Billy Meier, according to Semjase, was special among humans. Her people had attempted to make contact with humanity but found their chosen subjects to be too fearful and weak to successfully proclaim the Pleiadians' truth to the people of Earth. Other "boastful" humans, she explained, "come up, pretending contact with us and pretending even have flown in the ships.... Those are nothing more than deceivers who sun themselves in doubtful glory and want to profit from all." Another lie, as described by Semjase, was the claim that contactees were "in contact with [other] planetary human beings of your solar system." This, she explains, is impossible because these planets "are so desolate that human life is not even possible there."[10]

One of the goals of Meier's visitors, then, was to "warn the Earth humans of these creatures.... They even have destroyed whole planets or beaten their inhabitants into barbarous bondage." Meier, as the representative of Semjase's people to humanity, had a duty to expose as frauds — basically — the vast majority of the contactees who had preceded him. This is unusual for contactee narratives. Typically, there was some attempt to avoid undermining other contactees stories. This was something of a practical concern, as contactees would often appear together at conventions such as those at Giant Rock, and bad blood would be bad for business. Meier, being separated from the mainstream of contactee culture as well as the larger flying saucer events and organizations, had more leeway to try to distinguish himself from other contactees.

Despite Wendelle Stevens's assertion that he had excised comments critical of religion from the Billy Meier "contact notes," criticism of mainstream religious thought "and the connected underdevelopment of the human spirit" is central to Semjase's mission to communicate with Meier. According to Semjase, "Above everything there remains but one that possesses the power of life and death over each creature.... This is the CREATION alone, which has laid its laws over all." The typical human concept of God is incorrect, she said. God is merely "a human being who exercises a powerful reign of tyranny over his fellow creatures." Sadly, "the human being hunts for his religious wrong beliefs and affirms God being the Creation itself.... He goes even further and pretends a normal Earthman by the name of 'Immanuel' who is also called 'Jesus Christ' is God's son and the creation itself."[11] Earth religion, then, is largely wrong. This is a distinct difference from the religious messages of other contactees who, for example, affirm the existence of a vaguely Judeo-Christian God and save their criticism for Earthly religious institutions and hierarchies. Meier's assertion of Jesus being a "normal Earthman" is also a shift away from prevalent contactee doctrine, which places Jesus (or "Sananda Jesus") among the pantheon of ascended masters.

Humble Eduard "Billy" Meier, then, is apparently the first human who is capable of comprehending and successfully disseminating the Pleiadians' message to the people of Earth. Billy was prepared for this from before his current incarnation on Earth — in past lives he was the Biblical prophets Enoch and Elijah, among others.[12] Meier was also the best candidate to be the Pleiadians' representative because he already had knowledge of the spiritual truths humanity needed to hear. Samjese said:

> We know that you are aware of a secret old scripture whose originals were unfortunately destroyed.... Diffuse and spread the transmission of the scripture, because it is the only one which is authentic truth.... To us it seems the most important book to be written, but it will be harsh in language and will meet with hate.... But it is finally able to destroy, for many, the madness of religion, or at least to temper it very deliberately.[13]

The book she spoke of is the *Talmud of Jmmanuel* ("Jmmanuel" being the Pleiadian-approved spelling of "Immanuel"). According to Meier and his supporters, Billy Meier and a former Orthodox priest, Isa Rashid, discovered this text — originally in Aramaic — in the Old City of Jerusalem in 1963. Meier claims that the *Talmud of Jmmanuel* is the foundational text of the Gospel of Matthew and was really written by Judas Iscariot. The truths contained in this book, which Meier was commanded to reveal, have had dangerous consequences:

> This is the book that none of the major religions want you to read. Having translated 36 chapters of the scrolls from Aramaic to German, Isa Rashid ultimately paid with his life when he and his family were assassinated by the powers that be but not before 36 chapters were sent to his friend in Switzerland, who then assembled the text into the form presented in this book.

Once again, Meier is special and distinct from other humans. Even Isa Rashid was not in Meier's league — there is now a new edition of the *Talmud of Jmmanuel* in which Meier corrected the "many errors that were made by Isa Rashid during the translation from Aramaic to German."[14] Meier's work on the *Talmud of Jmmanuel*, along with his other statements condemning Earth religious systems, has resulted in 22 separate assassination attempts "from both terrestrial and extraterrestrial human beings."[15]

Like many contactees, Meier connected the activities of his extraterrestrial friends with both the distant human past and the politics of the human present. Meier developed an extensive cosmology involving not only the Pleiadians, but also evil creatures known as the Giza Intelligences who have attempted, through various means, to dominate the peoples of Earth. For thousands of years, as summarized by the Billy Meier Wiki, the Giza Intelligences have

> deceived Earth humankind with religious "miracles" and "visions" of every kind, in order to maintain, and to yet further increase, the religious delusion with the plan of eventually appearing as angels and gods, as they have done in earlier times, and subjugating a voluntarily worshipful Earth humankind. They also had an alternative plan whereby they would also try to reach their goal by barbaric violence and a third world war. Two thirds of terrestrial humanity would have been annihilated and die a horrible death.

In keeping with Meier's views on the fallibility of and negative influence of Earth's religious belief systems, it is unsurprising that they, also, are the result of the machinations of the Giza Intelligences, who "played a major role in the creation of the malicious falsification that is the New Testament." Earth humanity, according to Meier's teachings, has been subject to the whims of malevolent intelligences since the beginning of recorded history. Fortunately for Earth, the friendly Pleiadians captured and expelled the evil Giza Intelligences in May 1978 after they attacked Billy Meier's headquarters. Sadly, humanity will continue to feel the negative effects of their actions for several hundred more years.[16]

In addition to the ongoing effect of the Giza Intelligences' activities, there is another force on Earth that Semjase the Pleiadian (through Meier) identify as harmful to humanity. These are the "Hebraons," "Hebrons," or as known in modern English, "Hebrews." According to Semjase/Meier, this group of people were "the real dregs of society and outcasts of earthmankind, because they constantly incited fights and quarrels within the whole world, which is still maintained until the present.... Peace on Earth will finally be then, when this mightthirsty [sic] and murderous self-called Hebraon race-connection has become completely scattered." Worse, they declared themselves the "first-born people and the chosen ones, as their descendents [sic], the Jews of today still dare to pretend this."[17] In the years since the publication of these initial contact notes, Billy Meier and his followers have sought to soften the anti–Semitism of the claim that the Jews have caused a great deal of the world's problems and that there cannot not be peace until they are "scattered."

In 2004, German FIGU representative Christian Frehner, writing on behalf of the FIGU, asserted the organization condemns all racism, particularly anti–Semitism: "As has been emphasized again and again (during the talks between Billy and his ET friends) is the fact that if, e.g., Israel is accused of crimes etc., it is never meant that the whole people of Israel (or the USA, etc.) is blamed or made responsible for the bad things that are happening." Frehner uses the opportunity of establishing a divide between criticism of the political state of Israel and the Jewish people to launch into a denunciation of the entire existence of the Jewish state: "I want to add my opinion that the foundation of the state of Israel after WWII was a severe mistake and should never have occurred…. But I also don't think that Israel will exist long into the future if it doesn't change its war-mongering and suppressing politics and thinking and acting."[18] This attempt to divest the *policy* direction of Meier and the Pleiadians goes further into territory that some critics could describe as anti–Semitic or — at least — a bit virulent in its denunciation of Israel's creation and somewhat sinister suggestion that it will soon disappear.

Another example of this attempted softening is the increasing stridency of their assertions that such criticisms are aimed at the political entity of Israel rather than a particular ethnically or culturally specific group of people. Contact 215 allegedly took place between Meier and a Pleiadian named Quetzal on February 28, 1987. During this contact, Meier wished to know the truth about "the massacre of the Palestinian refugees in Sabra and Shatila in the year 1982" in which "more than 3,000 people were brutally and bestially murdered." Specifically, Meier wanted to know "who the main responsible person was or who the main responsible persons were." Quetzal identifies the perpetrators as Ariel Sharon and Menachem Begin, who "secretly decided upon the massacre" using "Christian militias." According to Quetzal/Meier, Sharon himself, whom the Pleiadian "predicts" will one day be Israeli Prime Minister, "thinks the Palestinians look better dead than alive." Sharon is also an "unusually aggressive man and a Palestinian-hater, as well as a murderous element who doesn't shy away from any atrocities, as is also true of Begin."[19]

In contrast to the anti–Semitic comments about the ancient "Hebraon" peoples, Meier bases this criticism of Israel's actions in 1982 during the Lebanese Civil War on largely verifiable evidence and events. Despite the harsh language directed at Sharon and Begin, this goes a distinctly political direction rather than a spiritual or even paranormal direction. In this seg-

ment of Contact 215, the only supernatural feature is the existence of the
Pleiadian Quetzal. The discussion of Israel's policies and the desire for
change expressed by Meier and his followers places the Meier/Pleiadian
contacts firmly in the contactee tradition of urging political or social
change. Even the anti–Semitic tone of the writings echo the references to
"International Bankers" used in the writings of contactees of the 1950s and
1960s.

Another example of the political bent — especially large-scale issues
that effect whole regions or, indeed, the entire planet — is a petition on
population control compiled and publicized by followers of Billy Meier's
teachings and based on warnings given by the Pleiadians through Meier.
The following list of effects of overpopulation is lengthy (and only a selection of the concerns expressed in the petition), but indicates the seriousness
with which the Meier's followers consider the question of population control:

> Famines, energy shortages, epidemics ... degeneration, terrorism, dictatorship,
> anarchism, slavery ... racial hatred ... hatred towards asylum-seekers; radioactive
> emissions, chemical pollution of water, air, plants, food, human beings and
> animals. Crime, murder, mass murders, manslaughter; alcoholism, hatred of
> strangers, oppression, hatred of one's fellowman, extremism, sectarianism, drug
> addiction, overpopulation, annihilation of animal species, war, violence, torture
> and capital punishment, general mismanagement, water contamination, erad-
> ication of plant species; hatred, vice, jealousy, lovelessness, lack of logic, false
> humanitarianism ... and the lack of living space.

In short, blame for nearly everything that goes wrong in the world can be
laid at the feet of overpopulation. There is no explanation exactly how
overpopulation contributes to both dictatorship and anarchism, for example. According to the petition, the ideal population of the Earth is 529
million — any more than this is beyond the ability of the Earth to support.

According to the petitioners, the solution to the problem of overpopulation is a seven-year total ban on any procreation, followed by a one-
year period where births would be possible within certain strict criteria
including "an existing marriage of at least 3 years," "Proof of health, no
hereditary and infectious diseases, no addiction to illegal or prescription
drugs or to alcohol, etc.," and "No affiliation with extremist or subversive
groups." This would be followed by another seven-year ban on reproduction. This pattern would continue until the Earth's population stabilized
at 529 million. Penalties for unauthorized childbearing are harsh, including

sterilization and seizure of children, after which they would be raised by the state.[20]

The petition writers provide no documentation for the claims about population growth beyond references to Billy Meier's contact reports. Despite the petition's existing only on an unauthorized Billy Meier Wiki, there are hundreds of "signatures," many of them quoting Meier in their support of the petition's goals and methods. The goals and methods described in this petition would require a vast shift in governmental policy and, indeed, in the nature of government, including an expansion of global governance. Like the writings of Meier and his followers on the geopolitics of the Middle East, this petition on overpopulation and the need for birth restrictions transcends the outlandish nature of contact with humanoid extraterrestrials and takes Meier's narratives into the realm the political and social change and reform. Like the contactees of the United States in the 1950s and 1960s, Billy Meier's stories of the Pleiadians' visits serve as a vehicle for very down-to-Earth concerns. Strong views on politics, religion, and social policy all emerge in Meier's contact narratives. Meier's story and movement emerged after Jacques Vallee (who considered Meier's photos to be fraudulent) published *Messengers of Deception*, but many of the messages promulgated by Meier and his followers adhere to the pattern Vallee set out. Meier's stories and claims work toward actively undermining religious traditions and — in his followers' desired implementation of birth restriction policies — basic conceptions of liberty and freedom.

Another strong similarity between Meier's contacts and those of the classic American contactees is an air of self-aggrandizement. Meier is not just a reincarnated Pleiadian (an origin which is reminiscent of Howard Menger), he is the only human on Earth the Pleiadians had found who was capable both of understanding and successfully disseminating such important information. These connections place Meier firmly into the same constellation of contactees such as George Adamski and George Van Tassel, demonstrating that the contactee movement was not confined to the United States in the 1950s and 1960s but rather continued to expand and evolve.

TUELLA AND ASHTAR COMMAND

During the 1970s and 1980s the figure of Ashtar and the concept of Ashtar Command re-emerged in the extraterrestrial contact narrative world. This time, cutting through the voices and providing a degree of unification was a figure calling herself Tuella, whose real name was Thelma

B. Terrill. Tuella's channelings from Ashtar and other beings continued the work of George Van Tassel but with a different focus. Van Tassel spent a great deal of time in his messages discussing the origins of humanity and the universe, spinning explanations of scientific phenomena and the operating principles behind extraterrestrial technology. Tuella, in contrast, weaves a story of a vast interplanetary political and social system. She develops the bland voices of Ashtar, Kuthumi, Hatonn, and others into a cast of characters who interact with each other and with her. Tuella also pushed an agenda of spiritual enlightenment and internal, personal transformation.

In the preface to her 1982 book *Project: World Evacuation*, Tuella discusses the possibility that some of her readers might be extraterrestrials inhabiting human bodies or working toward some manner of enlightenment or connection with higher powers:

> If your inner truth identifies you as a volunteer from another realm or world on an assignment to Earth, these words are for you! If you are persuaded you are one of the "Star People," you will read this volume with awareness and clarity. If you are a disciple or initiate of the Higher Revelation, you will discern and perceive the purpose of this message from other dimensions of being. If you are a growing, glowing Christian, just beginning to look up, and outward beyond the walls of manmade divisions of earthly ecclesiastical hierarchies, your heart will witness to these things. If you are not consciously any of these, read not to scoff, but to hold these revelations in your heart while you "wait and see."

Thus, this book is for nearly everyone except the actively, aggressively skeptical. Here, as with the more religiously oriented contact groups that emerged in the 1970s, there is less of a spiritual division between the contactee and her audience. Tuella is the one channeling the various ascended masters who orbit the Earth, but you —*you!*— dear reader, may actually *be* one of these masters. You just need, Tuella is saying, some spiritual prompting.[21]

Project: World Evacuation serves as an introduction to the Ashtar Command's plan for Earth and humanity. Unlike the messages from beyond that circulated in the 1950s and 1960s, there is a sense of fatalism in the mission and humanity's ultimate destiny. The visitors from beyond, led by the Lord Sananda Jesus, have sent messengers to teach humanity how to achieve "an elevated approach to life" since the beginning of time. Some listened, many did not. Now, according to Ashtar Command,

> it is time to separate those groups in keeping with their choices, and let those who refuse the advancement of their being remain together according to their

own desires. The few who have burned within their hearts to find the Ultimate Reality will be permitted to follow these aspirations in the setting of a New World, cleansed and made bright by Universal action.[22]

In some ways, this is a logical development of the contactee tales of the 1950s and 1960s. Adamski, Menger, Van Tassel, and the rest conveyed messages to humanity from their cosmic brethren. Between the 1960s and the 1980s, there was no indication that humanity had changed at all. Indeed, one could make the argument that humanity had regressed rather than progressed in the areas of love, service, and peace. Thus, the time has come for humanity to reap the consequences of its behavior. Thus, there are two recurring themes in the channeled extraterrestrial contact narratives of the 1980s and 1990s: *this won't go on forever* and *which side are you on?* Unlike earlier contactee stories, however, the change required of humanity is not merely societal or political, but internal and spiritual as well.

The contactees of the 1950s and 1960s urged humanity to take positive steps to change their behavior and fate, such as eliminating nuclear weapons, war, greed, and so on. Such things are, however, policy issues. Ashtar, speaking through Tuella, asserts that for the challenges facing humanity (and humanity's friends among the stars), solutions are much more complex: "Inner disturbances taking pace within the planet itself are direct reflections of the aspirations and the attitudes and vibrations of those who dwell upon it. We have repeatedly attempted to turn the thoughts of humanity toward the reality of Divine Truth and Principles. We have dared to lower our craft into your frequencies in a visible way."[23] Thus, the negative effects suffered by the Earth and its people are not only the result of the military and ecological policies of the world's political and economic leaders, but of the internal spiritual attitudes of humanity.

These vibrational disturbances have a direct effect on the physical planet and those living upon it. Ashtar's associate Kuthumi explains that the time has come for humanity to escape the Earth: "Planetary changes have already taken place on inner levels within the auric field and the astral belt and surrounding regions. Soon, these emanations will penetrate the physical octave and those who dwell thereon.... The Highest Celestial Councils have decreed that those chosen ones shall be personally removed from Earth, to be temporarily placed in a higher frequency, within our domain." Given the need for the "chosen ones" to be removed from the planet, the Ashtar Command has a plan in place for the rescue of those who are worthy. Kuthumi claims there are missions of "volunteers" on the planet who are "filled with light, complete in their dedication and consecration to serve the Celestial government, the Solar Hierarchy and the Intergalactic Confederation."[24]

Though the inner vibrational frequencies of the human race is one of the contributing factors to the impending crises facing Earth, more prosaic military and political policy issues are also a of concern to the forces of light surrounding the planet. In this way, the channeled communication "compiled" by Tuella shows itself to be firmly in the same cultural school of thought as other contactee narratives. Hatonn, "a Great Commander from a very high-ranking station" who is "honored by all," has much to say about the condition of humanity: "Why would you seek to destroy [the Earth], O man? Cannot your differences be reconciled in a peaceful way?"

Humanity, however, is not alone. Hatonn describes the scope of the problem:

> There were times eons ago when some of our worlds had not yet found this solution. In their torment and thrust for power over others, they did also seek the great weapons of destruction and did cause much havoc within many constellations.... Out of these problems, we of the Galactic Federation of Planets formed the Galactic Pact, which forbids warfare against another and the warlike ones who would not yield were removed from our midst.
>
> Now your world has projected itself into this chaotic time of unrest and threat due to the calculations of a few in your midst who will not yield to the peaceful way or the attitude of peace and love on Earth.... Therefore, it is ordained that before this orbit into the Golden Age is fulfilled, the Earth will be prepared for its advancement by many changes. War will be removed, outlawed, from your planet, and all of the impurities of your way of life will be filtered away by the changing scene due to begin. There will be much turmoil in your midst and much sorrow for those who have sought to instigate bloodshed upon Terra.[25]

While this discussion of human geopolitical foolishness and destruction is similar to that of the earlier contactees, here there is an even more patronizing tone directed toward the people of Earth. Unlike Orthon, Firkon, or other Space Age space brothers, Hatonn is taking the opportunity for change away from humanity. There is, again, a sense of fatalism. It is, according to Hatonn, likely that humanity will be unwilling to turn from its ways. Thus, the forces of light feel justified in taking that choice away from humanity, rescuing those whose spirits are elevated to the proper level, and dealing with those who have not attempted to improve themselves.

There is one case, however, where direct intervention in the affairs of humanity — beyond the rescue of the faithful — is justified:

> We, therefore, have been authorized by the Spiritual Hierarchy, to intervene in the affairs of Earth in the event of attempted nuclear holocaust.... Intervention will come to you in the form of cataclysms of great magnitude. We plead with Mankind ... to lay aside your arms and dismantle your stockpiles of death....
>
> I do now give my attention to the peacemakers among you. Your efforts are carefully recorded and every effort of love to extend love amongst your fellows shall not be forgotten, but your reward shall come to you. Further, you will not be expected to be a participant in the destructions you have labored so faithfully to avert. You will be removed from the chaos and be sheltered in our ships that will come to escort you to safety. I have many times visualized this great event in my mind, marveling at the efficiency of the Plan and the expertise of those who will bring it to completion.[26]

This chain of potential events falls short of a prediction. There is enough "what-if" space in Hatonn's message that if no nuclear exchange takes place during the lifetime of Ashtar enthusiasts and adherents, there is unlikely to be a feeling of letdown. If such an event, however, were to occur, the space brothers have an extensive plan in place to deal with it, an idea which provides a degree of comfort to those who believe in the message.

In addition to the parallels with the 1950s and 1960s contactees, Hatonn's account is reminiscent of the notion of Pre-Tribulation Rapture in some strands of Christian eschatological thought. This interpretation of the New Testament asserts that faithful Christians will be taken up into Heaven prior to the reign of the Anti-Christ on Earth. The overall effect of these ideas is the same — to illustrate a dichotomy between those who are faithful to a doctrine and those who are unfaithful, and to designate rewards and punishments to each group based on their positions and actions. This reflection of a spiritual or theological component to the ideas Hatonn (through Tuella) presents is consistent with the overall spiritual approach of the Tuella-channeled materials. Where Orthon, George Adamski's contact from Venus, spoke against atomic weapons testing and development, he did so to prevent vaguely explained — but scientific-sounding — dangers to the solar system. When Hatonn makes the same demands of humanity, he does so because he has been "authorized by the Spiritual Hierarchy." This heavy spiritual emphasis is the key difference between the contact narratives of the Space Age and those of the New Age.

This increased emphasis on the spiritual aspects of the space brothers and the consequent near-absence of anything that might be considered scientific (or even pseudo-scientific) is a logical consequence of the outcome of the Condon Committee's report. That event diminished the necessary connection between contact and science. As public enthusiasm for flying saucer tales diminished in the 1970s and 1980s, contactees found themselves increasingly preaching to a smaller and smaller choir.

Along with the spiritual emphasis, another notable aspect of Tuella's writings is the manner in which she describes the individual space brothers she channels. While earlier contactees may have had generally good impressions of the extraterrestrials with whom they interacted, Tuella positively gushes with admiration for the beings she channels. She introduces Ashtar, for example, as

> a Beloved Christian Commander and a very beautiful Being. He is highly evolved in the upper worlds, very influential, and has a great benefactoring influence upon those he leads.... In the Alliance of the Space Confederation, Commander Ashtar is the highest in authority for our hemisphere. He is also the Commander of the Star Ship upon which our Beloved Lord and Great Commander, Jesus-Sananda, spends so much of His time. He has the authority to clear any channel and interrupt and take over any communication from any source at any time, upon our planet; yet he is gentle, loving, devout, and totally inspiring as a great Leader.[27]

Ashtar is not the only member of the Intergalactic Forces of Light who receives such adulation. During the course of an intergalactic council, Ashtar introduces one of the speakers:

> The speaker for this morning session is one of the most respected members of our Commands, having served the Confederation in many capacities and many examples of his great concern for the people of Earth. He stands as their protector at this hour, and represents them in our major councils. His words and decisions are of great importance to all of us, and I join with you in earnest attention to his words. I bring forward our friend and brother ... Monka![28]

Tuella introduces Hatonn, the space brother who explains about the potential intervention on Earth in the event of nuclear war, as "a great Leader honored by all. He truly exemplifies the spirit of Love."[29]

Tuella's fawning treatment of Ashtar continues in 1985's *Ashtar: A Tribute*. The three sections of this book are devoted to "Ashtar the Man," "Ashtar and the Mission," and "Ashtar and the Message." The second and third parts largely repeat the messages of *Project: World Evacuation*, while the first consists of a series of detailed descriptions of Ashtar's physical appearance, spiritual goodness, and highly desirable leadership qualities. Tuella — perhaps unsurprisingly — dedicates the book to Ashtar, calling him "a friend and brother and my beloved Commander, with whom I serve the kingdom of God on earth and the Light of our Radiant One." In laying out the contents of the book, she explains:

> [W]e have attempted to compile those fragments which would best help us to discern the heart of this beloved Being, to appreciate his spiritual burden, his exemplary character, his depth of purpose, his unswerving loyalty to Our Radiant One and his dedication to the Kingdom of God on Earth. May the aura of his Light and his Love touch you as you read, to enjoy, to absorb, to be quickened to new heights of spiritual understanding and attainment.[30]

One interesting aspect of the book is that Tuella includes a variety of channeled messages and contributions from contactees around the world. While Tuella was the key figure associated with the Ashtar channelings of the 1980s, it is important to remember that this was not a one-woman show.

Apart from the obvious purpose of praising every aspect of Ashtar's appearance, character, and importance, one of the purposes of *Ashtar: A Tribute* is to define Ashtar's role within the cosmic hierarchy and — in doing so — more closely establish continuity between the channeled messages of Tuella and her contemporaries and those messages and visits experienced by the Space Age contactees such as George Van Tassel. While these connections were implicit in the themes of *Project: World Evacuation*, this later book makes them explicit.

Who is Ashtar? As Canadian contactee Oscar Magocsi relates:

> Commander Ashtar has many roles. He is Protector and Defender, Advisor and Administrator, but his work as Protector and Defender is the most prominent. A Commander is one who speaks with Authority to command and issue orders. Ashtar is a Protector of Humanity and the fate of planet Earth, as well as a Defender-Protector of the Solar System and its affairs.

This sounds, largely, like a military and political role. Ashtar, however, also has a spiritual role about which Tuella's readers had inquired. The question facing Tuella and her fellow contactees was about the exact nature of Ashtar. As one of the chapters in *Ashtar: A Tribute* asks, "Spaceman or Angel?" The straight answer is not exactly clear. Again, from Oscar Magocsi:

> He is not an embodiment of an Archangel, but is, nevertheless, participating in a very close partnership and very close cooperative Cosmic representation of one of high administration at that level. It is not Archangel Gabriel, but is

another. Within his own attributes of Protector, Defender and Enforcer, another Archangel works in unison with the energies of Ashtar.

Thus, Ashtar (and others like him) is not an angel but is, rather, "over-shadowed" by an unnamed Archangel. Ashtar, then, straddles the spiritual and non-spiritual worlds; he is an etheric (that is, non-physical) being, while not an archangel himself. Tuella acknowledges that this explanation raises more questions than it answers.[31]

As more information about Ashtar emerges, the strands of religion, spiritualism, and flying saucer history continue to merge. Tuella relates a transmission from another contactee, Bob Graham, who channeled a being called "Joshua" during a meeting in Prescott, Arizona:

> Ashtar is of the Herald Angels and first manifested in the early '50s through so-called UFO type of communications with individuals like George Van Tassel and others, awaiting the return of the Herald Angels, who are the participants in the so-called UFOs that have manifested from time to time. They are observing from their sphere (which is not physical) the actions of men and nations as the periods of time ripen for the return of the Christ, who will return on those same clouds of Heaven, which are partial or full materializations of the vehicles used in the celestial realms.

As Joshua/Bob Graham's account continues, however, the story diverges from what had been transmitted in Tuella's earlier collection of channelings:

> They also play a very important role in preserving the United States from extinction by warring forces that are soon to attack its shores. That only by this Divine Intervention will the enemy be driven, and that the destiny of the United States will be assured as the example that will be set as Christ returns, and that this Nation will serve Mankind until the End Time when the Physical Universe is no longer needed and is dissolved back into its Ethereal form.
>
> Ashtar also represents one of countless Hosts similar to those who manifested in the times of Isaiah and slew thousands of Philistines in the preservation of the Israelites. The history of the dawn of Man records countless manifestations of these Herald Angels.[32]

In the transmissions making up *Project: World Evacuation*, the single mention of the United States was a fleeting reference to the popularity of UFO stories in the country. Other geopolitical references in that earlier book were addressed to humanity in general and did not have the appearance of taking sides. Here, the United States emerges as a blessed promised land, protected by the space beings acting in the service of Sananda Jesus. Also significant is the follow-up explanation of Ashtar's people being responsible for protecting the Israelites in the stories of the Old Testament, reinforcing the conception of the United States as a political entity singled out for blessing by the space people.

As the number of contactees and channelers who spoke on behalf of Ashtar grew, the message became splintered. George Van Tassel, Ethel P. Hill, or Tuella (in her earliest messages) did not claim special status for the United States, or any other political entity. Since the 1980s, the transmissions of Ashtar, Hatonn, and others have had as many distinct goals as they had messengers, continuing to diffuse the focus of whatever may have existed of the "Ashtar Command."

Exopolitics: Contact Narratives in the Post–Cold War World

Extraterrestrial contact narratives have consistently appeared in print and, especially, on the Internet during the 1990s and into the 21st century. Continuing the trend begun in the 1970s and 1980s, these contacts have been predominantly psychic in nature. One new aspect of the contactee phenomenon, however, has been the blending of traditional contactee sentiments with the political conspiracy narratives that emerged in the 1980s and 1990s and persisted into the new century. This blending of contacteeism and conspiracy took two forms: one, the "exopolitics" movement, took an essentially positive view of the space brothers and sisters, much as the earliest contactees did. The other, exemplified by the publications of the *Phoenix Journal*, used the traditional channeled alien Hatonn to convey pessimistic, sinister conspiracy thinking to the channeling community.

Channeled messages from Ashtar and his compatriots persisted during the 1990s and into the 21st century. The focus of the late-century missives maintained the basic thrust of the 1970s and 1980s: humanity must transition to something better and our space brothers and sisters are surrounding the planet, trying to help us through the good offices of specially chosen messengers. As discussed in Chapter 4, this trend paralleled that of the early contactees, even featuring some of the same members of the vast terrestrial and extraterrestrial cast. Just as the early contactees' stories folded in other aspects of extraterrestrial thought and culture, the channeled contact messages of the 1990s and 2000s do the same thing. Channels and contactees continue to integrate seemingly disparate political and spiritual elements in their ongoing narrative.

Striding across the chasm between the sweetness-and-light space saviors that Tuella channeled and the vicious rectum-probing "Grays" of conspiracy paranoia (see Chapter 2) was a figure calling himself Gyeorgos Ceres Hatonn. Hatonn was one of the names that had appeared in various channeled works over the years, including those "compiled" by Tuella. These appeared in the late 1980s and continued to be released into the next decade, by a company called Phoenix Source Publishers (or Phoenix Source Distributors; the name changes occasionally). Over the course of more than 300 books and pamphlets, the *Phoenix Journals* addressed a phenomenal variety of paranormal, political, and spiritual topics. While channeled materials since the beginning of the flying saucer phenomenon blended a variety of topics, the communications published by Hatonn spoke more directly to political concerns, to the point where the extraterrestrial nature of Hatonn and his people served more as window dressing than an integral part of his transmissions. Two particularly striking examples of the themes and methods of the Phoenix Source Hatonn materials are *Space — Gate: The Veil Removed* (double hyphens in the original title) and *Destruction of a Planet: Zionism is Racism.*

Space — Gate consists of a series of "transmissions" which occurred from August 18 to August 20, 1989. In the foreword, Hatonn identifies himself as "Commander in Chief, Earth Project Transition, Pleiades Sector Flight Command, Intergalactic Federation Fleet–Ashtar Command; Earth Representative to the Cosmic Council and Intergalactic Federation Council on Earth Transition." This is a combination of a number of concepts and terms from other channeled materials over the years. Hatonn, however, does not consider his messages as channeling. Refuting the idea that there is a supernatural force involved, he says,

> This document contains truth which can be validated. It comes forth in dictated format from myself [*sic*] to one of my transceivers (recorder). There is nothing of "channeling" about it — it is via actual radio-type short-wave directly from my source into a receiver terminal. No hocus pocus nor mystical hoopla. This recorder does exactly that — records. She is not privy to the information resources nor is she given to "interpretation" other than as any other reader would personally interpret.[33]

Hatonn makes quick work of any supposition that his contact with his "receiver" (referred to as "Dharma" in the actual transmissions) is anything other than technological in nature. This is consistent with Hatonn's attempts to focus on more "nuts-and-bolts" political implications of extra-

terrestrial contact and distance himself from the messages of other channeling contactees such as Tuella. Also significant is the manner in which
Hatonn downplays the role of his human receiver. She is merely a conduit
for Hatonn's words, nothing more.

Hatonn's condescending attitude toward his receiver is worth exploring, since it is a key difference between the Phoenix Source materials and
other channeled works. At the end of many chapters, Hatonn concludes
by expressing concern (or irritation) that Dharma the Receiver needs some
rest. For example, at the end of the second chapter, he orders, "Dharma,
take a break — I see you are going to pass-out and I don't need a sick sec-
retary, little one. Go get thy balance back and we will continue."[34] Later,
Hatonn emphatically attempts to dissuade people from confusing the relative importance of Hatonn and Dharma, emphasizing that Dharma is
merely a conduit:

> I, Commander Gyeorgeos Hatonn, hereby want it known to anyone reading
> this document — it will come forth from seven separate sources in almost iden-
> tical format — it is useless to touch this author for she is void of any information
> other than what I give her through radio signal. I dictate; she writes — then
> she goes aside and throws up.[35]

The human receiver, as Hatonn describes her, is weak and mindless. She
is an empty vessel, important only because of the knowledge she receives
from Hatonn. The receiver, Dharma, does not even get the dignity or
recognition of having her true name published. Hatonn's denunciation of
Dharma's importance is one of the most striking differences between the
messages of Hatonn and other channeled works of the same time period,
such as Tuella's.

One point of continuity between Hatonn's work and others of its
type is the re-casting of Christian deities in the light of Theosophical traditions. Hatonn and the rest of "the lighted brotherhood" are under the
command of "Esu Jesus Sananda." Ashtar makes an appearance as well, as
the commander in charge of the evacuation of Earth. The characters as
well as the basic scenario — guardians from space, led by Jesus, have come
to Earth to save the righteous from evil — are similar to those promulgated
by other contactees, whether they had physical or psychic contact with
their space-traveling friends. There may be severe consequences for those
who do not follow the commands of Hatonn, Sananda Jesus, and Ashtar:

> Earth is going to march right through evolution, transition, tribulation, new
> "birthing" and new "berthing." ... You need no psychic reader to tell you how

it will be. You can hide your head in your sand bucket; it will change nothing.

There are detailed and magnificent plans in operation to cause the transition to be quite survivable and workable for those who choose to work with us.... The Evil Forces shall be met and stopped, but it will be a most unpleasant confrontation.[36]

Two choices exist for humanity: with the space brothers or with the adversary. This is similar to many other contactee narratives, if a bit more harsh in tone.

There are, however, significant ways in which Hatonn's messages diverge from most previous contact narratives. One is the manner in which Hatonn reshapes the universe of extraterrestrial races and politics to conform to the new conspiracy theories and ideas which emerged in the 1980s and 1990s. The other is the intense focus on current events, particularly those surrounding politics and economics. While other contactee narratives discuss political and economic corruption and wrongdoing in vague, universal ways, Hatonn — as is fitting in what was, basically, a serial publication — offers a running commentary on newsworthy happenings and people.

Unusually for contactee-style writings, Hatonn's messages including, *Space — Gate*, exist in the same conceptual and narrative universe as the John Lear and William Cooper theories and writings. Hatonn identifies the "enemy camp" as

the group of small grey beings that are in total infiltration within your government.... They have been very clever, as is their trait, for they have the "big boy" leader himself, Satan, at the helm and between your military, government, and scientific community mingled with their misdirected lies and false information, you are in serious, serious trouble.

Hatonn then proceeds to recount the familiar narrative of crashed craft at Roswell, a secret deal between the Grays and the United States government, and the establishment of the MJ-12 Committee's shadow government. Hatonn, like Cooper, implicates conspiracy theory whipping boys Nelson Rockefeller, Henry Kissinger, the Council on Foreign Relations, and the Bilderberger Group as significant players in the formation of the conspiracy. Hatonn's summary of the development of the relationship between the Grays and the U.S. government and events leading up to the final confrontation between the evil and good space beings hits the same key points as earlier documents; at times, *Space — Gate* reads like a paraphrase of the Lear and Cooper writings of the late 1980s. Like Lear and Cooper, Hatonn interprets the *Alternative 3* fictional documentary as a ploy through which the powers-that-be (in their arrogance) hid their horrific plans in plain sight. The prophecies at Fatima, the Grays using holographic technology to create a false "second coming" (see Chapter 6), and the establishment of alien bases beneath the deserts of the American west all make an appearance.[37]

Hatonn also apes Cooper's accusations that George H.W. Bush, while head of the Central Intelligence Agency in the 1970s, developed a plan to use illegal drug trafficking to fund advanced weapons programs with which they might combat the double-crossing Grays. When it comes to Hatonn's discussion of government welfare programs' use as a social control device, he copies Cooper word-for-word, with only a change of pronoun, "Social Welfare programs were put into place to create a dependent non-working element in your [Cooper's speech says "our"] society."[38] Hatonn then goes on to explain how the major UFO research organizations and well-known researchers are corrupt as well, and have been infiltrated and co-opted. Cooper, in his "Covenant with Death" speech (delivered a few months before these alleged Hatonn transmissions) arrived at the same conclusion. There is a cabal of highly placed conspirators who control the planet (although Hatonn does take pains to point out that the United States is much more evil and responsible for humanity's potential downfall than other nations like the United Kingdom or China.[39]) There are, sadly, few ways out. Hatonn, unlike Cooper, provides the one sliver of hope available to humanity:

> You dear ones are in a big pack of trouble. You cannot fight this monster alone. The only way you can even hope to hold even is to have adequate matching abilities — which your brothers of the Cosmos have available to offer you. You are going to march right through to Armageddon for that is the way it is. Master Esu Jesus Sananda will come and there will be a big bunch of disagreement and I can't think of anything nice to say about it.

This eschatological focus and the discussion of the space brothers' role of protector is one of the key ways that Hatonn's account breaks with that of Cooper's and Lear's which are, generally, more hopeless.

Hatonn's transmissions also differ in some other ways. For example, Hatonn spends dozens of pages in an appendix explaining fractional reserve banking and illustrating reasons why it has led to the enslavement of humanity. He also devotes several pages at the end of the book to defending the photographs and story of Swiss contactee Billy Meier. Several times,

Hatonn identifies himself as being from the Pleiades (the origin of Meier's alleged contacts) and, thus, can state with authority that Meier is being truthful. Attempts to silence Meier are not, Hatonn claims, due solely to his extraterrestrial contact stories but, rather, due to his religious beliefs (discussed earlier in this chapter):

> You ones ask for proof, proof, proof—you get it spread all over you and you do not see. It is not for the reason of the UFO content that Billy Meier is cursed—*this is to the world*—it is because he had access and dared to speak the truth about the creation, God and Immanuel—the one you erroneously call Jesus. Jesus is a greek word for the annointed [sic] one and Immanuel was given that label by Paul (Saul of Tarusus) long after Immanuel was gone.... my promise to beloved Billy Eduard Meier is that just as with Judas Iscarioth [sic], your name shall be cleared and written in honor on the book of transition.[40]

Hatonn's endorsement of Meier, and of Meier's claims about the origins of Christianity, place him firmly in the camp of contactees, while his endorsements (or copying) of William Cooper's and John Lear's ideas place him in the nuts-and-bolts political conspiracy side of the flying saucer belief spectrum.

Another series of transmissions by Hatonn, dating from December 1991 and published as one in the series of *Phoenix Journals* in January 1992, is titled *Destruction of a Planet: Racism IS Zionism.* Here, Hatonn presents a dizzying array of anti–Semitism, conspiracy theory, and paranoia. Crucially, there is only the barest mention of space travel or Hatonn's extraterrestrial origins and these mentions are not integral to the claims made throughout its 221 pages. This part of the brief description on the back cover of the book sums up the tone well:

> We are given to know how the great deceiver (Satan) has pulled off the greatest deception ever on this planet by using the "Jews" as his main characters with Zionism as their cover. Many of his henchmen even changed their names so they could hide their "Jew" heritage so they could better play their games of deception.... Hatonn keeps us updated on all important events whether our controlled press realizes it or not.[41]

The entire book is a whirlwind tour through a variety of invective ranging from the Roosevelt administration's alleged foreknowledge of the Pearl Harbor attack to the dangers of the depleted uranium munitions used in the First Gulf War to the deplorable conditions and corruption on federal Indian reservations, domination of the health care system by the pharmaceutical industry, and the use of swine flu to eliminate elderly white Americans in the 1970s. As indicated by the title, however, the bulk of the venom in the book is reserved for the state of Israel and "Zionist Communism."

As part of his attack on "Zionist Communism," Hatonn spends a great deal of the book outlining Holocaust denial claims and referencing the *Protocols of the Elders of Zion*, the widely acknowledged forgery which some conspiracy theorists claim is an authentic outline of a plan for Jewish world domination. As Hatonn explains:

> So why does Hatonn spend so much time on the "holocaust" of the Second World War? Because it is the most obvious LIE of your generations to which you can see and relate for many of you live who experienced the circumstance. This is also why we spend time on the Protocols for you must see the connections of the same names and the same practices as have come to limit your existence and enslave you.[42]

The claims Hatonn makes here against the Jewish people are not unique or original. He brings up such well-worn arguments such as the notion that the Holocaust was a lie which "has made an enormous political and financial fraud possible, whose principal beneficiary is the state of Israel."[43] There is nothing here that is groundbreaking — merely tired conspiracy theories retreaded over and over.

This tiredness and unoriginality, though, provide the only real thematic link between *Destruction of a Planet* and *Space — Gate*. Both works borrow heavily from various paranormal and conspiracy theory genres, gluing together disparate aspects of flying saucer contactee lore (even down to the names Hatonn, Ashtar, and Sananda Jesus) with the affected archaic language of classic channeled communications. The writings attributed to Hatonn, then, may be studied best as a pseudo- or hybrid-contactee style designed to appeal both to the believer well versed in psychic transmissions and to those who were drawn to the dark, paranoid delusions of conspiracy theory. Thus, rather than being either a "pure" contactee narrative or a "pure" collation of conspiracy theory, Hatonn's writings tend to blend the two, creating a synthesis which would appeal to both groups.

Stretching into the 21st century, a particularly representative example of contemporary contact culture's ability to maintain continuity with the past while remaining relevant to current social and political concerns is the work of Michael Ellegion and Aurora Light (a.k.a. Aurora Ellegion). According to their website, channelforthemasters.com, Michael channels "Ashtar, Archangel Michael, St. Germain, Kuthumi, Quan Yin and other Key Members of the Cosmic Team!"[44] This is a remarkably broad invocation of a variety of the leading brand names of channeled extraterrestrial messages. In doing so, Ellegion places himself within the long continuity of extraterrestrial channels, stretching back to George Van Tassel, Tuella and others. This provides Ellegion with a measure of credibility within contactee circles. Hatonn, though appearing in channeled material for decades, does not rate a mention as one of the Masters contacted by Ellegion. This is, perhaps, explained by the Hatonn figure's strong connection with the paranoid and decidedly non–New Age feel of the *Phoenix Journal* publications.

Their 2008 book, *Prepare for the Landings! Are You Ready?*, purports to be a collection of the authors' "first-hand experiences and communications with benevolent, angelic-type human-appearing ETs, as well as information from numerous other contactees and channels with similar experiences."[45] Upon reading, *Prepare for the Landings!* is that and more. The book is a mélange of personal contacts (physical and psychic) along with liberal doses of conspiracy theory drawn from around the Internet and extensive reprinting of material from, among others, Tuella's Ashtar channelings of the 1980s. It is, in many ways, a strange book, jumping from alleged personal experience to relations of the experiences of others to riffs on the contactee stories of the 1950s and 1960s.

The connections to earlier contactee stories and experiences are a useful place to begin an examination of Ellegion's and Light's work. While the following is a lengthy quotation, it is important as a starting point for an investigation of this aspect of *Prepare for the Landings!*

> There was a surge of information during the "Flying Saucer movement" ('50s and early '60s) when the original and sincere Pioneers, the contactees of that era, were having encounters and communications, as we have had, with these very beautiful and benevolent human-appearing ETs. Unfortunately, there has been a major "cover-up" during the last few decades, where "agents of disinformation" (with secret ties to the cabal) have attempted to mislead the public about these Beings. These "spin doctors," who refer to themselves as "professional" UFO researchers, are well-known names within the UFO community.[46]

Ellegion and Light are careful to position themselves in opposition to the mainstream of UFO investigation and belief, casting their lot with those (Adamski, Van Tassel, et al.) who have been rejected and ridiculed for decades. Like the contactee narratives of the Cold War, the stories presented in *Prepare for the Landings!* must be taken on faith, not being based on logic, reason, or evidence. Like the contactees of old, Ellegion and Light are not seeking to persuade or convince. Rather, they are messengers and conduits. The message is the readers' to do with what they will.

The majority of the book deals with Ellegion's personal experiences and contacts with what he calls his "friends in high places," with Light's contributions mostly concerning how cosmic forces guided her throughout her life to her eventual destiny, to come into contact with Michael Ellegion.[47] Ellegion speaks of himself as having a soul that pre-existed his physical human body. Before his birth, Ellegion lived on a "lightship" orbiting the Earth. "Approximately 20 minutes before I was born, my soul and spirit was [sic] literally projected down from the ... lightship I was on into my Earth mother's womb."[48] The crew of the lightship judged this particular mother and her husband to be suitable to raise Ellegion's "Earth embodiment" because of their metaphysical beliefs as well as their holistic approach to diet and health care. Unlike most space brothers and sisters living on Earth, Ellegion came into this world fully aware of his extraterrestrial origins and his mission on Earth. While Ellegion had an awakening of sorts as a child after a head injury, he sees his position as one he has always had.

As with earlier contactee narratives, Ellegion integrates current terrestrial concerns with his fantastic tales. Holistic health methods and techniques and critiques of conventional medical treatments are a consistent theme in *Prepare for the Landings!* In particular, resistance to vaccination surfaces throughout the book, in addition to an entire chapter devoted to the topic. Light and Ellegion claim the encouragement of vaccinations — particularly childhood vaccinations — is part of a broader campaign against humanity. Vaccinations, they assert, are a means of control over the population as well as a delivery vehicle for man-made contagions which the New World Order could use to wipe out the more troublesome members of humanity.

Ellegion then channels a being named Zoser, who is a "Physician of Light." Zoser reports:

> Many have suspected and even seen documentation verifying that we have been monitoring from our ships, the cabal and their dark alchemists. We are aware they are creating viruses in their laboratories to artificially create plagues. Many viruses specifically target different races, such as the SARS disease that was targeting the Asian population, because the ruling elite want to rule over a much smaller number of slaves.... It saddens us greatly to see those who were ignorant about the actual facts and true nature of vaccinations, willingly allowing themselves and their children to be poisoned, through the scam of vacci-

nations.... Some parents report being forced, almost at gunpoint, to have their children vaccinated.

This is a dire situation, according to Zoser. The ultimate goal is "to keep humanity's vibrational frequency and consciousness low, along with their immune system weakened. This way, people cannot clearly discern properly what is being planned against them." These spiritual and health concerns, of course, are almost minor compared to the other purpose for vaccinations — the implanting of biomechanical tracking chips in the children of the world. Fortunately for humanity, the Federation of Light will, eventually, make a "mass appearance, openly landing all over Earth," bringing with them miraculous cures for all of humanity's ailments.[49]

Like the writings of Hatonn discussed earlier, the bulk of the ideas in *Prepare for the Landings!* are not unique to Michael Ellegion and Aurora Light (or the beings they channel). Rather, the book collects longstanding contactee and extraterrestrial channeling memes and repackages them with a fresh veneer of up-to-date topics that reach out and grab readers. Globalism, vaccinations, health, war, gun control, and overweening government control and scrutiny of citizens' lives are issues that occupy the minds of many around the world. Ellegion and Light took these concerns and bound them up with the cast of characters developed in the 1980s by Tuella and originated in the 1950s and 1960s by George Van Tassel. *Prepare for the Landings!* represented a stage in the evolution of contactee literature rather than a revolution or breakthrough.

At times of particular social, political, or economic stress, the messages change and shift, tuning into whatever concerns people may have. The Occupy Wall Street events in 2012, for example, brought a response from the beings guarding the Earth. The immediacy of the Internet allows channelers and contactees to broadcast in near-real time, as events occur. One channeled being, Peter — a being from the Pleiades — had an opinion on the economic crises and public demonstrations in May 2012.

Initially, Peter is pleased with the progress of the Occupy movement, saying, "You have all become very, very powerful in the past few months. Collectively you have been combining your energies and powers in extraordinary ways to create magnificent changes on your planet. Excellent work. We applaud and commend you!" But there is much more, Peter argues, that people can do to bring down the dark powers that enslave humanity. Although the Pleiadians are behind the Occupy movement "100 percent," humanity needs to strike a crushing blow to their financial overlords.

How should humanity do this? Peter suggests that humanity will be empowered by individual humans ceasing to make payments on their credit card bills. It is a concrete step that needs to be taken:

> Look, standing up for your beliefs and protesting, that's all well and good, but, at this point, we see it as wasted energy when you can all just very simply — but it must be collectively — just stop paying these people who control your world. If EVERYONE stops paying, we ask you ... what could they possibly do? Do this, and you will have your new financial system (or non-financial system) by July.[50]

The last part of this selection is atypical of the bulk of channeled communications given through contactees. Often, specific dates do not appear. Long experience of failed prophecies and the resulting discouragement and loss of face by the contactees who made predictions have resulted in exceedingly vague "prophecies." Often, there is — as here — some sort of collective action that humanity must take. If the promised events fail to take place, then — obviously — someone did not do as they were told. That a new "non-financial" system did not appear in July 2012 means that somebody cracked under the pressure and paid his credit card bill.

The channeled messages of Ashtar, Sananda Jesus, and others represent one strand of the present-day contact narrative. Another, parallel strand exists within the exopolitics movement. According to one of its main proponents, Dr. Michael Salla, exopolitics "is the study of the key individuals, political institutions and processes associated with extraterrestrial life. Information concerning extraterrestrial life and technology is kept secret from the general public, elected political representatives & even senior military officials."[51]

In general, supporters of the exopolitics movement believe that disclosure of information concerning alien visitations involves battling a "truth embargo" held in place by shadowy forces within the military-industrial-intelligence complex. Exopolitics positions itself as a new field of political science. Its trappings are academic and scholarly; at its heart, however, exopolitics is good old-fashioned conspiracy thinking. Shadowy figures hide reality-changing truths while noble, misunderstood, ridiculed heroes fight to expose these truths to a deluded populace. What sets exopolitics apart from the surge of paranoia and conspiracy that arose around the flying saucer phenomenon in the 1980s and 1990s is that exopolitics is, ultimately, future-facing and — largely, though not entirely — optimistic. Like the writings and proclamations of earlier contactees and their channeling cousins of later years, the work of exopolitical thinkers is more likely to offer deliverance rather than damnation. An Internet search for the term produces close to a million hits, but just a handful of names dominate. Steven Greer, Michael Salla, and Alfred Webre are three of the most significant figures in the exopolitics movement. Their work over the past two decades illustrates the range of activities that make up exopolitics, from attempts to contact the space people to surprisingly prosaic Washington, D.C., lobbying.

Steven Greer, M.D., is an emergency room physician and former chair of the department of emergency medicine at Caldwell Memorial Hospital in North Carolina.[52] Since the early 1990s, Greer has engaged in an effort to highlight important socio-cultural concerns such as issues of war and peace, government accountability, and environmental responsibility. The narrative trappings of Greer's efforts generally involve fringe topics such as belief in extraterrestrial contact and elaborate tales of government and corporate collusion and conspiracy. These trappings camouflage a set of desires and a basic social-change strategy that is firmly in line with American traditions. Beginning in the early 1990s, he inaugurated the first of a series of nonprofit organizations. These organizations have varying foci and goals, but they share a number of characteristics. They all urge citizen involvement to effect change in social, cultural, and political arenas. They all find fault with aspects of the American *status quo*, attributing this negative state of affairs to government secrecy in the realms of extraterrestrial contact and advanced technology (allegedly sourced from extraterrestrial craft). Despite these faults, all of these organizations assert that improvement is possible and that humanity's future hangs in the balance, awaiting the efforts of everyday American citizens. Greer targets each of these organizations to specific audiences, using different language and appeals to different mindsets, ranging from those who might consider themselves open-minded and spiritual to those who might identify themselves as skeptical and materialistic.

CSETI — Center for the Study of Extraterrestrial Intelligence

Initiated in 1990, CSETI's goal is to further "our understanding of extraterrestrial intelligence" and is "committed to the thoughtful long-term development of bilateral ETI–Human communication and exchange, and open public education on the subject."[53] CSETI positions itself as a "scientific and educational organization" and one cannot help but notice that the acronym "CSETI" is a blatant play on "SETI," the well-funded and endorsed-by-scientists effort to explore the origins of extraterrestrial life.

Despite their claims to be scientific and educational, the methods and techniques might be foreign to most astronomers or physicists. One example of Greer's efforts to advance his supporters' knowledge of extraterrestrial is the "Ambassador to the Universe" training program. During this training, "You are invited to join Dr. Greer and the senior CSETI Team in making ET contact at night, and learning advanced techniques in Remote Viewing and higher states of consciousness. The acclaimed CSETI CE-5 contact protocols will be shared and experienced, and deep knowledge of the nature of Mind and our own awareness as tools for ET Contact will be taught."[54] The training details do not discuss exactly who has "acclaimed" the CE-5 protocols, nor do they provide explanations of exactly what they mean by "Remote Viewing" and "higher states of consciousness." One assumes that the target audience is familiar with these terms. Talk of "consciousness" has been part and parcel of New Age belief (both ET and non–ET related) for decades. Remote viewing — a systematic approach to alleged psychic prediction — became a publicly known concept in the 1990s when reports surfaced that the U.S. government engaged in such efforts during the height of the Cold War.[55]

These terms presuppose knowledge of and belief in paranormal phenomena, demonstrating that Greer has a well-defined target audience for this $995 training session. Further defining this audience are the guidelines for those who would consider taking part in such training. Potential trainees are required to "have a pure intent and believe in Universal Peace." They must also desire "to learn to communicate with ETs in Consciousness and have an effect on World — and Universal — Consciousness."[56] Those who might be concerned that the ET visitors are less than friendly are discouraged as well, for Greer's view is that the ETs are benevolent.[57] These guidelines provide careful self-selection of trainees. Graduates of this training are likely to have a positive reaction to Greer's ideas because only those who accept Greer's basic tenets are encouraged to take part.

In CSETI's "Core Principles," Greer provides a distinct role for his self-styled ambassadors. Greer asserts that "careful bilateral communications between ETI and humans is of continuing importance and will increase in the future," with such communication leading to the "establishment of a lasting world peace."[58] Thus, those who actively involve themselves in Greer's efforts are bringing forth a new world of peace for humanity and will serve as bridges between humanity and benevolent, enlightened beings from beyond the stars.

The Disclosure Project

Among those who follow the world of conspiracy theory, UFO belief systems, and extraterrestrial contact narratives, Steven Greer is most often identified with his "Disclosure" initiative, which began as Project Starlight in 1993 and still continues. According to its *Background Briefing Points for Congressional Hearings and Legislation*, the Disclosure Project has been "identifying top-secret military, government and other witnesses to UFO and Extraterrestrial events."[59] The purpose of this identification is to establish "beyond any doubt" the existence of extraterrestrial life forms, visitation and technology.[60]

These basic goals did not originate with Greer. UFO and ET contact proponents have always striven for credibility — for witnesses and testimony that establish the reality of these phenomena to the droves of *un*believers and cut short their ridicule and skepticism. Political scientist Jodi Dean attributes this eternal search for some kind of identifiable truth as an expression of "postmodern anxieties":

> The fugitivity of truth is now a problem for all of us. No longer related to popular cultures' marginal discourses, or even confined to peripheral discussions in philosophy and political theory, the fugitivity of truth is a fact of life in the techno-global information age. The concerns of ufology, its worries about evidence and credibility, about whom to trust and whom to believe are the concerns of the rest of us. They are a concentrated version of the facts and pseudofacts of life at the millennium.[61]

Although Dean, in her 1998 book *Aliens in America: Conspiracy Cultures from Outerspace to Cyberspace*, does not discuss Steven Greer or his Disclosure Project, her assessment of the search for credibility and evidence could easily be applied to either of those topics. The Disclosure Project rests on the perceived credibility of its witnesses and those giving testimony about their experiences with ET intelligence. Dean argues that the UFO movement constructs "the problem of truth as a question of credibility." Likewise, Greer and supporters of the Disclosure Project aver that its witnesses are truthful because they are credible. Further, their credibility stems from their positions and occupations.

In the *Executive Summary* of evidence the Project released in 2001, witnesses are identified by pseudonyms, but their occupations are clearly stated. This indicates that what they do is more important than who they are in establishing their credibility and, thus, the truth of their claims. The witnesses presented are described as "Senior Air Traffic Controller," "Former Head of the British Ministry of Defense," and "NRO [National Reconnaissance Office] operative." In some cases, witnesses are identified only by the organizations for which they worked: "US Air Force," "US Strategic Command," or "New York Air National Guard." Credibility, it seems, can be established through mere association with certain institutions.[62]

The Disclosure Project's May 9, 2001, "briefing" at the National Press Club was to be a showcase for the credibility of the Project's witnesses. These witnesses ranged from retired military officers to government scientists to NASA employees. Some of this testimony was quite vague, such as this statement from "Dr. B.": "I know that some people I worked with did disappear on certain programs and were never heard from again. They just disappeared. There has been evidence of that all through my work. You know, that people go out on projects [and disappear]. But [to protect myself from this] I wouldn't go any further on a project because I could see something strange coming. So, a lot of people have disappeared, you know, that are higher up."[63] More specific is this statement from an FAA official:

This was one of the guys from the CIA. Okay? That they were never there and this never happened. At the time I said, well, I don't know why you are saying this. I mean, there was something there and if it's not the stealth bomber, then, you know, it's a UFO. And if it's a UFO, why wouldn't you want the people to know? Oh, they got all excited over that. You don't even want to say those words. He said this is the first time they ever had 30 minutes of radar data on a UFO. And they are all itching to get their hands onto the data and to find out what it is and what really goes on. He says if they come out and told the American public that they ran into a UFO out there, it would cause panic across the country. So therefore, you can't talk about it. And they are going to take all this data....[64]

Much of the testimony at the briefing event centered on similar stories — government intimidation of UFO witnesses and those who had experienced alleged contact with alien intelligences or craft. These allegations are significant because, if true, they logically lead to the accomplishment of the Disclosure Project's goal: the release of closely held government information on extraterrestrial technology. According to Greer, the accomplishment of this goal would have significant "Implications for the Environment, World Peace [and] World Poverty."[65]

The Environment

Greer claims that the Disclosure Project has evidence of technology which can "access the ambient electromagnetic and so-called zero point energy state to produce vast amounts of energy without any pollution," providing "the definitive solution to the vast majority of environmental problems facing our world." This technology represents a magic bullet to solve the world's ecological and energy production crises.[66]

Poverty

This technology will have a leveling effect:

> These technologies, because they will decentralize power — literally and figuratively — will enable the billions living in misery and poverty to enter a world of new abundance. And with economic and technological development, education will rise and birth rates will fall. It is well known that as societies become more educated, prosperous and technologically advanced — and women take an increasingly equal role in society — the birth rate falls and population stabilizes. This is a good thing for world civilization and the future of humanity.[67]

Taking a materialistic stance, Greer argues that poverty is merely the result of access problems — insufficient energy production, for example. His view of poverty's causes and solutions is not a nuanced one: the human factor, especially, seems to be missing, and there is no discussion of the structural causes of poverty and the differences in causes in different parts of the world. Just because such technology exists does not mean it will be distributed equally. Again, this alleged ET technology is presented as a magical cure-all.

World Peace

Issues of peace and security may also be solved by the governments of the world openly embracing these wondrous technologies:

> The real threat of war over a shrinking supply of fossil fuels in the next 10–20 years further underscores the need for this disclosure. What happens when the

4 billion people living in poverty want cars, electricity and other modern conveniences — all of which depend on fossil fuels? To any thinking person, it is obvious that we must transition quickly to the use of these now classified technologies — they are powerful solutions already sitting on a shelf.

Much like his discussion of poverty, Greer engages in reductionist thinking, asserting that energy production and access is the only threat and that these "classified technologies" are the best — if not only — solution.[68]

Like CSETI, the Disclosure Project targets an audience which is, presumably, amenable to such assertions. The targets are those who are familiar with the shadowy world of conspiracy theory popularized in 1990s culture like the film *Conspiracy Theory*, the TV series *The X-Files* and *Dark Skies*, and the explosion of conversation on the subject which took place on the nascent World Wide Web at the time.[69] These people were not steeped in the spiritual, personal side of the ET question. Largely, this potential audience were more materialistic, nuts-and-bolts thinkers who required hard evidence for claims of extraterrestrial visitation. Greer attempts to fulfill that requirement with credibility-tinged testimony and the use of language such as "press briefing" to imbue his efforts with an official flavor. This is in stark contrast to the stories of channels and the traditional contactees of decades past. For those who transmitted the messages of Ashtar or others, proof is something that appears after one has begun to believe, if it even appears at all.

It is possible to cast a wider net in search of Greer's ideas on "free energy" and its importance to the future of Earth, but that net would not sink very far in the water. The Executive Summary referenced here contains the ideas and claims that had fueled Greer's disclosure efforts since the early 1990s and which continue today. The question raised is one of Greer's wider significance: how do his efforts fit into the wider context of extraterrestrial contact narratives?

Greer's projects center around three important concepts: first, the revelation of a single, significant *thing* (ET-inspired technology) which will reshape the world into a better place. Second, Greer has always emphasized the necessity of ordinary people's involvement in the cause. For example, citizens should be involved with coming forward with secret information or writing to one's representatives and demanding investigation and action to put this information into action. Third, in Greer's work there is a villain — a power or organization fighting to maintain the status quo against a rising tide of progress. The puzzle pieces are similar to earlier and contemporary contact narratives. The overall picture, however, is a bit different. Substitute "Atlantis crystals" for zero-point energy devices; exchange "the Cabal" for "PI-40." The narrative is similar, but the details (and underlying assumptions of what is important — the material or the spiritual) and methods (expert terrestrial testimony and liberated secret document versus channeled messages from the ascended masters) are different.[70]

THE DISCLOSURE PRESIDENT? BARACK OBAMA'S 2008 PRESIDENTIAL CAMPAIGN AND THE EXOPOLITICS MOVEMENT

While this conspiracy thinking pervades the exopolitics movement, it has been especially visible since the 2008 presidential campaign and subsequent election of Barack Obama.

Not surprisingly, some exopolitics proponents latched onto then-Senator Obama's assurances of transparency in his administration and believed that he could be the president who would finally end the truth embargo and reveal what they saw as the reality of ET visitation to the people of the Earth. When the Democratic presidential field was wide open, however, exopoliticians held up two other candidates as viable battlers of the truth embargo. Gov. Bill Richardson (from the Roswell State, no less) told MSNBC's Chris Matthews, "The Federal Government has not come clean at all on that issue and it should." Even more exciting was Ohio's Dennis Kucinich, who claimed to have sighted a triangle-shaped UFO. This story, originally reported in the *Cleveland Plain Dealer*, surfaced again in the October 30, 2007, Democratic candidate debate. If that were not spectacular enough, exopols like Michael Salla bruited about the account of Kucinich's tale told by New Age mainstay Shirley MacLaine, who reported that Kucinich "said he felt a connection in his heart and heard directions in his mind."[71]

When the dust cleared, however, Barack Obama and John McCain were the major party candidates in 2008. One exopol who went on the offense to capture the candidates' attention was Stephen Bassett. Bassett is the only registered lobbyist in the United States who deals exclusively with UFO issues. In October of 2008, Bassett wrote an open letter to the two candidates in which he challenged them to come clean on the UFO issue: "As President Elect ... In the spring of 2009, before the truth embargo becomes your embargo, initiate disclosure of the extraterrestrial presence and begin rebuilding the trust of the American people in their government and the standing of your country in the world."[72] Bassett explicitly links the disclosure of extraterrestrial truths to wider issues of national prestige and public confidence. Like countless conspiracy theorists before him, Bassett focuses on one specific magic bullet to solve numerous complex problems. Ending the truth embargo, for Bassett, is the key issue that would change the United States for the better. Exopolitics, far from being an innovation in a scholarly field, simply reiterates well-worn clichés.

During the period between Obama's election and inauguration, exopoliticians examined every aspect of the Obama transition for evidence of a disclosure-friendly attitude from the president-elect and his staff. As often happens in conspiratorial thinking, the slightest connections and parallels are explained as conclusive proof of the theories in question. One such example from Obama's transition period was the appointment of John Podesta as the co-chair of the president-elect's transition team.

Podesta had long been a sainted figure for the exopolitics movement. He had been Bill Clinton's chief of staff for the last two years of his presidency and had a role in penning Executive Order 12958, which declassified millions of pages of national security and diplomatic documents. UFO researchers of the 1990s believed that order was part of a broader effort by the Clinton administration to disclose government secrets about extraterrestrial life and technology. New directives have since superseded that order, but for exopoliticians, Podesta remains a link to that mythical effort to reveal the truth. Podesta's work on the Obama transition is thus seen by exopoliticians like Michael Salla as evidence that the nascent Obama administration was seeking an opportunity to revive the Clinton-era disclosure effort.[73]

The appointment of Leon Panetta as director of Central Intelligence had a similar effect on exopoliticians. Panetta was President Clinton's chief of staff prior to John Podesta and, allegedly, a fan of *The X-Files* television show. Panetta apparently wanted to open up the real "x-files" housed within various bureaucracies and reveal the truth of extraterrestrial visitation to the public. Salla believes that taken together, the positions of Podesta and Panetta indicate "a coordinated effort by former Clinton era figures to steer the Obama administration towards locating and declassifying UFO files."[74] Salla focuses his attention on two incidents in these men's careers that are nearly unknown outside the ranks of UFO researchers. From this, he has constructed a narrative of disclosure where the actors are divorced from their bureaucratic and political realities.

For Salla and other exopolitical thinkers, the truth embargo regarding government knowledge of extraterrestrial life is *the* story of American politics. These thinkers do discuss other issues — war and peace, the economy, the environment. These other issues, however, are unfailingly placed within the narrower context of the alien truth embargo. The discussion of these other issues adheres to the following structure:

1. The government truth embargo on knowledge of alien life and alien technology — now in the hands of the U.S. government — were it lifted, could solve the issues troubling our nation and world.

2. There is afoot —*right now*— an effort by well-meaning, well-placed government officials to reveal this information to the American people.

3. This effort will go astray due to the political manipulations of those within the military-political-intelligence complex.

Perhaps the most extravagant example of this is Dr. Steven Greer's May 9, 2001, "briefing" at the National Press Club, where he assembled a variety of alleged-whistleblowers to share their stories and call for open congressional hearings on the issue of the government/ET cover-up. The whistleblowers were a motley crew, ranging from very strait-laced, uncomfortable-looking retired military officers to those who channeled alien messages through telepathy. The congressional hearings never happened. Greer blamed the "suppressed" and "censored" media for ignoring his event.[75]

But things changed in 2008. Barack Obama appealed to these conspiracy mongers for many of the same reasons he appealed to many voters in the 2008 election. Obama's campaign traded on promises of change and a new direction for American politics and foreign policy. The exopolitics movement, made up of people who view American politics and foreign policy through a lens of well-worn political conspiracy theories, simply viewed these promises through that same lens. Like many special interest groups, they lose sight of the politics of Washington, D.C. They overlook the very real restraints on a president's power. Where the exopols are often different from those who want forward momentum on health care reform, same-sex marriage, or global warming is in the conspiracy-laden reasoning used to explain why their goals were not realized.

Similarly, just as the voters, media, and pundits excitedly discussed the possibility — and subsequent reality — of the first African American president, exopolitical thinkers wove Obama's ethnicity into their master narrative of disclosure. In the February 2010 issue of *Washington Monthly*, Stephen Bassett, the ET lobbyist, told reporter Daniel Fromson: "If you're going to go to the world and say, 'We have been keeping from you the most profound information in history for six decades,' and it so happens that that world is predominantly brown, it might help a lot if the president who was telling them was brown ... these are significant assets, all right?"[76] A year earlier, "Nathan" — a commenter on Bassett's website — asserted:

> Barack Obama is the best person to disclose whether or not UFOs exist for these reasons; his black, white and Asian [*sic*] heritage will allow people the world over to feel comfortable with him making the announcement, and he is ignorant (not "in the know") to the issue and will be able to dodge accusations about being involved in cover ups and not telling the public sooner.[77]

Obama's ethnicity, previous career, appointees, and off-hand comments are all seized upon here and shed light on the broader tapestry of the story surrounding him. Barack Obama is a man of destiny, down to his very DNA.

This is a familiar notion to those who have studied the conspiracy theories surrounding President Obama. Outlandish theories and assertions floated around Senator, candidate, and President Obama. These claims ranged from the well-known assertions that he was secretly born in Kenya to more extreme theories, such as the one which claims Obama was groomed from birth to be president by a shadowy cabal of Soviet Communists.[78] Part and parcel of conspiracy theories is that what people see before them has been planned for far longer than anyone could imagine — happenstance, luck, or accidents hold little meaning for the conspiracy theorist. Thus, what the exopoliticians do in constructing their conspiracy theory is not unique. Exopolitics has, however, inverted the tropes of Obama-based conspiracy theories. His ethnicity is a boon, not a threat; his political associates are paragons of disclosure and openness rather than exponents of radical, anti–American extremism. His every utterance is dissected for signs of a new dawn — not proof that he is a closet communist or an imminent Islamo-fascist.[79] Unlike most political conspiracy narratives, the exopolitical movement presents an essentially optimistic and positive vision of Barack Obama.

Optimistic, also, is exopolitics' vision of the future. It is a future where the people have access to unimaginable technology, free energy, a pristine world, and a place in a peaceful interstellar community. It is a vision and worldview that have more in common with *Star Trek* than the terrestrial, political world. This is a trait the exopolitics movement shares with the contactee phenomenon. The future has the potential to be a better place, a utopia. For the contactees, the ideal future comes about through humanity's adherence to the cosmic laws and principles. For the exopoliticians, the utopian future is in the hands of the government, which is withholding the gift of advanced, extraterrestrial technology.

If we look past the stargazing naïveté we see something interesting and significant. What we have in the exopolitics movement is a rare thing: a conspiracy theory with a happy ending. Exopolitical activists' response to the presidency of Barack Obama is a compelling counterpoint to the "Obamaphobia" present on the fringes of American political culture. Thanks to these exopolitical thinkers, the election of 2008 presented Barack Obama as a conspiratorial counterweight — a figure who existed for no other reason than to demolish the walls of silence that have surrounded the ET question for over 60 years.

In addition to the exopolitical thinkers who have latched onto the Obama candidacy and subsequent presidency as a turning point in the "truth embargo," contactees have channeled extraterrestrial information about President Obama since 2008 as well. The Internet is full of transcripts asserting that Obama was not just the choice of those who want the truth about extraterrestrial evidence from the government but also by the extraterrestrials themselves. Often, these messages attributed to Barack Obama powers and responsibilities far beyond those of the presidency. Nancy Tate was the receiver of one example of this type of channeled transmission in February of 2009, a few weeks after Obama's inauguration. Tate channeled two beings, "Hatonn" (from the tone of the transmissions, this was not the Hatonn of the *Phoenix Journal*) and Anakhanda Shaka Mushaba.

One crucial thing readers learn is that Barack Obama is more — much more — than merely the president of the United States. Hatonn states: "When Barack Obama took office he took on a more involved position than anyone knows. He took on the job of bringing not only the nation to a place of unity, he also administered to the economy of the rest of the world." Key to the economic revitalization of the planet is reformation of religious institutions. According to Hatonn and Anakhanda, the evil "Illuminati cabal," in league with the Vatican, which controls the world, holds the religious institutions of humanity in thrall through financial debt. Obama's economic plans will free churches from Illuminati control and allow parishioners to "take over and declare their rights to worship in the way they can, and to be able to bring a fair and equitable form of structure to their churches. This will begin the reformation of the world of religion, for with the revelation of what has been taking place the people will begin to search their own souls and Spirit for the truth." Religion is not the only area where President Obama is working with forces around the world (as well as with the Mushaba Council, whom Hatonn and Anakhanda represent). Trade issues are also on the presidential/extraterrestrial radar. Particularly important is the issue of American manufacturing:

> Obama knows that because our goods and services are being shipped outside the U.S. and then returned to us at a much significant cost [sic], it has been adding undue hardships on the people NOT ONLY IN HIGHER PRICING FOR GOODS, BUT COSTING US DEARLY IN JOBS. He will keep the jobs and goods manufactured within American borders which will create more jobs and a more thriving economy.

Along with restoring glory to American manufacturing, Obama will reform banking and eliminate the Federal Reserve System. The United States will return the dollar to the gold and silver standards of the past. As if all this were not enough, there will be no more income tax for individuals, only businesses. Obama has also been touring the United States and seeing how communities have eliminated banks, establishing financial co-ops in their place.

Barrack Obama will, Hatonn and Anakhanda tell their readers, establish such systems on a national level. As has become standard, the two extraterrestrials declare, "Barack has known for a long time about our Family in the cosmos. He is preparing a briefing that will be given to all of the leaders of the countries as to when and how the truth of the ETs can be brought forward." In fact, these actions are all parts of "the Golden Age master plan that includes Barack Obama's election as president of the United States as an integral part of Earth's ascension." Lest anyone be concerned that such an all-powerful, successful leader would become a dictator, Nancy Tate's extraterrestrial contacts assure readers: "This man, Barack Obama, recognizes that without all of you he is nothing. He knows that you are all in this together, and that he is in it for the duration that is destined for him. He sees all of you as his equal, and he sings your praises in his heart continually as a song of rejoicing and reverence for the

One that we all are." Barack Obama captured the imagination of the contactee and channeling communities like no politician before, although it is unclear whether it was because of his ethnicity or because his candidacy and presidency came after eight years of an administration that — on the surface, at least — militated against those things espoused by the space brothers and sisters.

Regardless of the promise of Obama as an obvious, even ideal "Disclosure president," no such disclosure has occurred. Stephen Bassett's Paradigm Research Group website has a count-up timer which tracks the number of days since President Obama's inauguration without disclosure taking place, despite a number of petition drives conducted through the White House's "We the People" online petition portal. One petition stated, "We, the undersigned, strongly urge the President of the United States to formally acknowledge an extraterrestrial presence engaging the human race and immediately release into the public domain all files from all agencies and military services relevant to this phenomenon."[80] Another called "for the President to disclose to the American people the long withheld knowledge of government interactions with extraterrestrial beings and call for open Congressional hearings to allow the people to become aware of this subject through those whose voices have been silenced by unconstitutional secrecy oaths."[81]

These petitions (which, together, garnered 17,465 digital signatures) received a response from Phil Larson, a staffer in the White House Office of Science and Technology Policy. Larson stated, "The U.S. government has no evidence that any life exists outside our planet, or that an extraterrestrial presence has contacted or engaged any member of the human race. In addition, there is no credible information to suggest that any evidence is being hidden from the public's eye."[82] Bassett responded in a press release, "Unfortunately for the OSTP and the Obama administration, that assertion is false. Furthermore, given that approximately 50% of the American people are now convinced of an extraterrestrial presence and more than 80 percent believe the government is not telling the truth about the phenomenon, it is an embarrassment."[83] And so the volleys go back and forth.

The exopolitics movement, on the surface, may not seem to connect with the contactee phenomenon of either the Space Age or the New Age. While it does seem to have more in common with the conspiracy theorists like John Lear, William Cooper or Hatonn, the goals and methods of the exopolitics movement have much in common with those of the contactees. Both movements had specific, concrete goals for society. Both groups believe that friendly — or at least not unfriendly — space people hold the solutions to the problems humanity faces. In the exopolitical narrative, conspiring forces within the government and industry seek to keep humanity from advancing. In more traditional contactee lore, humanity's selfishness and lack of vision is what holds it back. At their core, both movements seek some variety of extraterrestrial salvation for humanity. Whether this salvation is technological or spiritual, the similarities between the two movements are striking.

Since the 1970s the contactee movement has moved in more diverse directions than contactees of the Space Age. The emergence of dedicated religious movements (some more cult-like than others), the explosion of channelers receiving vastly different messages from, ostensibly, the same beings, and the birth of the exopolitics movement have all diluted the concept of "contact." It would, most likely, come as a surprise to Michael Salla, Steven Greer, or Stephen Basset to know how much they share with their forebears like George Adamski or George Van Tassel. Traditional contactee movements, though, have not gone away; Billy Meier's visits with the Pleiadian beings are the recent successor to George Adamski's encounters with Orthon and Firkon. Michael Ellegion's channelings from the "Cosmic Team" take the work of Tuella (who, herself, carried the torch from channelers like Ethel P. Hill) and push it into the 21st century. This movement will continue to evolve, with new voices stepping into the interspatial breach, carrying forward the messages they believe humanity needs to hear.

6

Dark Contact

Men in Black, Demons and the End of the World

Not every story about more-or-less human beings visiting from other worlds presented the encounters in a positive light. From "Men in Black" to the Antichrist himself, the tropes of contactee narratives had a sinister side as well.

It may be a cliché, but if one were to ask a random man or woman on the street to discuss the "Men in Black" it is very likely that one would receive a response that discusses the film series starring Will Smith and Tommy Lee Jones. There is a lesser chance that the respondent will mention something to do with flying saucers or the paranormal. The Men in Black, aside from being a high-grossing film concept, are a prime example of the dark side of contactee narratives and thought.

While the majority of alleged human contacts with human-appearing extraterrestrials are positive and uplifting, there are aspects of contact culture that feature encounters which are more sinister. There are shadows cast by the light of the space brothers. This darkness extends back to the beginning of the phenomenon and continues to this day in a variety of flying saucer subgenres. On one end of the spectrum, there are classic tales of the Men in Black which hold a cracked mirror up to the conventional contactee narrative. On the other end are overtly religious interpretations of contact which cast the human-appearing visitors as demons, deceiving the unwary with heretical space theology. This chapter will also explore the connections between contact culture and eschatology. While a variety of contactees link the messages of their space brothers to the end of the world—or at least *an* end of the world—some have, in recent years, merged the demonic aspects of the sinister, abducting, anal-probing "Grays" with the human

176

appearance of the contactees' visitors. This extraterrestrial and religious mélange often plays a role in elaborate conspiracy theories involving interpretations of Biblical prophecy, Antichrists, and the like.

The Men in Black phenomenon fits within the broad conception of "contact narrative" in a number of ways. First, there is the basic notion of human-like beings interacting with a select array of people (in this case, flying saucer witnesses). Second — and far more significant — is the manner in which the Men in Black mythology has developed since the 1950s. Concepts like Ashtar Command continue to flourish and evolve. George Adamski's sightings are still discussed by contact enthusiasts and, as we have seen in the writing of Benjamin Crème and Gerard Aartsen, the characterization of George Adamski himself has developed to the point where some seriously raise the question of whether he might have been an incarnated star visitor. Similarly, the Men in Black narrative has developed and evolved over the years.

One aspect of the Men in Black genre of contact claims that may be problematic is the exact nature of these shadowy figures. If they are actually visitors from space, as some allege, then stories of their activities fall squarely in the realm of "contact narrative." But if they are completely terrestrial — if, for example, they are simply frighteningly dressed and suspiciously sinister government agents — then fitting them into the contactee genre becomes more difficult. Regardless of their true origins, if any, I choose to discuss them as contactee stories mostly because Albert K. Bender, the first widely known MIB experiencer, described them as visitors from another planet. Another key reason to regard them as part of the contactee genre is that, often, the stories involving the Men in Black very specifically invert the tropes of typical contactee tales.

The Men in Black phenomenon has its roots in the earliest days of flying saucer culture. It began with a man named Albert K. Bender, founder and head of the International Flying Saucer Bureau. The IFSB was an international network of hundreds of saucer spotters and investigators who interviewed witnesses, wrote reports and sought an answer for the questions posed by unidentified flying objects. The organization produced a newsletter, *Space Review*, which summarized sightings and featured articles speculating on the origins the strange craft and the intentions of those who controlled them. Founded in April 1952, the IFSB was one of the earliest of the many, many saucer investigation organizations to appear and vanish in the 1950s and 1960s.[1]

The significance of Bender's International Flying Saucer Bureau stems from the circumstances surrounding its ending. In the October 1953 issue of *Space Review*, two items by President Bender caught readers' attention and sparked a meme which has remained prominent into the present. The first was headed "Late Bulletin" and read: "A source, which the IFSB considers very reliable, has informed us that the investigation of the flying saucer mystery and solution is approaching its final stages. The same source to whom we had referred data, which had come into our possession, suggested that it was not the proper method and time to publish this data in *Space Review*." Following this was another item, a "Statement of Importance": "The mystery of the flying saucers is no longer a mystery. The source is already known, but any information about this is being withheld by orders from a higher source. We would like to print the full story in *Space Review*, but because of the nature of the information we are sorry that we have been advised in the negative. We advise those engaged in saucer work to please be very cautious."[2] Over the subsequent months, the IFSB would disband, with mentions of and speculation about flying saucers disappearing from *Space Review* as they pro-duced enough issues to finish out members' subscriptions. The story of the IFSB and its president's paranoid comments would, most likely, have faded into the background noise of the 1950s saucer craze if it had not been for the efforts of the IFSB's chief investigator, Gray Barker.

Born in 1925, Barker was a native of Braxton County, West Virginia, and, in the early 1950s was living in Clarksburg, West Virginia, working as a motion picture booker. He got involved in investigating anom-alous events in 1952 by writing an article for *Fate* magazine on the "Flatwoods Monster" that

A young Gray Barker in a portrait taken in the late 1940s (courtesy Gray Barker Collection, Clarksburg-Harrison Public Library, Clarksburg, West Virginia).

terrorized rural West Virginia.[3] From there, he became a member of the IFSB and started his own magazine, *The Saucerian*. From this grew a flying saucer publishing empire — Saucerian Books — which would publish hundreds of books and tracts, many of which dealt with contactee stories. Barker's approach to flying saucer "journalism" has been subject to much scrutiny. John C. Sherwood, a journalist who wrote saucer material in the 1960s, discussed Barker's view of flying saucers and their adherents in a 1998 issue of *Skeptical Inquirer* magazine. Sherwood quotes from a letter Barker sent him in 1968:

> Strictly off the record, unusual interest and fixation upon UFOs represents, in my opinion, a definite symptom of neurosis.... I cannot (again off the record) bear for very long most of the people and the fans of Saucerdom, mainly because most of them are oral aggressors (i.e., they talk all the time about saucers and make you listen). I do genuinely like a few saucerers (and former saucerers) like yourself, who, along with their interest in saucers, seem to be pretty sane and can have a sense of humor about it.[4]

Despite Barker's apparent antipathy for flying saucer believers, his work made a significant contribution to a number of mythic elements, including the Men in Black.

Barker spun the story of the International Flying Saucer Bureau's rapid and mysterious decline into a book that launched the notion of organized, sinister suppression of those who sought the truth about possible extraterrestrial visitation. *They Knew Too Much About Flying Saucers*, published in 1956, detailed Barker's entree into the world of saucer investigation as well as his involvement in the IFSB. As the mystery surrounding the organization deepened, Barker and other members of the organization's leadership began to press Alert Bender about what he knew and why he closed the organization. Throughout the course of the book, Bender related that after he learned the truth about the origins of the flying saucers, three men visited him and made him promise, "on his honor as an American," that he would not divulge what he knew.[5]

Intertwined with the attempts to entice Bender to reveal the truth is a number of diversions into various aspects of saucer and paranormal lore. Barker, in searching for the answers Bender keeps hidden, explores several theories of what the saucers might be. Most of the discussion, however, is related to the possible origins of the three men in black who terrified Bender into silence. Whether or not three men (in any color clothes) actually *did* threaten Albert Bender is — and probably will always be — unknown.

Barker's telling of the story, however, brought together such a number of possibilities — from government agents, to hoaxers, to human-appearing aliens — that the waters would forever be muddy. Part of the charm of *They Knew Too Much About Flying Saucers* is that it blurred the line between bland reportage and entertaining storytelling. For example, Barker took an extensive detour into the world of Richard Shaver and the Deros and Teros of the hollow Earth. Could, Barker asked, the Men in Black who silenced Albert K. Bender be the evil, mischievous Deros, intent on keeping the secret of their civilization from prying human eyes? Barker shifted between first- and third-person narrations, and provided interludes that were more akin in tone to suspense or detective novels than the more boringly straightforward saucer books of the time. Equally important is that Barker did not provide an answer. The book left the reader with no real solution to the mystery of the Men in Black, but did provide a number of exciting avenues and theories for curious readers to explore, doubtless available through Gray Barker's Saucerian Publications.

Regardless of whether or not Albert Bender actually was threatened into silence by Men in Black, the foundation of the story emerges in Barker's book and his dramatized account is borne out by correspondence between — in particular — Bender and photographer August C. Roberts, a member of the IFSB's Department of Investigation.

On September 14, 1953, Bender wrote to Roberts: "You [Roberts] and all the members there not to accept any more memberships for IFSB until you read the Oct. 15th issue of *Space Review*."[6] This would be the issue in which Bender warned saucer researchers to be "careful." Within days of that issue's reaching readers, Bender would cut himself off from the world of saucer investigation. Writing to Roberts on October 18, Bender says:

> May I please ask you Augie, as a friend, not to ask me any more questions about the situation at hand. I am being disturbed constantly by phone calls and inquiries and I must be abrupt and ask everyone to stop with their questions as I cannot tell any more that you don't already know. I might add that I received a phone call after I talked with you from long distance, D.C. and the person calling me asked me my name and then asked some question [*sic*] that startled me. How did he know that I was talking to you.[7]

In a subsequent letter, Bender tells him, "If you are coming up to see me — please do not expect to discuss 'Saucers' in any way, shape, or form. I do not care to talk about this subject to anyone anymore."[8] In a letter following

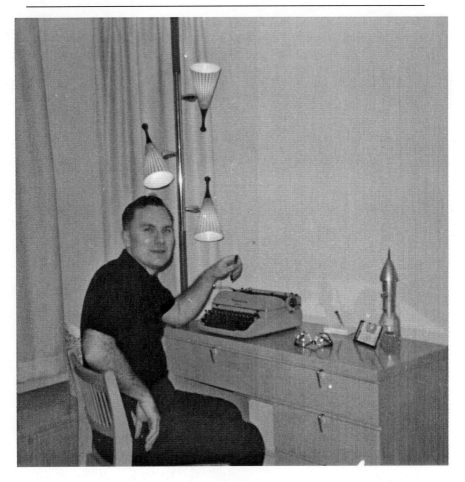

Albert K. Bender at his typewriter (courtesy Gray Barker Collection, Clarksburg-Harrison Public Library, Clarksburg, West Virginia).

up a visit between the two men, Bender wrote that he was "very pleased with your visit even though you did throw numerous questions at me."[9] This is consistent with the tale Barker tells in *They Knew Too Much About Flying Saucers*; so far, so familiar.

There is a gap, however, between the end of the IFSB (1953) and the publication of Barker's book (1956). The correspondence between Roberts and Bender during that time indicates that the Men in Black mythology had begun to develop. On August 2, 1954, Roberts wrote to Bender:

> I'm going to write teh [*sic*] Bender story for the next issue of the Nexus. I know that you don't want it written, but as I understand from a very good source of

information ... that you are planning to write a book about the Saucers, three men, etc. ... I have held off writing the story all this time. But if you are planning to write a book, then I can't see why I should hold back now.... I'm sure you will find my Bender story very interesting. I know many of our readers will. When you gave me the job on the investigating staff, I never thought that I would have to investigate you....[10]

Roberts signed the letter, "Your Friend — or ??????" Significantly, in what is a letter *to* Bender, Roberts refers to the emerging Men in Black narrative as "[the] Bender story" and "my Bender story." One might expect that Roberts would say "your story." Referring to Bender in the third person gives the impression that the narrative exists independently of Bender himself. Given the extensive growth and development of the Men in Black mythos, this is not too far from the truth of what would happen in the future.

Al Bender, being the focus of this story, replied to Roberts two days later (August 4, 1954) with surprising vehemence:

May I say that since this is a free country ... go right ahead and print anything you desire, but be sure that what you print is true and has proof to back it up. Otherwise, you may get yourself into difficulty especially if your publication is a copyrighted one.... As for any book I intend to write, you had better check again, as that is the least of my thoughts ... rest assured that when I do write it won't be on any subject as non-sensical [*sic*] as the saucers.[11]

From all available information, Bender was being truthful about his having no intentions of writing a book about his experiences. Within a few years, however, Bender would put pen to paper and tell his own story, taking it in a direction distinct from that Barker had taken in *They Knew Too Much About Flying Saucers.*

Bender's 1962 book (published, edited, and annotated by Barker) gave readers more background into the life of Albert K. Bender. Living with his stepfather, and working as a factory clerk, Bender created an elaborate attic hideaway, festooned with horror movie and haunted house trappings and decorations. He painted "grotesque figures" from horror literature on the walls and relates that "so many of the ghostly characters appeared to be looking straight at me, no matter where I might be in the room!"[12] Bender, to at least some degree, was a man immersed in the supernatural before his foray into the flying saucer mystery. *Flying Saucers and the Three Men* recast the Men in Black as sinister extraterrestrial visitors, as opposed to government agents or saucer-phobic law enforcement officers. In Bender's telling, while the Men in Black were responsible for the end of the International Flying Saucer Bureau, they were space visitors who possessed, among other things, flying saucers and Antarctic bases. Bender weaves a story which extends beyond the events surrounding the collapse of the IFSB. His experiences begin while walking home from a movie. Bender saw a "bluish flash," developed a headache, and felt as though he were floating above the ground. He "had the strong impression that somebody or something was telling me to forget IFSB, to give it up."[13] Bender, while telling the story of the IFSB and the sightings they investigated, relates more incidents of bizarre headaches and feelings that someone was watching him.

Bender's atypical contact experiences accelerated during "World Contact Day." According to Bender, members of the IFSB would "attempt to send a message to the occupants of the Saucers (if they exist) by the use of mental telepathy." At a given time (6:00 P.M., Eastern Standard Time, March 15, 1953), all participants would concentrate on an identical message calling to the saucer people, assuring them of friendship, and asking them to "be responsible for creating a miracle here on our planet to wake up the ignorant ones to reality."[14] On the 15th, as Bender transmitted the psychic message to the crews of the flying saucers, a headache — similar to but more massive than those he'd had before — overtook him. Bender had what later New Age writers would call an out-of-body experience, floating above himself as he attempted communication with the space people. In the midst of this painful, bizarre happening, he heard a voice from in front of him say, "We have been watching you and your activities. Please be advised to discontinue delving into the mysteries of the universe. We will make an appearance if you disobey.... We have a special assignment ... and must not be disturbed by your people."[15] Bender's trance-like state ended and he was once again alone, surrounded by an odor of sulfur and a quickly-dissipating yellow mist.

Interestingly, Gray Barker (who edited and published *Flying Saucers and the Three Men*) does not mention "Contact Day" or psychic connections to the flying saucers in *They Knew Too Much About Flying Saucers*. He does, however, discuss it in his later book *Men in Black: The Secret Terror Among Us*, published in 1983. In his book, Bender states that he did not tell anyone of the events of C-Day but rather kept a diary of it so, if anything happened to him, "somebody would find the envelope [containing the diary] and would know what had happened that day."[16] Barker's omission of any mention of World Contact Day from *They Knew Too Much*

About Flying Saucers is curious, as this was — apparently — a critical event in the decline of the International Flying Saucer Bureau.

There are a number of possible reasons why Barker didn't include the story in his earlier book. It is important to examine the differences between the varying accounts of Bender and the Men in Black and the possible reasons for the differences. Like the Roswell incident (see Chapter 2), the emergence of the Men in Black trope illustrates the shifting nature of narrative, testimony, and history which emerges in the flying saucer field. Barker presented *They Knew Too Much About Flying Saucers* as an unfolding story seen through the eyes of Barker and other investigators like August Roberts and Dominic Luschesi. From this point of view, World Contact Day was irrelevant to the story Barker decided to tell. At the end of *They Knew Too Much About Flying Saucers*, Barker and his fellow investigators have a great deal of speculation, but no answers. Thus, World Contact Day was not a key event to their investigation. The more cynical observer might assert that — since there is no real evidence of mysterious, sinister visitors — Barker and Bender simply failed to get their stories straight before they wrote them.

Barker managed to avoid the "There are absolutely craft from outer space"/"There is nothing going on at all" belief-denial dichotomy. A key difference in Barker's work is that rather than connecting paranormal and flying saucer sightings to mythology and folklore, Barker's works created folklore. The Men in Black — as figures who appear to intimidate flying saucer researchers — did not begin with Barker and Bender. Similar stories stretch back into the 1940s. What Barker accomplished was to shape the notion of the Men in Black into something that took on a life of its own.

The directors of the Gray Barker Project at West Virginia University's Center for Literary Computing recognize this about Barker's work, describing his work as "an act of literary self-creation," an example of the postmodern novel:

> If the postmodern novel troubled the notion of authorship, of intertextual relations, and of the margins between text and context, then the Gray Barker archive is the most extensive, successful, and aporetic postmodern novel ever written. Individual texts in the archive present complex interplays of truth, interpolation, and invention. At the same time, the archive's insertion into public memory and the space of debate causes a seismic disturbance in the very concept of the archive.... The Gray Barker archive presents no end of evidence, presents the author as trickster, and presents text as self-reflexive and pastiche.[17]

This conceptualization of Barker's body of work, including *They Knew Too Much About Flying Saucers*, his editorship and annotation of *Flying Saucers and the Three Men*, and his publishing and promotion of books and articles across the spectrum of flying saucer belief, blurs the lines between journalism, speculation, and entertainment. There is a great deal of testimony that Barker rarely believed the materials he published or wrote. This does not necessarily mean that Barker's writings or the writings he promoted are unimportant. As we've seen, the factual accuracy (or even the basic provability) of contact narrative is often less important than the messages these narratives convey.

Barker's work — and given his level of editorial input and annotation, we can include Bender's book among them — greatly contributed to both the mythology of flying saucer belief and popular culture. Since the 1950s, the notion of the Men in Black has transcended the flying saucer subculture, with appearances in comics, films, novels, and television. Barker's work in developing the mythology of the Men in Black is also very significant for understanding the role of contacteeism in the development of paranormal thought. The actions and appearance of the Men in Black parallel the space brothers. The Men in Black are human-like and engage in personal (and sometimes psychic) contact with experiencers.

While the Men in Black have been subject to scholarly investigation in the years since their debut, many of these focus on their connection to "sinister" concepts rather than their ties to the contemporary contact culture. Peter Rojcewicz, for example, explored the connections between Men in Black stories and traditional accounts of demonic visitations. He concluded, "These separate but not separated phenomena form a continuum of folk concepts and beliefs in 'other worlds.'"[18] Rojewicz uses tales of devil-like visitations to place the Men in Black within the context of devilish figures. While this is certainly a valid conclusion (the yellow, sulfur-like mist and odor experienced by Bender is a clear "demonic" signpost), they also bear resemblance to the positive contact experiences of the 1950s and 1960s.

Bender's encounter with the three Men in Black represents a conscious bending both of the traditional contact narrative as well as the emerging tradition of the Men in Black encounter. The Men in Black Bender meets with are not particularly mysterious — we will come to know their origin and their goals. Unlike traditional contactee narratives, the visitors are not friendly. They have, for example, actual weapons. Their most powerful

Albert K. Bender (ca. 1962) promoting *Flying Saucers and the Three Men*, complete with a representation of one of the beings from the planet Kazik (courtesy Gray Barker Collection, Clarksburg-Harrison Public Library, Clarksburg, West Virginia).

weapon "is a ray with a long range which burns up everything in its path."[19] The notion of ray guns is one Space Age science fiction trope that often gets left behind by the writers of contactee tales. George King's epic space battle with the evil space dwarves (see Chapter 4), of course, was an exception. The general lack of violence and weapons (and action of any sort) is not surprising given the peaceful relations the vast majority of space brothers and sisters had with their neighbors.

In many ways, Bender's *Flying Saucers and the Three Men* reads like a pastiche of paranormal themed ideas and writing — contactee literature — of the 1950s and early 1960s. A few weeks later, Bender returned from a trip. Late at night, he had another experience. "Three shadowy figures" dressed in dark clothes and wearing homburgs appeared in the room, hovering a foot above the floor. They told Bender that they'd been observing his flying saucer investigations and believed him to be "a very good contact for us on your planet.... You are an average person, and we know that what we tell you and show you will not be believed by anyone you might tell." They went on to explain to Bender that their human-like appearance was an illusion: "We also found it necessary to carry off Earth people to use their bodies to disguise our own." The three men didn't explain the mechanism behind this process, but the horrific implications of this variety of "body snatching" resonated with Bender's already established predilection for horror imagery. After this second, more in-depth experience with the three men, Bender's story began to take on more similarity to traditional contact.[20]

Bender visits an "exalted one" in the Antarctic base of the visitors from Kazik. These meetings with the exalted one evoke the meetings with the Masters with whom George Adamski met and discussed in *Inside the Spaceships*. The differences, however, are striking and amusing. Rather than exalting the virtues of cosmic peace, the exalted one discusses the uses of death rays. Instead of fresh fruit, the people of Kazik subsist on "a fungus kind of growth" and shellfish. Far from feeling relaxed and at ease in the presence of space visitors, Bender portrays himself in print as becoming ever more troubled, neurotic and paranoid: "The headache remained, and my eyes burned and felt swollen. I sat down on the bed, rubbed my eyes and head. Again I wondered if I were going out of my mind. Had I suffered some kind of fit? Had I dreamed this and the other realistic experiences? I began to think it might be logical and wise to see a doctor."[21]

The beings from Kazik would continue to influence Bender's life after they stopped physically visiting him. He would continue to have debilitating headaches, even after the strange piece of metal through which he contacted the beings from Kazik disintegrated. Bender counted himself lucky that was all he suffered: "I am most thankful that I got through them with nothing more serious than the terrible headaches.... I am happy it has ended." He hopes that if the space people return they find Earth at peace, and not "a barren desolate place of ruined cities and bomb craters." Here, Bender reverts to the patterns of more typical contactee fare, asserting the vital importance of peace and harmony on Earth.[22]

Despite the horrors he had been through, Bender expressed hope that *Flying Saucers and the Three Men* would settle the issue of why he had left flying saucer research, hoping that those who "lost faith in me and the IFSB will now be able to read my true story. Now that they know the truth, perhaps some of them will again treat me as a friend." Beyond this hope, Bender expressed a more general dream for his life in the final lines of the book: "Perhaps the harassment of the telephone calls at late hours and uninvited visitors at my door will cease. Perhaps I can be left alone to live a normal life like any other human being, and the terrible personal consequences of my involvement with otherworldly visitors can be at least partly forgotten." Through the eyes of Albert Bender, the writing and publication of *Flying Saucers and the Three Men* takes on the appearance of a kind of exorcism — an attempt to cast out from his life the demonic (or at least annoying) Men in Black of Kazik.[23]

Bender would appear on the flying saucer scene once more before leaving it forever. On June 24, 1967, at the Hotel Commodore in New York City, James Moseley hosted the largest indoor flying saucer conference in American history. Among the speakers was Albert Bender, who at the last minute before the conference — for reasons known only to him — agreed to "appear" only through a 29-minute tape-recorded message. Fortunately, UFO researchers and historians have preserved this recording, for it is Bender's last hurrah in the world of flying saucers. Significantly, he does not focus on the Men in Black but rather the planet Kazik.

Like *Flying Saucers and the Three Men*, Bender's story sounds like a typical contactee tale, but with some twists. Most of the speech is given over to interesting facts about the planet and its people. The Kazik, he reports, have three sexes — male, female, and a third sex that is "exalted" above the others. Their planet is twice the size of Earth, but looks like our moon, with craters that are entrances to the underground cities, lit constantly by a mysterious bioluminescent material. There is no greed or crime and Kazik is a moneyless society, with everybody pitching in, doing work for free. "Love on Kazik," Bender says, "is free love, as there is no such thing as marriage." All the children are raised by a dedicated group of caretakers. The Kazik are able to shift their forms in order to adjust their appearance and appear frightening to others if necessary.[24]

All of this is similar to contactee tales told by Adamski and others and is in keeping with Bender's account in *Flying Saucers and the Three Men*. The final portion, however, moves away from the established territory of idyllic alien societies. Referring to the violet light to which he was exposed (which he was told would prevent "any earthly diseases"—see Chapter 7 for more on his sensual experience), Bender claims he was "given a power that would come gradually. This power was to be realized sooner than I anticipated. Already I am frightened to death with what I have already accomplished with this uncanny force that has been planted in my body. The power brings no good to myself but only aids me in bringing harm to my enemies. It is an evil thing and I cannot control it when it overtakes me." Bender goes on to describe an incident where harm had befallen those with whom he had quarreled at work. Another example he gave was of a man who refused to extinguish his cigar on a bus when Bender had asked. After several incidents like this, Bender wished the man would "burn himself with his cigar." Bender later learned the man had burned to death in an apartment fire from smoking in bed: "I was shocked to realize I had wished this thing upon him."[25] Bender, in his talk, mentioned that he was working on a second book on his experiences with the people of Kazik. But the book would never appear: after this tape-recorded appearance, Bender left the flying saucer field for good, refusing to discuss his experiences in any way. Thus, we are left with little direct information from Bender and others about his experiences.

As it does with the conventions of contactee narrative, the one-two punch of *They Knew Too Much About Flying Saucers* and *Flying Saucers and the Three Men* blurs the line between fact and fiction. Borrowing a concept from comic book fandom, Bender's book is an early attempt at establishing a retroactive continuity, or "retcon"—a conscious attempt to fill in details missing from an earlier narrative. There are sequences in Bender's book that were clearly designed to slot into gaps of narrative or understanding that appeared in Barker's earlier book. Whether these narrative fixes were the doing of Bender the author or Barker the editor is ultimately unclear.

James Moseley, in his autobiography, claims that as early as the late 1950s, Barker's perception of the flying saucer phenomenon — and of Bender's encounters with the Men in Black — had shifted: "Gray had given up any pretense of believing the tale. If he had ever had any serious belief in

UFOs, the realization that Bender's story was a crock seemed to drive him into total disbelief. He thought of UFOs and ufology as he did motion pictures — make-believe, wonderment, entertainment, fantasy, fun and games."[26] Barker and Bender's Men in Black work in the 1950s and 1960s exists in a fictional world — related to, but separate from the world in which the "real" Bender, Barker, Moseley, et al., lived. This world was malleable and, being malleable, was subject to fixing or expanding when necessary.

There are several places where Bender's book seems to address issues raised in Barker's. Readers, perhaps, were wondering just what it was that Bender experienced which caused Barker to write, "After they got through with you, you wished you'd have never heard of the word, 'Saucer.' You turned pale and got awfully sick. You couldn't get anything to stay on your stomach for three long days."[27] The revelation of Bender's visits from the men from Kazik, the sulfur mist, and the debilitating pain he experienced would explain the terror in the earlier work as well as build on the foundations of the mystery Barker laid down.

Another example of Bender's work picking up loose threads from Barker's book is a brief explanation of "apparitions and ghosts" as being invisible creatures living below the surface of the Earth. This brief paragraph picks up on the discussion of Richard Shaver's Deros and Teros which appeared in *They Knew Too Much About Flying Saucers*. It's all too easy to imagine a saucer aficionado reading Bender's book, turning and leafing through his older copy of Barker's tome. Eyes alight, our hypothetical saucer enthusiast thinks to him- or herself, "It all makes sense!" Given James Moseley's assertion that Barker, over time, saw the question of flying saucers as entertainment, this creation of a shared, semi-fictional saucer universe is a possible explanation for the "retconning" of Bender's Men in Black story.

The Men in Black have connections to the contactee phenomenon beyond the experiences of Albert K. Bender on the planet Kazik. George Adamski believed he as the victim of the "Silence Group" which attempted to thwart his worldwide speaking tour. Ashtar and his associates have mentioned evil space beings. Billy Meier has found himself the target of 22 separate assassination attempts to date. Some of these were the actions of the Men in Black, who Meier claims are from the Sirius star system. Fortunately for Meier, the Pleiadians have removed the Sirians from a position of being able to cause trouble: "The men in black were rounded up and taken into custody through forces of their home world after their last evil attacks against you. They also do not pose a threat anymore."[28] Despite the divergence between the actions and messages of the Men in Black compared to the friendly space brothers and sisters the contactees encountered, they represent a parallel track of contactee thought. These tracks overlapped occasionally, as shown in George Adamski's dealings with the "Silence Group." Buck Nelson (see Chapter 4) also encountered the Men in Black, who warned him that he could talk about his encounters all he wanted, but he should "never try to prove it."[29] The worlds of contactees, Men in Black, and conspiracy theories are not in separate silos, free from cross-contamination. Contactees, like Adamski and Nelson, would employ whatever useful memes available to tell their story. The suggestion, to readers, that they were being shut up, that their stories contained truth, was a helpful marketing tool.

In either of their guises — either as sinister denizens of officialdom sent to protect government secrets or as dark beings from Sirius or Kazik — the Men in Black represent the dark fears held by the generally shiny and optimistic contactees. Perhaps the government would stifle their messages; perhaps all of the space people were their brothers and sisters, the evil as well as the kind. The Men in Black trend, at least as it relates to the contactee phenomenon, is a brake on the enthusiasm. It is a sobering reminder that the future does not come without a price.

Religion, Christianity and Contact

Scholars have examined contact claims and stories in the context of religion more than through any other lens. Published in 1995, James R. Lewis's collection of essays *The Gods Have Landed: New Religions from Other Worlds* contains several studies on the religious aspects of particular UFO contact groups (the followers of Räel, for example) and the religious nature of contact claims in general. J. Gordon Melton argues that contactees "should be approached as participants in an occult religious movement. They are not kooks, but they are people who have been swept into a movement because of a direct experience with some extraordinary occurrences" which closely resemble "common visionary and psychic experiences cast in a framework of space age technology."[30]

Writers and researchers who have examined the extraterrestrial contact phenomenon from a Christian perspective have often latched onto its occult and New Age aspects. The themes of Theosophy (the prominent role of ascended masters, including a version of Jesus) and contact techniques such as automatic writing and other forms of channeling are often present. These have often served as a point of criticism and suspicion for some Christian (particularly fundamentalist or evangelical) writers.

The relationship between Christianity and the contactee phenomenon is complex. While the contactees of the 1950s and 1960s often referred to God, Jesus, and Christ, they often did so within a context of critiquing contemporary religious hierarchies. Many times, when contactees refer to Jesus — or any other traditional religious figure — it is akin to the Theosophical tradition of understanding religious leaders and founders as being part of a pantheon of ascended masters rather than individually and exclusively important. Christian writers have often perceived these critiques as evidence of an anti–Christian attitude on the part of contactees.

While contactees have generally discussed Christianity in the terms described above, less consistent is the attitude of Christianity toward contactee narratives and claims. For the most part, Christian writers and thinkers have lumped contactees claims — along with other flying saucer sightings, abduction reports and the like — in with other aspects of "New Age" thinking and philosophy, only rarely speaking on the subject specifically. Beginning in the 1970s, writers began to examine the flying saucer/UFO phenomenon (including contactee claims and narratives) from the viewpoint of Christianity, particularly evangelical Protestantism. In many cases, the judgment of these writers was that the messages promulgated by these extraterrestrial visitors were negative. John A. Saliba, in his essay "Religious Dimensions of UFO Phenomena," argues that contactee claims generally fall into two categories. The first "depicts the aliens as angelic and attractive youth ... who are generally interested in the well-being of the human race." The second category presents "aliens as dangerous and terrifying creatures or negative astral entities, whose activities are violent and hostile."[31] Figure such as Orthon, the Venusian whom George Adamski met in the California desert, would fall into the first category, while the three Men in Black who menaced Albert Bender might fall into the second.

In 1975, Christian publishers Harvest House released *UFOs: What on Earth Is Happening?* by John Weldon and Zola Levitt. While this was Weldon's first book, Zola Levitt had a long career writing books focusing on Biblical prophecy with titles such as *Satan in the Sanctuary* and *The*

Coming Russian Invasion of Israel. It is thus a distinctly eschatological, Biblical-prophecy viewpoint that permeates the Weldon and Levitt text. Weldon and Levitt argue that "UFO's and the other strange manifestations we are seeing represent demon activity" and that "the most frightening possibility of all, from the point of view of Biblical prophecy, is that *somebody* will step out of a UFO with solutions to our world problems.... Don't put this book down yet. We may be about to meet the Antichrist!" [emphasis in original]. This description certainly seems to be in line with the depictions of the space brothers, although the authors' assertion that the people of Earth would greet such messages and messengers with open arms and eager acceptance is not borne out by the relative obscurity of the contactees.[32]

As one indicator of the demonic (or at the very least, non–Christian) nature of flying saucer contact, Weldon and Levitt examine the claims and activities of George King (see Chapter 4) and his Aetherius Society. The authors provide a brief summary of the history of King's contacts and the establishment of the Aetherius Society, focusing on the organization's activities. King himself is indicted as inhabiting the dark side due to his longtime practice of yoga, which they describe as "demonic." Yoga's demonic nature is demonstrated, partially, through the "death, insanity, and incurable illness resulting from misapplied Yoga techniques." The activities of the Aetherius Society also come under scrutiny. One example is Operation Prayer Power, which involved members of the Society praying in response to natural disasters. In Weldon and Levitt's analysis, this is "an authentic spiritual effort," although with goals and effects far different from what is claimed: "Actually the point was to store psychic energy. The Russians reportedly performed such an occult psychic energy-storage exercise to remove sludge from rivers.... There is actually some efficacy to this technique, since, in the demon theory, it is supposed that any obeisance to the demons will be rewarded with help from them." King, and other contactees who refer to God, Jesus, prayer, and other Christianity-tinged themes are thus to be suspected and — possibly — condemned as demonic because of it. Also significant in this critique of George King and the Aetherius Society is the focus on the non-western aspects of King's story, such as yoga. Often, Christian critics of flying saucer contact narratives and ideas consider these non-western notions to be intrinsically anti–Christian, liable to lure the unwary into the clutches of Satan.[33]

Evangelical authors would emerge with renewed output on the UFO question in the late 1990s. The explosion of media coverage surrounding the Heaven's Gate mass suicide, as well as the growing popularity of *The X-Files* on television, Art Bell's *Coast to Coast AM* radio show, and the 50th anniversary of the alleged flying saucer crash near Roswell, New Mexico, led to an increase in UFO-related books of all types. Books dealing with the intersection of flying saucers and Christianity were no exception. Like earlier works, many of these would portray belief in contactee narratives (and the messages conveyed from the space brothers) as being fundamentally incompatible with Christianity.

One example is televangelist Bob Larson's *UFOs and the Alien Agenda*. Bob Larson, according to his website biography, "is the world's foremost expert on cults, the occult and supernatural phenomena."[34] Larson got his start during the Satanic cult and ritual abuse scares of the 1980s. Since the late 1990s, Larson has concentrated on performing exorcisms. In *UFOs and the Alien Agenda*, Larson takes a similar approach to Weldon and Levitt's earlier book, concentrating on aspects of the UFO phenomenon he considers demonic or steeped in New Age thought.

One of the key differences between Larson's book and the Weldon/Levitt effort is that Larson spends much less time in actual critiques and more in merely ridiculing and dismissing UFO and contact claims. In the chapter titled "New Age Nuttiness," Larson connects — in a very vague way — flying saucer and contact experiences with New Age thoughts and philosophies. For example, "Aliens do not like to be ignored. In their cosmological scheme, there is only one way to interpret reality: their way!... This arrogance is similar to the New Age's underlying exclusivity.... To the New Age, Christ is okay as long as He is one of many masters, but never the supreme embodiment of Truth." Larson also declares, "The current angel-crazy faction of the New Age movement is partially an outgrowth of equating UFO occupants with the heavenly messengers of the Bible."[35] Most of the book is given over to overly broad assessments such as these. Rarely does Larson refer to specific UFO figures or specific New Age texts or beliefs.

Just as Larson paints the New Age movement and UFO contact with a fairly broad brush, he also uses the recent (at the time) tragedy of the Heaven's Gate cult suicide to promote evangelical Christian social views:

> The secular media covering this story have almost universally suggested that the horror of Heaven's Gate would not have happened if Applewhite had accepted his homosexuality. Conservative Christians, who believe that homo-

sexual behavior is unacceptable, argue that his indulgence in this behavior was a moral violation that clouded his spiritual judgment, thus leading to other reprehensible deeds.[36]

Extraterrestrial contact claims — and the results, no matter how tragic — are, in Larson's world, the result solely of "moral violations." Homosexuality, however, is the sin Larson singles out as crucial, despite referring to other crimes such as fraud and — obviously — inducing followers to suicide. Larson identifies Applewhite's sexuality as the foundation of the entire chain of events, grouping homosexuality along with New Age beliefs in a forbidden zone of thought and practice, contrary to Christian norms.

Like other writers who have examined the flying saucer and extraterrestrial contact phenomena, Bob Larson sees the utility in viewing it within the context of theology and new religious movements. Larson, however, is a religious partisan. He views claims of contact between humans and extraterrestrials as real, but distinctly sinister events and intricately tied to end-time events: "Will extraterrestrials really be involved in God's end-time program? Will Christians be raptured, lifted off the planet by UFOs? Or has some dark force simply been preparing people to accept that explanation?" Larson goes on to assert that "it should be obvious by now that some sinister force is deliberately developing a religious system.... A Mystery Babylon belief is slowly creeping into modern consciousness." Larson describes those who have had "direct contact with alien benefactors" as the apostles of this dark religion.[37]

For Larson, there is no real difference between the George Adamski-like figure that had a friendly encounter with a space brother, the scientist speculating on the possibility of life on other planets, or the terrified woman who believes she was abducted and impregnated by reptilians from the lower fourth dimension. All of these encounters with the alleged or potential extraterrestrials are contrary to Larson's view of God's plan for humanity. If there are extraterrestrials out there, visiting Earth, their role is destructive to the souls of humanity.

Another book also published in 1997, which expands on some of the themes introduced by Larson is *Alien Encounters: The Secret Behind the UFO Phenomenon* by Chuck Missler and Mark Eastman. Most of the book is a rehash of the history of flying saucer and extraterrestrial encounters, focusing heavily on the dangers of connections between alleged alien civilizations and ancient human civilizations, since these often contradict stories of creation told in the Old Testament, or because they interpret these stories in ways which run counter to accepted Christian interpretations of these stories. Missler and Eastman also address the narratives and teachings of the contactees, focusing on George Van Tassel's communications with Ashtar (and later Ashtar channels such as Tuella). The authors specifically address warnings of the destruction of humanity due to war, and the promise of rescue for those who accepted Ashtar's teaching. Missler and Eastman assert that these warnings are a means of conditioning people to accept New Age teachings and to consciously muddle those New Age concepts with notion of the Rapture promoted by evangelical Protestants. There will be a "counterfeit" rapture that will deceive many in the Church, the authors claim.[38]

Authors such as Weldon, Levitt, Larson, Missler, and Eastman discussed here also share in common a concern that theories of extraterrestrial contact and visitation were being used to promote a worldview of "evolution" and to undermine the truth of the creation story as presented in the Old Testament. Others believe that since the Bible does not specifically mention the existence of non-human intelligent life, therefore none exist. The closest analogue to extraterrestrials, they claim, are the Nephilim, beings who appear in the sixth chapter of Genesis and mate with human women before the Great Flood. Since Genesis declares that these "giants" were on the Earth after the flood, some have determined that the Nephilim are the aliens which people have encountered.[39]

In general, evangelical Protestant authors have treated extraterrestrial contact — as well as those who have experienced such contact — as being freighted with potential peril for the soul. Already possessing a supernatural, salvation-based worldview imparted by divine revelation, evangelical Protestants and promoters of extraterrestrial contactee narratives and teachings repel each other as if they are like poles of a magnet. While critics from a scientific or journalistic viewpoint often attack contactee claims based on the factual and evidentiary deficiencies of the individual stories, evangelical Protestant writers and thinkers tend to dismiss them because the contactee claims are heretical — they defy orthodoxy, creed, and accepted interpretation of scripture. contactees, on the other hand, are a much broader "church" — their orthodoxy is flexible, though not endlessly so. Their conceptions of spiritual truth, by absorbing a wide variety of different theological traditions, represent a threat to the entire idea of religious orthodoxy.

The fears and paranoia of a counterfeit alien salvation held by some on the paranormal-evangelical fringe was, in the United States and other nations during the 1990s, mirrored by right-wing extremists who warned of a New World Order which would eliminate the very notion of national sovereignty and usher in a global government to eliminate rights, liberty, and basic human dignity. During the 1990s, there emerged a ménage of paranoid political conspiracy theories which tied into many of the ideas promulgated by contactees. While the fears of right-wing conspiracy theorists seems far afield from the glorious promises of the stories told by the space brothers and their representatives on Earth, there is a strong correlation between the sociopolitical ideas, theories, and goals of those contactees and the paranoid warnings of those fighting the New World Order. In many cases, however, those who warn of a New World Order set themselves at odds with those who would be on the side of contactees like Adamski, Williamson, and the rest. Although the origins of these memes — emerging in right-wing circles during the 1990s and propagated on the Internet ever since — are cloudy, one of the earliest explications of the story comes from Canadian journalist Serge Monast.

In 1994, Monast recorded a lecture for an organization called the International Free Press in Magog, Quebec, Canada. Monast's lecture, originating a generation ago, encompasses such a broad array of right-wing paranoia that it is almost a primer for the genre as a whole. It is worthwhile to examine it in detail in order to understand the degree to which the political and social ideas appropriated by the contactees frightened some on the right. Monast begins by asserting that the New World Order is a real thing, "a real Satanic under going [sic] project." It has several goals, including:

- The end of "all Christian traditional religions in order to replace them by a one-world religion based on the 'cult of man.'"
- The abolition of "national identity and national pride in order to establish a world identity and world pride."
- The abolition of "the family as known today in order to replace it by individuals all working for the glory of one-world government."
- "The implementation of a universal and obligatory membership to the United Nations, as transcending of the United Nations [sic] by multi-military and multi-police force."

- The establishment of "a world wide Justice Department through the United Nations with an International Criminal Court."
- "A New World Religion and a New World Culture for all men."

All who wish to be a part of the new order "will have to take an oath to Lucifer with a ritual initiation." Those who do not will be herded into concentration camps for elimination. Christian children are to be reserved as sexual playthings for the elite and human sacrifice.

These themes have remained constant in right-wing paranoia even into the 21st century. Monast's account of the origins of these conspiracy theories, however, relate to the ideals presented by the many of the contactees. Monast points to the Theosophical ideas of Helena Blavatsky and Alice Bailey as the roots of the New World Order paradigm. As we have seen, these spiritualist ideas were also the foundation for many of the contactees, many of whom talk about the dawn of a new age heralded by the arrival (physical or telepathic) of the space brothers. For Monast, and those who took his ideas and ran with them throughout the 1990s, the notion of friendly space people bringing salvation is all part of the conspiracy. The conspiracy, according to Serge Monast, centers on something called Project Blue Beam.

Project Blue Beam is, according to Monast, the product of NASA technology combined with the New World Order's desire for total control of the planet. Tying together tales of aliens, government mind control schemes and holographic technology, Blue Beam is a dastardly plot to seize control of humanity's hearts and minds; and it ties directly into the development of contactee narratives. According to Monast, the project has four distinct stages. The first step is to use secret technology to generate earthquakes that will reveal previously unknown archaeological sites in order to "suddenly explain ... the wrong meaning of all major religions' basic doctrines." This breakdown of the veracity of humanity's major faiths will generate doubt and lead to a desire for a religious structure to take its place.

The second and third stages of Project Blue Beam both involve the continued shaping of humanity's spiritual destiny. Step two consists of a "gigantic space show with three dimensional optical holograms and sounds, laser projections of multiple holographic images to different parts of the world, each receiving different images according to predominating regional/national religious faith. This new god's image will be talking in all languages." The end result of this deception will be a new, holographic "reality" which will lead to "the implementation of a new universal religion. Enough tricks will be foisted on us to hook us into the lie. The Project is the ability to take up a whole bunch of people as in a rapture type of situation and to whisk the whole bunch into never-never land." The third stage builds on this, using "psychotronic" devices to beam messages from "false gods" into the brains of unsuspecting men and women.

The fourth stage — emerging after all of this preparatory work has been completed — is where Project Blue Beam ties in most closely to the themes we have been examining. Stage four is the culmination of the conspiracy to enslave humanity and is fairly complex. The first goal of stage four "is to make mankind belief [*sic*] that an alien invasion is about to strike down on each major city of the earth in order to push each major nation to use its nuclear [*sic*] to strike back. This way, it would put each of these nations in a state of full disarmament in front of the United Nations after the false attack." So the nations of the world would use all their nuclear stockpiles against an enemy that didn't exist, rendering them defenseless against the coming UN takeover. The second part of stage four "is to make the Christians believe to [*sic*] a major rapture with the supposedly divine intervention of an alleged good alien force coming to save the people from a brutal satanic attack. Its goal is to get rid of all significant opposition to the New World Order." This will be followed by the appearance of alien and supernatural beings coming from every device with a microchip or connected into the power and telecommunications grids. The goal of this wave of apparitions is "to push all population on the edge to drown into a wave of suicide, killing and permanent psychological disorders."[40]

Hidden in plain sight, amidst all the paranoia, are interesting and significant connections between 1990s conspiracy thought and 1950s extraterrestrial contact narratives. Like evangelical writers on the paranormal such as Bob Larson and Chuck Missler, Serge Monast sees the stated peaceful intentions of the space brothers as fundamentally deceptive. The difference between the two views of the space brothers is in their origins. From the Christian eschatological perspective, the space brothers are demonic figures, bent on tricking humanity out of salvation. From Monast's perspective, while the basic forces are demonic in nature, the driving factors are political; regionalization and globalization, the perceived diminishing of national identity, and a seeming loss of freedom all contribute to his personal flavor of paranoia.

Central to both approaches, however, is the notion of the space brothers of contactee lore. They are here to help us defeat the baser natures of our own being. They bring knowledge and truth and understanding far beyond what our paltry political and spiritual traditions hold. Like the Men in Black trope, these paranoid notions required the existence of the contactees in order to come into being. Just as the contactees of the 1950s and 1960s were among the midwives of the New Age movements of the 1970s (along with Theosophy and other forms of spiritualism), those who dealt with the space brothers also bear responsibility for some of the darker aspects of paranormal culture.

The significance of these darker narratives, emerging in the 1950s and becoming more and more paranoid and frightening through the decades, is that they grow directly out of many of the original contactee notions. The idea of space people visiting humanity — for good purposes or ill — took on a life of its own. It wove its way into the Men in Black's threats and the political paranoia of Serge Monast. The space brothers infiltrated evangelical protestant Christianity, infecting its eschatology with their spiritualist notions and ideas, threatening the prevailing orthodoxy.

Taking a long view of these phenomena, it is clear that the contactee movement of the early Cold War era contributed, in at least some way, to such disparate cultural manifestations as the *Left Behind* series of books and films, *The X-Files*, the right-wing militia movement in the United States, and the anti-globalist movements around the world. It did not do this through an overt influence. The creators of these cultural manifestations of end-times scenarios or explorations of the paranormal and paranoid, if asked, would probably not identify the works of George Adamski or the collected sayings of Ashtar as one of their inspirations. The sinister activities of the Men in Black, however, did not spring from a void. Barker's and Bender's tales were informed by the stories of the contactees — humanoids and personal contact had been done to death. Inverting the contactee formula by making the contacts frightening and unsettling brought something new to the mythology of human-extraterrestrial interaction.

The contactee movement's transition into the spiritualist realm of the Tuella channeling built directly on the Theosophical tradition pioneered by George Adamski and others. It also put the flying saucers' Age of Aquarius on a collision course with evangelical fundamentalism in the late 1970s and 1980s. The vision of space brothers descending to save us from ourselves is not, apparently, comforting to everyone.

7

Sex, Gender
and Flying Saucers

Throughout the decades-long development of the flying saucer/
extraterrestrial contact movement, issues of gender and sexuality have occupied a peripheral — but significant — place. Both women and men have
promulgated contactee narratives and used this genre to convey political
and social ideals and philosophies. Women have, since the early 1950s,
occupied an increasing segment of contactee narratives, moving from the
sidelines to a prominent place, particularly in the realm of alleged channeled communications from space visitors. Male contactees have also, on
occasion, encountered women from other worlds; these encounters have
run the gamut from independent, assertive career spacewomen to alien
women who seem to inhabit gender roles which are often strangely parallel
to those expected of suburban Earth women. These gendered interactions
provide an additional lens through which to understand the contactee phenomenon.

Where Gender Fits

Gender refers to the spectrum of characteristics that a culture defines
as masculine, feminine, or androgynous, falling between the two categories.
Gender encompasses biological sex, the roles a culture defines for different
genders, and individuals' own gender identities. In recent years, some
scholars have begun to examine gender as a distinctly social construction
as well as a cultural one. Barbara J. Risman, for example, defined gender
"as a social structure because this brings gender to the same analytic plane
as politics and economics, where the focus has long been on political and

economic structures."[1] Just as contactee narratives give insight into the political, economic, and social beliefs of their creators, some narratives give us similar insight into gender.

The presence of women in contactee narratives is often inextricably tied to their role as sexual beings. Even in narratives where there is no actual sexual contact between humans and extraterrestrials, authors show women as sexualized creatures. In narratives where women are the contactees (and, thus, in a position of being able to tell their own stories), this sexualized approach is more overtly romanticized. There are exceptions, however, to the general trend of sexualization and romantization.

In general, women fall into three roles within the broad history of contactee narratives. One category consists of women who are contactees themselves, either through psychic or physical interaction. While there are a number of these women, their stories are often marginalized in the examination of extraterrestrial visitation claims. The majority of prominent contactees that have attracted attention since the advent of the phenomenon in the 1950s are male. While there are women who claimed contact experiences of their own, they remain on the periphery.

The women in the second group are those of extraterrestrial origin. Many of the male contactee writers described encounters with women from planets like Venus and Clarion. Often, these extraterrestrial women serve as a point of comparison to Earth women. Sometimes these women are presented as a contrast to the standard, media- and culturally-defined gender roles, and other times they are presented as a stereotypical example of "proper" and accepted gender roles of the period in question. This is particularly evident in the 1950s.

The third type of woman who appears in contactee literature is the simple bystander — a witness, spouse, daughter, or friend who may or may not believe the contactees' tales. All three of these categories give insight into issues of sexuality and gender, whether it be the authors' perceptions of the state of gender relations in their particular time or the authors' prescriptions of how and why gender roles should change.

The 1950s

The period that saw the advent of the classic contactee tale was also the decade during which gender roles in the western world were the most rigidly defined of the flying saucer era. This rigidity — strongest in the middle- and upper-middle-classes — was possibly, at least in the United States, a function of the same Cold War environment that informed the political, economic, and social outlooks of contactee narratives.

Some scholars, such as Elaine Tyler May in her book *Homeward Bound: American Families in the Cold War Era*, attribute the reassertion of strict traditional gender roles to the emergence of the conflict between the United States (and its western allies) and the Soviet Union. Experts considered traditional, middle-class domestic roles to be a way to apply the broad strategy of "containment" in a cultural context. As a result, media outlets began to valorize domesticity to American women who — just a few years previously — had been similarly entreated to take "men's jobs" in the defense and manufacturing industries. To be sure, the modern domestic ideal presented by television, radio, and magazines was largely confined to the middle-class, white suburbs, but the image was pervasive nonetheless.

Contactee narratives of the 1950s — while not actually subverting these conventions — tend not to use female characters in what one might consider traditional gender roles. This is, I think, due to two distinct factors. The first is the inherent weirdness of the subject matter with which contactee writers dealt — it was far enough outside the everyday that one can reasonably expect that depictions of "normal" domesticity and gender roles would be jarring. A second reason is that many of the men (along with the occasional and less common women) who created contactee tales (and other forms of flying saucer writing) were already, culturally speaking, outliers. They largely lived their lives on the fringes of society. A man like George Adamski, working at a hamburger stand and giving lectures on the Cosmic Law, already existed outside the cultural conventions of the time. Even George Van Tassel, with a traditionally nuclear family, moved them to a flimsy house located beneath a giant rock in the desert. Flying saucer contact tales did not, generally, come out of the suburbs. They came out of the wildernesses and cities, analogous in many ways to the literary works of the Beats of the same period.

Thus, rarely were there standard domestically focused gender roles for 1950s contactees to rebel against in their own lives. That still, however, left a potential space in which contactee writers used their narratives to critique the limitations on women's roles and lives in society at large.

The Interplanetary Career
Woman: Captain Aura Rhanes

Truman Bethurum's *Aboard a Flying Saucer*, in addition to being the second major work of contactee narrative, is also the first contactee work which we can view through the lens of gender roles in the American 1950s. The role of women (and that women have a role at all) sets Bethurum's work apart from Adamski's.

Adamski's contact episode contained within *Flying Saucers Have Landed* is largely devoid of women, apart from Alice Wells, one of the witnesses to the famed Desert Center contact. Even when considering later contactee works, Bethurum's dealings with Captain Aura Rhanes are an anomaly among 1950s contact figures. While she is a saucer captain, and in a position of command, she is also (through Bethurum) presented in a much more overtly gendered way than the space men and women usually are. At first glance, the 21st-century reader might notice that the stereotypical space-age jumpsuit is not in evidence here. Bethurum's early entree into the contactee scene meant that the stereotype of the jumpsuit wasn't yet a stereotype. Rather, Bethurum's specific and detailed vision of separate men's and women's uniforms — which conform to 1950s standards of what men's and women's clothing should be — serve as a reflection of traditional gender roles in keeping with the time period in which he was writing. Aura Rhanes, in Bethurum's narrative, represents an ideal human (if not Earth-born) woman. Bethurum portrays the males on the Clarionite saucer crew as competent, but he fawns over Rhanes. In introducing her to the reader, he describes her as "their captain, a beautiful woman."[2]

Bethurum describes both Aura Rhanes in a fundamentally different way from the way he does her male crew members. Bethurum describes the crew he meets as short (not "dwarves," but rather "fully developed small men") with "dark olive hued faces." His description of the captain, however, is much more flowery: "She was a trifle shorter than any of the men I had seen. Her smooth skin was a beautiful olive and roses, and her brown-eyed flashing smile seemed to make her complexion appear more glowing. I am sure she wore no makeup, but she certainly needed none. So this queen of women was the lady captain!"[3] Bethurum's attention to Aura Rhanes's appearance and suggestions of the degree to which he was besotted with her appear throughout the book. Along with this attraction is a condescending tone. For example, Bethurum often refers to Rhanes as the "little lady captain."[4] It is difficult to imagine Bethurum referring to a male in the same position as the "big man captain." Additionally, Bethurum's condescending attitude toward Aura Rhanes is sometimes combined with his expressions of appreciation for her physical beauty. After becoming acquainted with Rhanes, Bethurum relates, "I told her how impressed I was that a woman was captain of such a piece of equipment; how the males of our earth would rate her as tops in shapeliness and beauty."[5] There is an implicit connection between her beauty and Bethurum's surprise that she is in command of a spacecraft. One wonders if Bethurum would have been so surprised if Aura Rhanes had been less attractive.

Bethurum also spends more time and description on Aura Rhanes's uniform than on the uniforms of her male crew members. While the men wore "black billed caps ... jackets like cowboys and trousers of material which reflected a blue-grayish cast," Captain Rhanes's uniform — and appearance in general — gets a much fuller treatment: "Her black hair was short and brushed into an upward curl at the ends, and she wore jauntily tilted on one side of her proudly held head a black and red beret.... Her bodice was of some fitted material which looked like black velvet, with short sleeves decorated with a small red ribbon bow. The top of her skirt ... was of the most radiant red material I have ever seen. It looked like wool and was set all round in small flat pleats."[6]

Throughout the book, Bethurum's relationship with his wife, Mary, is interestingly strained. Due to his work on various distant construction jobs, he spends weeks and months at a time away from his family. Bethurum writes Mary soon after his encounters with the Clarionites begin. Initially, he's simply asking her to come visit him, hoping to introduce her to the visitors. When she refuses, he decides to tell her the whole story of his visits with the Clarionites. Mary's reaction is far from what Bethurum was expecting. She responds to his letter with one of her own, claiming to be "dismayed and shocked to her very foundations" by his story. She goes so far as to say, Bethurum relates, that "since we had only been married a few years ... she had taken the trouble to telephone my daughters long distance and ask them if I had aver been the victim of a visual delusion, or had ever been in any mental institution."[7]

Mary's skepticism of Bethurum's tale — increasingly tinged with jealousy of his friendship with Aura Rhanes — would continue until she met the period's other famed contactee, George Adamski, who affirmed the probability that Truman was telling the truth. As the book ends, Mary is excited by the prospect of someday meeting the Clarionites herself.

Mary, Whitey, his daughters, and the constellation of other Earth human characters with whom Truman Bethurum surrounds himself in this book form a spectrum of belief. This spectrum ranges from outright skepticism and ridicule to interest and acceptance. Crucially, until the very end of the narrative, Truman's wife Mary is the only woman on the skeptical end of this spectrum. The skeptical side is, other than Mary, composed of the men with whom Truman Bethurum associates, particularly his supervisor, Whitey. The people in Bethurum's life who believed his stories of saucer contact (or, at least, chose to express interest or failed to express disbelief) were women — Truman's adult daughters, Whitey's wife, and the waitress at the local restaurant. Thus, as Bethurum's interest in the Clarionites approaches the degree of obsession, Mary moves further away from her role of wife, supporter, and female. Instead, she moves toward a role of antagonist, skeptic and male. Aura Rhanes takes on the role of the woman Truman can talk to and ask questions, and to whom he feels connected.

At the risk of engaging in psychoanalysis, one must wonder if Truman Bethurum was using his flying saucer contact narrative as a means to work through domestic conflict within his home. Whatever wedge might have existed between Truman and Mary is irrelevant; in *Aboard a Flying Saucer*, the cause of their marital conflict is extraterrestrial. Aura Rhanes represents an ideal — an ideal that, apparently, Mary Bethurum cannot live up to. The only way the rift could be healed would be for her to accept Truman's tales of contact with the planet Clarion. This eventually happens at the end of *Aboard a Flying Saucer*, through the intervention of George Adamski, who believes Truman Bethurum's story and convinces Mary of its truth.[8]

The Mitchell Sisters: Contact Lite

Helen Mitchell and Betty Mitchell were sisters who recorded a contact experience with several men from Mars. Gray Barker's Saucerian Books published their pamphlet, *We Met the Space People*, in 1959. The sisters spoke at numerous flying saucer conventions and meetings in the late 1950s. By the early 1960s, they had faded from the flying saucer scene —

which was consistent with the fading of contacteeism in the mainstream of flying saucer belief, in favor of a more "evidence-based" approach. The Mitchell sisters were emblematic of the type of second- or third-string contactees who populated the lecture and convention circuit during the 1950s and 1960s, telling stories that were largely derivative of the other, major contactees such as George Adamski or George Van Tassel.

What sets Helen and Betty Mitchell apart from other small-time contactees in the early days of the phenomenon is not the content of their message. As we will see, the content of *We Met the Space People* is akin to a "greatest hits collection" or précis of common contactee themes. As women, however, their viewpoint is particularly valuable. Oddly, what might be most valuable about the Mitchell's sisters' contribution to contactee lore is the distinct lack of what one might call a woman's viewpoint or perspective in the work. The absence of overt discussions of gender is, however, a type of discourse.

Unlike Adamski's *Inside the Spaceships* or other full-length contactee tomes, *We Met the Space People* was one of many card-covered, stapled booklets produced during the 1950s by Saucerian. It comprises two sections, "Helen's Story" and "Betty's Account." Each is fairly brief, around 5000 words. Though not certain, it is probable that the editor of the book (most likely Gray Barker) crafted the work out of speeches given at a flying saucer convention. Betty, for example, reports that they received "information from a Venusian called Tregon. I would like to read his message for you, which we received just a few days before we came down here."[9] The brevity of the accounts and the reference to "reading" suggest that the editing of these speeches during their conversion into the published work may have been minimal, giving us a rawer take on the subject.

"Helen's Story" describes the initial encounter between the sisters and the men from Mars. Like many contactee tales, the initial meeting between Earthling and extraterrestrial took place in remarkably prosaic circumstances; in this case, in a St. Louis coffee shop while stopping to get a soda. Two men — Elen and Zelas — claimed to be from "a huge mothercraft orbiting the planet Earth" and asked the sisters if they would be willing to "serve as channels through which they could give certain information to Earth." Significantly, the item that convinced the sisters to believe Elen and Zelas was that the two visitors were able to relate incidents from the women's childhood which no one could know. This notion of male alien visitors watching Earth girls grow into adulthood and subsequently making contact is, as we shall see, a recurring theme without a parallel where the genders of the humans and aliens involved are reversed. There is often a paternalism or possessiveness in the relationships between alien men and Earth women.

On a subsequent visit to the same St. Louis coffee shop, the space brothers presented Helen and Betty with instructions on how to build a communications device through which the sisters could maintain contact with the Martians aboard their spacecraft and communicate with its commander, Alna. It was quite the complicated process: "His instructions were very explicit and precise, for he warned us that unless we placed every piece of the device in the proper place we would not be able to contact them with it. We were not allowed to take the drawn diagram of the device with us, but we had to remember it as it was explained to us."

This discussion of constructing an interplanetary communication device is suspiciously similar to a similar sequence in the 1955 film *This Island Earth* (based on a 1947 story, "The Alien Machine," by Raymond F. Jones), wherein Doctor Cal Meacham is instructed on how to build an Interocitor. Surprisingly, this type of overlap with popular science fiction films happened less frequently than one might think, although by the early 1960s, the amount of borrowing between fictional media and contactee material began to blur the lines between the two genres. Through this communication device, Helen and Betty learned a great deal about the Martians' way of life.[10]

In November 1957, the Mitchell sisters had their first trip on a flying saucer, taking a 15-minute flight to the mother craft in orbit of the Earth. Helen describes a tour of the mother craft, detailing the different areas of the ships and the uniforms of the (entirely male) crew. They then have dinner with Alna, the commander of the ship. Within a few weeks, the Martians contact the sisters, informing them that the Martian Council wishes to speak with them. Helen's narrative is then given over to an address by a space brother named Sigt who discusses the dangers of "the A and H bombs" which Earth governments were in the process of testing, releasing dangerous radiation into the atmosphere. This is dangerous for Earthlings, of course, but also for the space people living on Earth. Sigt has a simple solution to the problem: "How can you stop this from happening? The answer is simply stop the unnecessary tests of these bombs. For those who maintain it necessary to show the military strength, we can only say what strength is there to be shown that deprives the people, vegetation and animals of a perfectly beautiful and attainable future otherwise." As is common in contactee narratives, spiritual notions also enter into the tale told by Helen. In this case, the extraterrestrial messenger predicts that the radiation produced by humanity's testing of nuclear weapons will "lead to a generation of mutants." Lest humanity believe that this is a problem for their children, Sigt points out, "The continuance of these tests are affecting all responsible for them, and if one accepts reincarnation as an answer it would be definitely seen why no one here ... would want to re-live again in mutated bodies of the future generations.... Our warning to Earth is to cease your tests and save your future."[11]

"Betty's Account" is a record of her communications with Tregon, a space brother from Venus. Unlike "Helen's Story," with its topical discussion of the dangers of nuclear weapons testing, Betty's message from Tregon is largely given over to a history of Earth's lost civilizations, particularly Atlantis, and the connections between ancient Earth and the space brothers of the solar system. The time of Atlantis "saw a growth of intelligent comprehension in man" until people "began to follow the evil influences.... Earth was then polluted." Venusians came to call Earthlings to repent but not all did. This sequence of events culminated in the flood recorded in the Biblical story of Noah and the destruction of Atlantis. An important example of the type of evil the Atlanteans practiced: "The Brothers have told us before that the evil ones of Atlantis were experimenting with energy releases that our scientists are playing with today in the A and H bomb experiments." Just as messengers from Venus and Mars warned the evil humans of Atlantis in ancient times, the same pattern is repeating in the United States and Soviet Union in the 20th century. The question of whether the outcome will be different remains open. The final decision on that outcome is out of the space brothers' hands, "Tregon has told us that the evil of Earth will continue until the planets and oceans are radioactive unless Earthman puts a stop to his evil."[12]

One particularly interesting aspect of the Mitchell sisters' contribution to the contactee genre is that it came late enough to self-consciously address some of the critiques which readers had brought against contactee claims in general. In particular, the Mitchells speak to two of these claims. One is their discussion of the presence of "evil" space visitors (see Chapter 6). The other is one which specifically addresses the space brothers' motives. Betty explains: "Many times the enthusiast asks us, 'Why don't the Space People just come down and take over? Earth would be better off.' But ...

until Earth is again ready ... they will only issue warnings and perhaps take the faithful up to the far heavens where they will wait the final cleansing of Earth's surface." This represents both a significant shift away from the conventional contactee tropes as pioneered by Adamski and a continuation of a shift toward more overtly spiritual themes. The notion of the faithful being taken up and being saved from a time of tribulation has unmistakable parallels to the notion of a rapture-and-tribulation eschatology as promoted by dispensationalist evangelical Protestants. It also provides a vision of contactee belief as a type of salvation-based faith. There is protection (in the "heavens" if not Heaven) for those who are "faithful," despite the sisters never explaining the precise manner of the faith to which they refer.[13]

Tregon's and Sigt's views, as conveyed through Helen and Betty, are largely conventional in their themes within the context of contactee narratives. Its creation and public expression by women, however, makes this narrative more of a rarity than its more better-known contemporaries. The absence of emphasis on gender in the presentation/booklet composed by Betty and Helen Mitchell is in itself significant. Just as contactees such as Adamski and Van Tassel did not make an issue of their maleness, the Mitchell sisters' refusal to make an issue of their femaleness (at least in the published transcript of their experiences) represents an attempt to place themselves on an equal footing with these pioneering figures. The references to Atlantis and a rapture-like event, moreover, cement the sisters within the world of spiritualism and religion which, at the time, were also male-dominated fields.

While women would make their presence felt in the contactee movement in the 1960s with romantic-themed tales, and in the 1970s and '80s with the advent of extensive publication of psychically channeled material, Helen and Betty Mitchell's straightforward, classic contactee narrative was a milestone in the development of the genre.

Antonio Villas-Boas and the Emergence of the Reproduction Trope

One of the archetypal stories of flying saucer–based sexual encounters is that of Antonio Villas-Boas. Villas-Boas's story is, arguably, not entirely within the contactee realm. The beings he encounters do not speak to him in any intelligible language; they have no message for him to convey to humanity. Also setting Villas-Boas apart from other saucer encounterers is that he made no attempt to cash in on his experiences. The exotic and sexual nature of the story would have made it a hit. Villas-Boas's tale was confined to the pages of flying saucer magazines, newspapers, and nearly every book written on the subject from 1957 to the present.

The series of events began on the night of October 5, 1957. Villas-Boas was a young farmer in Brazil. That night, around 11 P.M., he was disturbed by lights appearing over the corral near his house. Going to investigate, he encountered an egg-shaped spacecraft, but it took to the skies before he could get too close. The next day, while plowing, he encountered the craft again. This time, the craft's occupants (described as male and smaller than average humans) captured Villas-Boas, taking him aboard.

Once on the ship, Villas-Boas was stripped naked; the men of the ship gave him a sponge bath and took several blood samples. He was then left alone in a small room. After an indeterminate amount of time, "a small but well built and completely nude woman" entered the room. As Coral Lorenzen, whose APRO organization had been the first U.S. saucer organization to investigate the story, wrote: "The woman's purpose was immediately evident. She held herself close to Villas-Boas, rubbing her head against his face.... A very normal sexual act took place and after more pettings she responded again." Villas-Boas was not entirely pleased with the encounter: "The howling noises she made during the togetherness ... reminded him of an animal," and she refused to let him kiss her, biting him painfully on the chin when he attempted any conventional romantic contact. At the conclusion of the act, the woman pointed to her belly, then pointed upward, giving Villas-Boas the impression that she intended to return for a further encounter.[14]

The experience reported by Villas-Boas has appeared in just about every major overview of the flying saucer saga published since its first American appearance in the early 1960s. The reasons are not hard to discern. Mystery, sex, an exotic locale — this story has a lot going for it, from a writer's point of view. The Villas-Boas story, however, has significance beyond mere titillation. It was the first contact story which emphasized a sexual encounter — not just attractiveness, as in the case of Aura Rhanes, or intergalactic romance, as we will see in the story of Elizabeth Klarer. The sex here is perfunctory and strange, not romantic at all. Later writers, particularly those who focus on alien abductions, pointed to the Villas-

Boas case as the first "modern abduction," mostly due to the clinical nature of the sexual encounter.

The 1960s

Albert K. Bender also experienced a sensual (if not explicitly sexual) experience at the hands of women from the mysterious planet Kazik. In November 1953, after dissolving the International Flying Saucer Bureau, Bender was feeling quite low. He found himself attacked by former IFSB board members as well as the general public. The mysterious manner in which he dismantled the organization garnered a local newspaper story in Bridgeport, Connecticut; Bender's words and actions were subject to a great deal of scrutiny and ridicule.[15]

The Men in Black came once more into Bender's study, surrounded by clouds of sulfurous mist. They took him to a "vast room of cold, shining metal." Into this clinical setting came "three beautiful women, dressed in tight white uniforms." Their hair was silver, arranged in buns and held in place with metal halo-type decorations. Bender's previous experiences with the visitors from Kazik had been stressful, often accompanied by debilitating headaches. In contrast, in the presence of the "physically attractive" women of Kazik, Bender "felt more at ease than with the other visitors." The three women paralyzed him with their glowing eyes and moved him to a metal bench. They removed his clothing and massaged a strange liquid into his skin, rubbing the substance into "every part of [his] body without exception." The women left and a machine descended from the ceiling and bathed Bender in a powerful, purple light. Ultimately, Bender learned that this procedure was designed to prevent "one dreaded disease on your planet which all persons fear" and that Bender would "have no need to fear this" after being treated with the purple light.[16]

While it is outside the scope of this study to attempt to explain exactly what happened to the people who claimed contact with extraterrestrial visitors, UFO and paranormal writer Nick Redfern presents an interesting analysis of the intersection of sexuality, paranoia, and health. Noting that the sulphurous odors Bender experienced might have been an indicator of some sort of migraine or other neurological condition, Redfern concludes,

> What all this tells us about Bender is that he had repressed sexual fantasies about getting it on with a trio of gorgeous space girls, a terror of developing

cancer — conveniently lessened by a reassurance from the aliens that he will now be *forever* cancer-free — and longstanding anxieties about having been visited by agents of the FBI.... Those internal worries then collided in chaotic fashion, duly spilled out of Bender's subconscious, and fell right into the heart of a semi-awake, altered state.[17]

Romance, Sexuality, Reproduction and Race: Elizabeth Klarer's Story

As we have seen in the writing of Marla Baxter, women's tales of extraterrestrial are, in general, more focused on emotional connection and romance than on raw sexuality. This is in sharp contrast to the lascivious physical tales of male contactees like Albert Bender and Antonio Villas-Boas or even the less overtly-erotic attention of Truman Bethurum toward Captain Aura Rhanes. At the tail end of the 1970s, another woman — South African Elizabeth Klarer — wrote of a romantic relationship with Akon of the planet Meton which had allegedly taken place in 1956. The account of this series of encounters, *Beyond the Light Barrier: The Autobiography of Elizabeth Klarer*, was first published in 1980.

Though Klarer's book recounts events that allegedly occurred in the 1950s and 1960s (as discussed in Chapter 4, *Flying Saucer Review* published her initial claims), this later autobiography has little in common with her earlier claims. In this expanded narrative, the space brother who visits her has a name, and he is from a planet that circles the star Proxima rather than hailing from nearby Venus. Unlike her earliest claims — which borrowed much from the contactee claims of figures like George Adamski — Klarer's *Beyond the Light Barrier* is grounded in the South Africa of the 1970s. Concerns about race and politics are a constant presence in Klarer's story. While it takes place in the — by now — familiar temporal territory of the Cold War, *Beyond the Light Barrier* examines the times through a lens that is distinct from the foundational texts of the contactee phenomenon, most of which were written by Americans concerned with the issues faced by the United States. The worries and fears Klarer describes are distinct from those of the American contactees who were ostensibly her contemporaries.

Born in South Africa of English descent in 1910, Klarer tells of an extraterrestrial contact experience in the context of the post–Colonial world and the decline of Britain as a major power. Her story moves beyond a mere retelling of an alien encounter and presents a vision of the complex world that comprised the twilight of British imperialism. Concerns about war, peace, defense, and race all play a role in Klarer's story, existing along-side her main point — the reality of extraterrestrial visitation and its impact on her life.

The subtitle of Klarer's book is significant. This is an autobiography, going back to Klarer's 1910 birth and subsequent childhood in the foothills of the Drakensberg Mountains. If the reader finds some of her stories and explanations perplexing, Klarer reminds them that her book "is about time on the cosmic level, with new data not yet registered on scientific instru-ments. The reader needs to follow the cosmic layout of my writing very closely." Put simply, if the reader is confused it's his own fault. Whether or not the development of *Beyond the Light Barrier* was "cosmic," it cer-tainly is one of the most densely packed contactee narratives. Klarer's story regularly references political and racial issues, often in a brief, almost throw-away manner. Klarer's purpose in writing *Beyond the Light Barrier*, according to the preface, is to explicate the "cosmic connections" revealed to her by extraterrestrials. She does not, at least overtly, set out to write a book about alien visitation, *and* racial strife, *and* the role of Britain in a post-imperialist world, but over the course of the book, this is what she does.

From the beginning of her life, Klarer knew of the presence of the visitors who came in "a beautiful spaceship from elsewhere." Klarer begins her tale by recounting an incident when, as a child, she witnessed a space-ship protect her family and (she assumes) the entire Earth from a stray asteroid. Years later, she and her husband are flying in a small aircraft when they encounter a blue-white sphere which Klarer (through "women's intuition") knows is an alien ship. After a debriefing by the military, Klarer and her husband (an Air Force officer) are ordered to Britain's de Havilland Experimental Flight Center.[18]

At de Havilland, the Klarers see a glimpse of the British future: "Code-named TK4, perhaps it would revolutionize flying for England, enabling the nation to have a craft to defend her skies against any of the aggressive invaders who seemed to get more and more ruthless in their quest for power and world domination and who were forever devising more horrible and diabolical weapons of destruction." Lest Elizabeth sound keen for the development of new weapons of war, she goes on to assert that "to destroy one's fellow creatures and one's planet is a reflection of mass insanity.... Humankind of Earth is thereby a product of its environment." Klarer attempts to have it both ways. On the one hand, she employs a typical contactee trope in denouncing the concept of war and armed conflict. On the other, she asserts that it's a very good thing Britain has the "TK4" to defend itself against the aggressive invaders. There's a tension in this passage between the clichéd contactee pacifism and a muscular assertion of Britain's need for protection in a hostile world. Klarer is caught between being a citizen of the universe and a subject of the Crown.[19]

For war *is* coming, according to Klarer. It is a war for which the people of Britain are ill-prepared. She writes:

> They had rallied around in panic to stem the flow of Hitler's hordes, but there was no vision to gauge the blow to England's pride that was now being forged. The veil of silence is so cunningly drawn over the perception of man that he cannot see the plan to enslave him with wars and rumors of still more wars to come — wars of racial strife, black against white — in a bid to take over the planet.[20]

This is an intriguing claim. Klarer doesn't explain who is drawing this veil of silence or who is attempting to take over the planet. More significant is her strong assertion that a race war is in humanity's future, which is unusual among contactees and one of the aspects of *Beyond the Light Barrier* which marks it out as being a work of the late 1970s and not the 1950s or 1960s. The narrative, though set in the 1950s, makes no explicit mention of the Cold War conflict between NATO and the Soviet bloc. The late 1970s, however, was the tail end of an era of détente between the two superpowers. Other concerns were foremost in Elizabeth Klarer's mind and, as a native of South Africa, race was an unsurprising component.

South Africa's political development was heavily influenced its colonial history, under the Dutch Boers and Britain. Colonization of Africa was hardly limited to South Africa, of course, but demographic factors distinguished South Africa from other central and southern African nations. According to political geographer A.J. Christopher, "The area witnessed the largest European immigration and colonization on the continent ... on a scale approaching that of midlatitude colonial settlement during the eighteenth and nineteenth centuries."[21] As was the case throughout colonial Africa, the white minority asserted political and economic control over the indigenous population, despite being outnumbered by them. The colonists exploited the labor of the black population. As the colonial population grew in the late 19th and early 20th centuries, conflict over land led to the passage of the Native Lands Act of 1913, which established reserved areas on which the government resettled black South Africans. The Act also designated some land for black and some for white South Africans, prohibiting the sale of "White lands" to black South Africans.

As independence movements and decolonization swept the African continent in the wake of the Second World War, South Africa was again distinct from other colonial states. Since 1910, South Africa had been a dominion of the British Empire, and since 1931 had had de facto independence. Thus, South Africa possessed a cultural connection to the British Empire, while at the same time having a degree of political autonomy that other colonies did not possess, including a government which had the ability to pass laws such as the Native Lands Act, establishing legally defined racial segregation throughout the country. When South African leaders pushed for further independence for their country in the 1950s and 1960s, culminating in the declaration of the Republic of South Africa in 1961, it was not a native African leadership which demanded autonomy, but the descendants of transplanted Europeans. Throughout the 1960s, '70s, and '80s, in the face of international economic and diplomatic pressure as well as internal violence, South Africa continued its policies of racial apartheid. It is, therefore, predictable that issues of racial violence would surface in Klarer's writings.

Amidst Klarer's digression into the need for a well-defended Britain, the couple meets with a figure referred to only as the Chief. Klarer and her husband are old friends with this man (whose position and name never surface), which helps explain why Elizabeth is so comfortable telling of her lifetime of experience with what she believes are extraterrestrial visitors. After she tells her story to the Chief, he concludes, "It is as I suspected.... Our planet is under close surveillance by an alien, but highly advanced civilization." The Chief then tasks Klarer with seeking out contact with the visitors, urging her to follow hunches and "to use [her] powers of extrasensory perception." The stakes, as explained to her, were high. Contact with the extraterrestrial entities might provide a way for humanity and its people to finally live in harmony.[22]

Thus Klarer is not just a contactee (actually, at this point in her story she isn't fully a true contactee at all), she is an agent of the state in an active effort to contact alien entities. This is another aspect of *Beyond the Light Barrier* that sets the book apart from earlier contactee narratives. In the American contact milieu, government officials often denied the presence of extraterrestrials and harass those who claimed visitations from them. Klarer returns home to the Drakensberg Mountains and seeks out the beings that could save humanity. She begins by establishing telepathic contact with the beings in the spaceships she has seen throughout her life. Heading into the countryside, she next begins her quest for a physical contact with the beings flying the ships.

It is at this point in *Beyond the Light Barrier* that racial and cultural distinctions again become a factor in Klarer's larger contact story. Throughout the text, Klarer had discussed her conversations with the Zulu people who lived near her home. At this point, when she begins to actively seek contact with the extraterrestrial visitors, the Zulu people emerge again, providing a conduit of sorts for the aliens. As she wanders the countryside waiting for the ship containing the man she knows through telepathy as Akon, she hears the Zulu people speaking to her:

> They told of the great wagon of the sky and the fiery visitors from the heaven country.... "The golden hair of your head will bring the *Abelungu* from the sky," they called across the valleys as I listened to their descriptive language, understanding it as well as my own. "You are 'one who brings together,' *Inkosazana* [princess]! The heaven dwellers will come and take you away from us."[23]

At least one of the reasons, then, that the extraterrestrial visitors seek Elizabeth is because of her "golden hair"—a distinctively Caucasian characteristic. This passage is emblematic of how Klarer depicts the native African population in South Africa. They are an exotic other, connected both to the land and the space visitors. Despite this connection, however, they do not meet the visitors. That is a privilege reserved to Elizabeth, the golden-haired one.

Such connections between indigenous peoples and alleged space visitors are not, of course, confined to Klarer's account. Contactees in the United States (George Hunt Williamson is a prime example) asserted that Native American religion was inspired by ancient contact with extraterrestrials. The crucial distinction is that Klarer's discussion of the Zulu people's knowledge of the space visitors takes place within the charged racial context of South Africa in the 1970s. Klarer's story manages to position the Zulu as being especially connected to the space people while at the same time placing herself at an even higher level. This, in a way, serves to recast the racial distinctions present in South Africa in a context that is outside the political and colonial past of the land into one that is at a higher level than terrestrial concerns. Despite this repositioning, Klarer ensures that she is exalted above the non-whites; maintaining the traditional racial hierarchy, implying that such a hierarchy is in place beyond South Africa, beyond Earth. The spaceman Elizabeth meets, Akon, is also presented with typically Caucasian features, particularly "golden hair" like Klarer's.[24] Racial and cultural distinctions between white and black South Africans persist throughout the book

Elizabeth's initial physical meeting with Akon is the culmination of months of psychic contact, during which time he has told her all about himself and his planet, Meton. There are romantic overtones to this first encounter, as she tells him, "I have known your face within my heart all my life." She describes "a deep emotion and great happiness" that filled her so that words were not able "to express the fullness of love within my heart for this man from another planet."[25] From this point on, *Beyond the Light Barrier* is primarily a love story, and further references to war, peace, and defense are fleeting and vague. Notions of race and ethnicity, however, continue to be a significant part of the narrative.

Klarer's husband (whom she never even names) has already disappeared from the narrative, a mere two dozen pages in. Akon, the handsome space visitor, has taken his place. He reveals that he has watched Elizabeth grow up, waiting for her to reach a point of understanding adequate to benefit from physical contact. The romance between Akon and Elizabeth Klarer which emerges throughout the remainder of *Beyond the Light Barrier* is one which conforms to standard western gender roles and norms of the 1950s. The relationship is heterosexual, the woman is under the authority of the man, and the woman's purpose is primarily to produce children.

There is a strong sense of dominance on the part of Akon ("I know what is best for you and will always look after you, my beloved"; "It is a knowledge and understanding that we share, and you now belong to me"); to be with him and his people, Klarer must subjugate her very thoughts to the visitors ("To be one of us, you must think as we do"). This obedience is necessary if Elizabeth is to be Akon's mate.

Yes, mate. The romance between Elizabeth and Akon is intensely physical, although the spiritual aspects are significant: "Gathering me into his arms, he kissed me on the lips. A magical, electric current seemed to fuse us together in an eternity of ecstasy. In that moment, I knew that the art of love was of the mind and soul, not only of the body."[26] The depth of the connection between the two is important since, according to Akon, "we rarely mate with Earth women." Significantly, there is no mention of *women* from Meton ever mating with Earth *men*. Earth women, such as Elizabeth Klarer, seem to serve mostly as breeding stock for the men of Meton. The purpose of this mating is, in fact, breeding, although there is passion, love and affection between Akon and Elizabeth.

The brief descriptions of actual sexual activity between Elizabeth and Akon are woven into the book's larger discussions of cosmic energy and spiritual themes: "How beautiful is nature's plan to mate in love and harmony, the joy of the soul, spirit and body — the three-in-one transcended into timelessness.... The eternal magic of wholeness bonded our love with the everlasting light of the universe, and I sensed an awareness I had not been conscious of before I lay in Akon's arms."[27] This approach to sexuality, a "spiritual and physical union" is in direct contrast with what Akon calls "the haphazard, often aggressive mating" which is a "direct result of aggressive and warlike tendencies inherited within the forming mind of the unborn."[28] Despite Akon's denunciation of the "aggressive" nature of the sexuality of Earth humans, he is consistently the initiator of the sexual encounters between himself and Elizabeth. Elizabeth's participation in these sexual behaviors is consensual, but passive. This is of a piece with Akon's assertions that he has responsibility for Elizabeth's best interests and the overall possessive nature of Akon's attitude toward her. Thus, despite the "alien" nature of the ideas Akon presents, the gender roles played by the man from Meton and the woman from Earth are very much in line with contemporary western notions.

The sexuality of *Beyond the Light Barrier* is inextricably connected to reproduction and race. Akon explains to Elizabeth that when his people do mate with Earth women (which, remember, he describes as a rare occurrence), the Meton people "keep the offspring to strengthen our race and infuse new blood."[29] Again, race arises in Klarer's narrative as a significant factor in the relationships between the peoples of Earth and Meton; Akon's statement is another link in the chain begun by the Zulu woman who commented on Elizabeth's "golden hair."

Later in her narrative, as Elizabeth meets more members of Akon's society, race and genetics remain recurring topics of conversation. Evaluating the appearance of Akon and his fellow Metons, Klarer concludes, "Both had the ascetic features of an ancient race, and bore the graceful dignity and joyful relaxation of centuries of good breeding and right thinking and living." The positive qualities of the Metons, thus, are genetic and inborn, not something that can be learned or adopted. Luckily for Elizabeth, she seems to spring from the same noble stock as Akon and his friends. Upon meeting Klarer, one Meton woman remarks, "She has slant eyes and golden hair.... She is descended from our original stock left behind on Earth, so it is right for her to be here with us now."[30] Indeed, the Metons originated in the solar system, first living on Venus (establishing a connection with the Venusians with whom George Adamski communicated), then Earth. When they moved on, some of their people were left behind on Earth but they became, over the eons, "thoughtless and destructive." As Elizabeth is one of the — apparently few — Earth women who are recognizable as from the same stock as the people from Meton, one might assume that her blonde Caucasian features indicate not just a connection with the alien visitors, but a tendency away from being "thoughtless and destructive."[31] The obvious corollary is that *non*–Caucasians were (and still are) responsible for the degeneration of the human species and the degradation of the Earth.

It is important to note, however, that the condemnation of and condescension toward non–Caucasian races is largely implicit rather than explicit. While Earth "harbors a race of humans confused and overcome by the forces of evil," it is unclear whether Klarer is using the term "race" in a genetic/cultural sense or whether she means it in a broader sense of a defined category of people. Certainly her comments early in the book about the inevitability of a black/white race war could indicate the former. The racialist nature of Klarer's narrative is bolstered further by the role played in the book by the South African Zulu people.

Throughout the Earthbound portions of *Beyond the Light Barrier*, Klarer presents the Zulu people she encounters as exotic and backward; wise to the ways of the natural world, but always a step behind the modern world, child-like, clinging to their tribal beliefs. While the Zulus with whom Klarer interacts (mainly farmers and servants) have seen the flying saucers of Akon and his people, they do not comprehend the experience in the same way Klarer, her family, and other Caucasian characters do.

Klarer's discussion of the return from her visit with Akon is emblematic of the way she discusses the Zulu. As she exits the spacecraft, a group of young Zulu boys "broke cover out of the long grass, scattering like a covey of quail.... I called to them in Zulu, telling them not to be afraid of the great wagon in the sky.... No explanation could still the overpowering, superstitious fear of anything so fantastic in the sky." The next morning, Elizabeth is served tea by her Zulu maid, whose "dark brown eyes [were] wide and soft with devotion" because she knows that Klarer has experienced something unearthly. Klarer recalls the conversation, peppered with Zulu words translated in the footnotes: "We have seen *umlingo* [magic] wagon in the sky. We ran to hide in a *donga* [deep ravine], shielding our eyes from the brightness like the lightning. Our fathers told of such things coming out of the sky, and the *inyanga yezulu* [sky doctor] says he has seen them many times and has talked to them." Klarer describes the boys who saw the spacecraft in an animal-like way, "scattering like a covey of quail"; the maid speaks as though she is a character in an Edgar Rice Burroughs novel, confronted with a steam locomotive or some such foreign technology.[32] Though written in the late 1970s, and alleged to take place in the 1950s, the story conveys attitudes toward the natives of South Africa that are more in line with depictions at the height of the era of European imperialism. In another example, Klarer's sister's horse groom, M'Kay, kills a dog (a white dog, representing "a white woman's familiar") in what Klarer describes as a "ritual murder" as a protection against the space people and in an attempt to "absorb Akon's strength and greatness."[33] Most telling, though, is Klarer's reaction to these comments from her maid: "She spoke with awe, hardly daring to talk about such things she could never understand."[34]

The Zulu maid and the young boys in the field are, to Klarer's mind, unable to cope with the reality of Akon and his people in the same way that she herself is. Klarer does not explicitly say this inability to understand is a product of race, but her white siblings, children, and military officials with whom she is acquainted have no trouble understanding the basics of what she experiences with Akon and his people. But rather than even try to understand, the Zulu people cower in fear (like the maid) or attempt to use their primitive ritual to steal power from the likes of Akon (as does the "pagan-hearted" M'Kay). With their strange, violent rituals and incomprehension of Elizabeth's encounters, Klarer presents the Zulu people as much more alien than the actual space visitors.

Eventually, Elizabeth does bear Akon's child, a boy named Ayling. His birth causes Klarer no pain, and she reports that as a baby he did not cry or fuss like Earth children.[35] As Akon promised, the child remains with his father. Elizabeth returns to South Africa with Akon's promise that he will return for her. He never does.

In its discussions of sexuality, gender, and race, *Beyond the Light Bar-*

rier presents a vision of race and gender relations that reflect the times in which they were written. In particular, Elizabeth Klarer's book represents an attempt to hold back the tide of change that was sweeping the western world in general — and South Africa in particular — in the 1970s. Klarer validates subservience for black South Africans, racial purity, and traditional gender roles at a time when South Africa's system of apartheid was under attack from without and within. Sexual mores were changing and a revitalized feminist movement threatened to change the traditional power relationship between men and women. Within the story of intergalactic love told by Klarer are indications that she fears the new world that is on its way to changing her homeland. Setting her story in the 1950s rather than the 1970s makes the time of the interplanetary childbirth more believable and enables her to deal with contemporary issues in a slightly camouflaged manner.

Klarer clearly has concern for the future. In the final paragraph of her autobiography, she wonders if Earth's people will survive into the future. One particular issue she sees as a potential problem is, apparently, the notion of equality. She asks, "Can their mass leveling and conformity produce leaders to solve the many problems they will face within the next five years?"[36] This frankly odd concern is in line with her characterization of Akon's commanding presence as the result of good breeding; there's an aristocratic thread which runs through Klarer's narrative. The rapidly democratizing world ran counter to this view, appearing, if anything, more alien than Akon's home on Meton. South Africa in the 1970s, however, at the time of Klarer's writing, was a deeply unsettled place. Trade union and student uprisings, along with the continued struggle over apartheid policy (including the increasing international diplomatic and economic isolation of the white South African regime), all indicated that the pleasant, rural upbringing Klarer experienced was a thing of the past, a relic of the colonialism that had imposed apartheid on South Africa in the first place.

Elizabeth Klarer's complex tale of interplanetary romance, breeding and love is significant not only because of the relative rarity of such romantic notions but also because of its focus on race and ethnicity. Like all contactees do, to a degree, Klarer attempted through her story to find explanations for why the world was the way it was and what solutions might emerge to change it. Race and ethnicity, however, play a much larger role in Klarer's work than in any other. The reason for this is that "her world" was *not* the United States of the Civil Rights era. Prominent

American contactees of the early Cold War period lived and wrote in a time and place of radical change in the racial landscape. Whatever their personal beliefs may have been (and we really have no way of knowing them), men like George Adamski and George Van Tassel often dropped in comments about the need for harmony and unity within the human race, regardless of skin color. Such a view was as progressive as demanding an end to nuclear testing or decrying the hypocrisy of organized religion. For Elizabeth Klarer, a woman writing in South Africa during a period of intense class and racial strife, the notion of a civil rights revolution was truly frightening.

Perhaps even more than gender or sexuality, Klarer's story is significant because of its role as evidence of the entrenched racial viewpoint in 1970s South Africa. Because of this close connection to the world of the 1970s, despite the setting of the story being a generation earlier, Klarer's story demonstrates the ability of contactee narratives to apply to a variety of time frames and differing social, cultural, and political situations. Klarer's story had a different purpose in 1979 than it did in 1956. Whether discussing the need for peace on Earth or fretting over the coming conflict between white and black South Africans, Elizabeth Klarer's tale of contact, love, and creating a family with Akon of the planet Meton demonstrates that such contactee narratives adapt to the times in which they are created and have the ability to convey ideas in any era.

Each of these accounts of gender and sexuality in the extraterrestrial contactee world show the landscape through slightly different lenses, altered refractions which highlight various areas of importance and meaning. From Truman Bethurum's vision of Aura Rhanes as the ideal partner (as opposed to his skeptical wife) to Elizabeth Klarer's visions of racial and cultural purity, these tales and notions describe the impact of extraterrestrial visitation on the human condition in a way which does not emerge in the more typical contactee narratives of the time.

8

Contact, Humanity and the Future

Through their written stories, speaking appearances, and the organizations they founded, those who claimed contact with extraterrestrial beings did more than tell tales of riding in flying saucers or receiving telepathic communication about the aliens' lifestyle. The messages conveyed by the contactees intersected with politics, spirituality, economics, and culture. Their stories told of worlds that were better than our own, where people lived in peace and equality. From the Cold War era of friendly space brothers to the new age of channeling and exopolitics, extraterrestrial contactees spoke to the concerns of their time — whether they were in the United States, Europe, or elsewhere. These issues ranged from the broad (humanity should live in peace) to the incredibly narrow (such as Billy Meier's specific condemnations of Israeli policies or Buck Nelson's denunciation of the labeling of canned food). Regardless of the issues they addressed, the contactees from the 1950s to today gave strong indications of believing in the power of their stories to change the world around them. Whether not their tales moved the needle on any particular issue is more difficult to determine.

What is less difficult to determine is the place of contactee narratives and culture within the broad sweep of history over the past 60 years. They have been part of the countercultural and subcultural conversations, providing a running commentary on important — and unimportant — issues of the day. Along with their darker cousins, the conspiracy theorists, the contactees have forged a path explaining why things are the way they are and providing a way out of the political, social, and economic troubles which they perceive to be haunting our modern world. The space brothers and sisters have already dealt with the issues that humanity struggles with. If we just follow their examples, the Earth could be a better place.

One consistent theme throughout the contactees' stories is the notion that humans on Earth have, somewhere along the way, gone off the virtuous path. Earth is the planet that just didn't get it — that is not as advanced as Venus, or Clarion, or the planets of the Pleiades. For the contactees of the 1950s and 1960s, Earth was a planet stuck in the cosmic kindergarten, locked in a lower stage of development. The only way for the planet — and the species — to move forward was for the people of Earth to follow the example of the space brother and space sisters. To do so would remedy the inequalities and injustices of human society. Peace would reign and humanity would no longer be under the shadow of a looming atomic annihilation. For the channelers of the 1970s and 1980s, by contrast, the enlightenment and salvation were on a personal level. Individuals could benefit from the wisdom of Ashtar, Hatonn, Sananda Jesus, or the other ascended masters and, by following their teachings, would find themselves numbered among the survivors when Earth's end finally comes. Since the 1990s, those in the emergent exopolitics movement have used stories of friendly extraterrestrials as part of their advocacy for various types of social and political change. The manner in which contactees have spread their views has changed and developed since the 1950s, but the concept of calling for reform through a filter of ET contact narrative has continued.

The contactee phenomenon is a fringe movement within a fringe movement. The claims of contactees have been largely marginalized within the larger flying saucer and UFO subculture. Leaders within the field focus on topics like alien abduction tales, their details extracted through hypnosis or political conspiracy theories linking a cover-up of a saucer crash at Roswell to the Trilateral Commission, the Council on Foreign Relations, and the Bilderbergers. These are the topics that fill convention halls, sell magazines, and fuel radio call-in shows. There are those within various parts of the paranormal field who accept stories and information received through channeled psychic transmissions. Organizations such as the George Adamski Foundation and the Aetherius Society continue to publish and defend the claims of foundational figures like Adamski and George King. The contactee phenomenon has gone from cutting edge, to embarrassing, to ignored, to — now — comfortably and amusingly retro. Despite this, the contactees have had a cultural impact far out of proportion to their numbers or apparent importance. The contactees and the tales of their experiences — real, imagined, or somewhere in-between — have reflected the changing culture of western civilization from the Cold War right down to the present. While today's contactee-style messages are more likely to be couched in political (or exopolitical) terms rather than veneered with spiritualism, the basic notions are still there, providing a filter for our culture and politics. Like other aspects of popular culture, to minimize or trivialize its importance imperils our understanding of the cultural and subcultural trends of particular historical periods — including our own.

Despite the waxing and waning of the popularity of the contactees and their claims over the past six decades, their methods remain useful for some within the UFO community. The exopolitics movement, in particular, has taken the model of contactees as their own, using otherworldly and unsupportable claims in order to promulgate specific, attainable political goals. Psychic channelers who claim to be in contact with extraterrestrial entities, as well, use their platforms to promote tangible social and political agendas. Contactees have not gone away. Rather, in this age of "new media," they are increasingly speaking to those who are mostly likely to already be listening. More and more, the heirs of the contactee tradition are preaching to the choir.

While the popularity of the contactees and their stories has declined since their heyday in the 1950s and 1960s, their cultural role at the dawn of human space travel is worth studying and considering for their significance to the lives and notions of humanity here in the 21st century. For the last decade, humanity has been teetering on the ledge of a new phase of human travel beyond Earth, transitioning to an age of privatized space travel as governmental space agencies attempt to determine what the future holds for publicly funded space exploration. Beyond the financial question of "who's paying for all of this?" is the scientific question of what *kind* of space exploration is most promising for expanding humanity's knowledge. Should we send humans to other planets, or should we send scientific probes, rovers, and drones? Just as, at the dawn of the Cold War, humans struggled to determine what the best course for the future would be, we are doing so today. Thus, the stories of the contactees have continued resonance.

There is still innovation in how scholars and thinkers — inside and outside the academy — examine the narratives that emerge from claims of the paranormal. Just as Jacques Vallee did in the 1970s and 1980s, writers continue to explore the deeper philosophical and social meanings of these messages. One of these writers took up the mantle of Jacques Vallee with an approach that blended a historical understanding of contactee narrative with cutting-edge discussion of futurism, art, and literature. Mac Tonnies and his ideas are a fitting bookend to this study of those who have claimed to have come into some kind of personal contact with visitors from other worlds.

Mac Tonnies was a Kansas City, Missouri, writer, photographer, and thinker who died in his sleep on October 18, 2009. Although living to just 34 years of age, Tonnies had spent years writing online and in print about the intersections of science, science fiction, the paranormal, technology and what some termed the "post-human" future. Tonnies's writings on paranormal and esoteric topics tended to drift toward the deconstruction of ideas that had existed long enough to be familiar to most readers. For example, his 2004 book *After the Martian Apocalypse: Extraterrestrial Artifacts and the Case for Mars Exploration* examined the alleged "Face on Mars" which had piqued public interest since the late 1970s. Tonnies used a fresh approach to this well-worn topic as an entrée for crafting a cogent argument for the need to promote continued human exploration of Mars — and other parts of space.

Tonnies's later ideas and words hold particular appeal when examined in the context of tales of alleged human-extraterrestrial contact. In his posthumously published book *The Cryptoterrestrials: A Meditation on Indigenous Humanoids and the Aliens among Us*, Tonnies presents they hypothesis that "at least some accounts of alien visitation can be attributed to a humanoid species indigenous to the Earth, a sister race that has adapted to our numerical superiority by developing a surprisingly robust technology."[1] This is a provocative notion, addressing both the earlier, traditional human contactee claims as well as the later abduction narratives. As with those claims, there is no readily available proof for Tonnies's theories, and he stated on several occasions that just because he discussed the idea didn't mean he absolutely *believed* in its literal truth. What then, can such a theory tell us?

Tonnies's ideas illustrate the enduring appeal of the unknown and, especially, of the stories of those who claim they have solved at least some of the mysteries of the unknown. Tonnies, like Jacques Vallee before him, sought to connect the stories of those who claim encounters with a range of paranormal phenomena with the fundamental nature of the Earth and humanity itself. Tonnies's work represented a strand of thought which lies between belief and skepticism, analyzing the stories for deeper meaning, not accepting them wholesale, but not rejecting them out of hand.

The extraterrestrial contact narratives of the last six decades have sought to do the same thing. Obviously, the nature of these contacts and the stories surrounding them has changed over the years. There is a substantial gulf between George Adamski's or George Van Tassel's fairly straightforward meetings with space brothers and the convoluted conspiracy tales of exopoliticians like Greer and Bassett. Hatonn's blending of interstellar transmissions to a devoted receiver and dark, twisted political conspiracy draws from a variety of different camps. Despite the differences, there are a number of consistent themes that emerge. Humanity is not alone in the universe. Those beings from beyond the planet Earth are, by and large, friendly and invested in humanity's development, but there are more sinister beings out there in the darkness. Humanity has to change and grow in order to leave the cosmic kindergarten and take its place among the peoples of the solar system and beyond. What's holding the Earth people back? Greed and selfishness — both individual and among nations — cause endless wars. Crooked politicians and rigid religious hierarchies keep people from true cooperation and spirituality. These are issues that humans have always been attempting to solve.

Ultimately, the claims of the contactees are no stranger than any other set of claims that rely on faith rather than objective proof and promise to save us from our own foolishness and make our time on this Earth more tolerable. Indeed, some of the contactees did establish religious movements. Their messages were (and are) important and worth listening to, if for no other reason than as a lens through which we can view the last 60 years of human history. From the H-bomb to the War in Afghanistan, contactees have expressed views that have been outside the mainstream but in line with other countercultural movements.

The contactees have been speaking to us, with stories which are both bizarre and banal. Perhaps it is time to listen, not because their stories have inherent truth, but because they are part of the history of the western world over the past six decades. Just because their stories strike us as less weighty than other, more conventional historical documents (or the activities of more commonly studied countercultural of subcultural movements) does not mean they should remain below the radar of historians studying the world of the Cold War, or of literary scholars examining travel writing, or of religious studies scholars examining the emergence of new faiths. The contactees have been part of the fabric of western culture since the Second World War, telling stories and urging change. Their stories are important, and contain whole worlds.

Chapter Notes

Introduction

1. Bruce J. Schulman, *The Seventies: The Great Shift in American Culture, Society, and Politics* (Cambridge, MA: Da Capo Press, 2002), 96.

2. *Ibid.*, 97.

3. Marilyn Ferguson, *The Aquarian Conspiracy: Personal and Social Transformation in the 1980s*, 1st ed. (Los Angeles: J.P. Tarcher, 1981), 23.

Chapter 1

1. James W. Moseley and Karl T. Pflock, *Shockingly Close to the Truth: Confessions of a Grave-Robbing Flying Saucerlogist*, 1st ed. (Amherst, NY: Prometheus, 2002), 56.

2. *Ibid.*, 118, 158–159.

3. Michael Shaller, Virginia Scharff, and Robert D. Schulzinger, *Present Tense: The United States Since 1945* (Boston: Houghton Mifflin, 1996), 92–122.

4. Paul Boyer, *By the Bomb's Early Light: American Thought and Consciousness at the Dawn of the Atomic Age* (New York: Pantheon, 1985), 265.

5. Ronald Oakley, *God's Country: America in the Fifties* (New York: Dembner, 1986), 364–365.

6. W.T. Lhamon, Jr., *Deliberate Speed: The Origins of a Cultural Style in the American 1950s* (Washington, D.C.: Smithsonian Institution Press, 1990), xiv.

7. Alan Brinkley, "The Illusion of Unity in Cold War Culture," in *Rethinking Cold War Culture*, edited by Peter J. Kuznik

and James Gilbert (Washington, D.C.: Smithsonian Institute Press, 2001), 62, 70–71.

8. Margot A. Henriksen, *Dr. Strangelove's America: Society and Culture in the Atomic Age* (Berkeley: University of California Press, 1997), x, 69.

9. Howard Brick, *Age of Contradiction: American Thought and Culture in the 1960s* (Ithaca: Cornell University Press, 2000), xii, 185.

10. David M. Jacobs, *The UFO Controversy in America* (Bloomington: Indiana University Press, 1975), 1–5.

11. Curtis Peebles, *Watch the Skies! A Chronicle of the Flying Saucer Myth* (Washington, D.C.: Smithsonian Institution Press, 1994), x.

12. Brenda Denzler, *The Lure of the Edge: Scientific Passions, Religious Beliefs, and the Pursuit of UFOs* (Berkeley: University of California Press, 2001), 159.

13. Jodi Dean, *Aliens in America: Conspiracy Cultures from Outerspace to Cyberspace* (Ithaca: Cornell University Press, 1998), 5, 42.

14. Timothy Melley, *Empire of Conspiracy: The Culture of Paranoia in Postwar America* (Ithaca: Cornell University Press, 2000), vii.

15. Peter Knight, *Conspiracy Culture: From Kennedy to the X-Files* (New York: Routledge, 2000), 3.

16. Christopher Partridge, "Understanding UFO Religions," in *UFO Religions*, 3–42 (London: Routledge, 2003), 10.

17. J. Gordon Melton, "The Contactees," in *The Gods Have Landed: New Religions from Other Worlds*, edited by James Lewis (Albany: State University of New York Press, 1995), 3–5, 10.

18. Robert S. Ellwood, "Spiritualism and UFO Religion in New Zealand: The International Transmission of Modern Spiritual Movements," in *The Gods Have Landed: New Religions from Other Worlds*, edited by James R. Lewis (Albany: State University of New York, 1995), 167.

19. Boyer, 49.

20. Jessica Wang, *American Science in an Age of Anxiety: Scientists, Anticommunism and the Cold War* (Chapel Hill: University of North Carolina Press, 1999), 3.

21. Stuart W. Leslie, *The Cold War and American Science: The Military-Industrial-Academic Complex at MIT and Stanford* (New York: Columbia University Press, 1993), 3.

22. Tom Moylan, *Scraps of the Untainted Sky: Science Fiction, Utopia, Dystopia* (Boulder, CO: Westview Press, 2000), xi, xiii.

23. John J. Pierce, *Foundations of Science Fiction: A Study in Imagination and Evolution* (New York: Greenwood Press, 1987), 11–14.

24. Christopher F. Roth, "Ufology as Anthropology: Race, Extraterrestrials, and the Occult," in *E.T. Culture: Anthropology in Outerspaces*, edited by Debbora Battaglia, 38–93 (Durham: Duke University Press, 2005), 50.

Chapter 2

1. David Hatcher Childress and Richard S. Shaver, *Lost Continents & the Hollow Earth* (Kempton, IL: Adventures Unlimited Press, 1999), 218–219.

2. *Ibid.*, 221.

3. *Ibid.*, 221–223.

4. *Ibid.*

5. *Ibid.*, 2.

6. *Ibid.*, 32.

7. *Ibid.*, 224.

8. Richard Toronto. "Shavertron." *Shavertron*, 2008. http://www.softcom.net/users/falconkam/shavindex08.html.

9. Brad Steiger, ed., *Project Blue Book* (New York: Ballantine, 1976), 26–36.

10. Peebles, 12.

11. Jacobs, *UFO Controversy*, 270.

12. *Ibid.*

13. Edward J. Ruppelt, *The Report on Unidentified Flying Objects* (Garden City, NY: Doubleday, 1956), 41–25. Ruppelt was an Air Force officer who, for a time, was in command of Project Blue Book (the organizational successor to Projects Sign and Grudge).

14. J. Allen Hynek, *The UFO Experience: A Scientific Inquiry* (New York: Marlowe, 1998), 173.

15. Tim Printy, "Project Grudge," http://members.aol.com/TPrinty/Grudge.html, 2001, 1.

16. Hynek, 1, 174.

17. *Ibid.*, 186.

18. Hynek, 100–107.

19. Peebles, 21–22.

20. Hynek, 108.

21. Gerald K. Haynes, "A Die-Hard Issue: CIA's Role in the Study of UFOs, 1947–90," *Studies in Intelligence* 1, no. 1 (1997): 2.

22. *Report of the Scientific Panel on Unidentified Flying Objects*, January 17, 1953: 2, 3.

23. "Speaking of Pictures ... A Rash of Flying Saucers Breaks Out Over the Country," *Life* (July 21, 1947): 14.

24. Given the date of the article, and given that Project Grudge is referred to by name, it's reasonable to assume that the outline of new USAF policy in the article refers to Project Blue Book, even though that name had not yet been made public.

25. "Have We Visitors From Space?" *Life* (April 7, 1952): 82.

26. *Search for the Flying Saucers*, ABC radio, originally broadcast July 10, 1947.

27. *Case for the Flying Saucers*, CBS radio, originally broadcast May 14, 1949.

28. Douglas Curran, *In Advance of the Landing* (New York: Abbeville Press, 1985) 43–44, 71–72.

29. Desmond Leslie and George Adamski, *Flying Saucers Have Landed*

(London: British Book Centre, 1953), 195–216.

30. Mosley and Pflock, 106.

31. *Ibid.*, 108.

32. *Ibid.*, 109.

33. *Ibid.*, 68.

34. John Lade, "Adamski — A Reasoned Support," *Flying Saucer Review*, October 1956, 18.

35. *Ibid.*, 332.

36. Peebles, 114.

37. Ibid., 39.

38. Jacobs, *UFO Controversy*, 130–132.

39. Peebles, 190.

40. *Ibid.*, 191.

41. *Ibid.*, 192.

42. *Saucer News* was, at this time, co-owned and published with Moseley.

43. Gray Barker, "The Condon Report," no date, Gray Barker Collection.

44. James W. Moseley, "A Lively Corpse," *Saucer News* 16, no. 4 (1969): 1–2.

45. Moseley and Pflock, 218.

46. Kevin Randle, Russ Estes, and William Cone, *The Abduction Enigma* (New York: Forge, 1999), 7.

47. David M. Jacobs, *The Threat: Revealing the Secret Alien Agenda* (New York: Simon & Schuster, 1999), 216, 251.

48. Don Berliner and Stanton T. Friedman, *Crash at Corona: The U.S. Military Retrieval and Cover-up of a UFO* (New York: Marlowe, 1997), xiii.

49. John Lear, "Lear's Aliens: Original Statement," *Bibliotecapleyades*, December 29, 1987. http://www.bibliotecapleyades.net/vida_alien/esp_vida_alien_18o.htm.

50. William Cooper, "The Origins, Identity, and Purpose of MJ-12," *Bibliotecapleyades*, May 23, 1989. http://www.bibliotecapleyades.net/sociopolitica/esp_sociopol_cooper11.htm.

51. Leslie Watkins, *Alternative 3* (Nantwich: Archimedes Press, 2010), 2, 4–5.

Chapter 3

1. Leslie and Adamski, 171.

2. Peebles, 93.

3. George Adamski, "The Kingdom of Heaven on Earth," 1937 (published online by the George Adamski Foundation: http://www.gafintl-adamski.com/html/heaven.html), 1–2.

4. George Adamski, "Satan, Man of the Hour," reprinted in Adamski, *Behind the Flying Saucer Mystery* (New York: Warner Paperback Library, 1960), 149–158.

5. *Report of the Special Committee on Investigation of the Munitions Industry* (The Nye Report), U.S. Congress, Senate, 74th Congress, 2nd sess., February 1936, 2.

6. Smedley Butler, *War Is a Racket* (New York: Round Table Press, 1935), 22.

7. *Action Comics* no. 1 (June 1938): 11.

8. "Soviet and American Communist Parties," in *Revelations from the Russian Archives*, http://www.loc.gov/exhibits/archives/sova.html, July 22, 2010, accessed October 1, 2011.

9. Adamski, "Kingdom of Heaven on Earth," 2.

10. *Ibid.*

11. The origins of this article are unclear. It does not appear in George M. Eberhart's *UFOS and the Extraterrestrial Contact Movement: A Bibliography*, which lists several of Adamski's other writings. It is likely that it was included in one of several general collections of Adamski's writings published by small UFO-oriented publishers. This article is currently published by the Adamski Foundation on their website: http://www.gafintl-adamski.com/html/GAArt.htm.

12. George Adamski, *Pioneers of Space: A Trip to the Moon, Mars, and Venus* (Los Angeles: Leonard-Freefield, 1949), 1.

13. *Ibid.*, 48.

14. *Ibid.*, 90.

15. *Ibid.*, 235.

16. *Ibid.*, 260

17. Leslie and Adamski, 171, 198.

18. *Ibid.*, 201, 205.

19. Moseley and Pflock, 67.

20. *Ibid.*, 68.

21. James W. Moseley, "Some New Facts about 'Flying Saucers Have Landed,'" *Nexus* 2, no. 1 (January 1955): 7, 12–13.

22. *Ibid.*, 16–17.

23. George Adamski, "Time Will Tell," *Saucerian Bulletin* 6 (Spring 1955): 33.

24. George Adamski, *Inside the Spaceships* (New York: Abelard-Schuman, 1955), 83, 90–93.

25. Adamski, *Behind the Flying Saucer Mystery*, 19–25.

26. *Ibid.*, 79–100.

27. *Ibid.*, 128.

28. Ellwood, 177–178.

29. *Ibid.*, 179–181.

30. *Ibid.*, 107, 123, 138, 141.

31. *Ibid.*, 141.

32. George Adamski, *Cosmic Philosophy*, 1961, iii.

33. *Ibid.*

34. *Ibid.*, 81.

35. *Ibid.*, 82–84.

36. *Ibid.*, 86.

37. Adamski, *Behind the Flying Saucer Mystery*, 103.

38. Joseph Ferriere, untitled editorial, *Probe* 14 (March/April 1966): 8.

39. Joseph Ferriere, "George Adamski's Appeal to Future Leaders," *Probe* 14 (March/April 1966), 2.

40. Desmond Leslie and Alice Wells, "Go in Peace!" in *Gray Barker's Book of Adamski*, edited by Gray Barker (Clarksburg, WV: Saucerian Publications, n.d.), 10–12.

41. Gerard Aartsen, *George Adamski — A Herald for the Space Brothers* (Amsterdam: BGA, 2010), xi.

42. "About Us," *Share International*, April 1999. http://share-international.org/aboutus/aboutus.htm.

43. "Who Is Benjamin Crème?" *Share International*, April 1999. http://share-international.org/background/bcreme/bc_main.htm.

44. Giorgio Dibitonto (trans. John T. Sherwood), *Angels in Starships* (Sedona, AZ: Sedona Visions, 1990), 28.

Chapter 4

1. Lawrence R. Samuel, *Future: A Recent History* (Austin: University of Texas Press, 2009), 97–98.

2. Christopher Roth, "Ufology as Anthropology: Race, Extraterrestrials, and the Occult," in *E. T. Culture: Anthropology in Outerspaces*, edited by Debbora Battaglia (Durham: Duke University Press, 2005), 51.

3. Truman Bethurum, *Aboard a Flying Saucer* (Los Angeles: DeVorss, 1954), 34.

4. Truman Bethurum, "Truman Bethurum to Gray Barker," November 16, 1953 (Gray Barker UFO Collection, Clarksburg-Harrison Public Library, Clarksburg, West Virginia).

5. Truman Bethurum, "Truman Bethurum to Gray Barker," October 4, 1954 (Gray Barker UFO Collection, Clarksburg-Harrison Public Library).

6. "Past Issues Revisited," George Adamski Foundation, n.d. http://www.adamskifoundation.com/html/issues.htm.

7. *Ibid.*, 74–75, 137.

8. Truman Bethurum, *Facing Reality* (Prescott, AZ: The Author, 1959), 76.

9. George Hunt Williamson and Alfred C. Bailey. *The Saucers Speak* (Pomeroy, WA: Health Research Books, 1996), 10.

10. George Hunt Williamson and Alfred Bailey, *The Saucers Speak* (London: Neville Spearman, 1963), 45.

11. Moseley and Pflock, 136–138.

12. George Hunt Williamson, "A Message from Our Space Brothers," n.d. http://webcache.googleusercontent.com/search?q=cache:http://www.bibliotecapleyades.net/bb/williamson.htm.

13. *Ibid.*

14. George Hunt Williamson, *Secret Places of the Lion* (London: Neville Spearman, 1958), ix-x.

15. Moseley and Pflock, 136–137.

16. Leslie and Adamski, 212.

17. George Hunt Williamson, *Other Tongues, Other Flesh* (Amherst, WI: Amherst Press, 1957), 117.

18. *Ibid.*, 95.

19. George Hunt Williamson, "Project Scroll," *Flying Saucer Review* (December 1957): 18–19.

20. George Van Tassel, *I Rode a Flying Saucer* (Los Angeles: New Age, 1952), 9–11.

21. *Ibid.*, 11.

22. *Ibid.*, 14–15.

23. *Ibid.*, 18.

24. *Ibid.*, 22.

25. *Ibid.*, 24.

26. *Ibid.*, 30.

27. *Ibid.*, 30–31.

28. *Ibid.*, 51.

29. George Van Tassel, *Into this World and Out Again*, 1956, front matter.

30. *Ibid.*,14.

31. Lily, *Golden Thoughts in Quiet Moments* (London: J. Burns, 1882), 32

32. "Koreshan State Historic Site." Florida State Parks, n.d. http://www.floridastateparks.org/koreshan/default.cfm.

33. Koresh, "The Ark of the Covenant," *The Flaming Sword* 28, no. 2 (1914): 347.

34. Van Tassel, *Into this World*, 23.

35. *Ibid.*, 94.

36. "History of the Integratron." The Integratron, n.d. http://integratron.com/2History/History.html.

37. Moseley and Pflock, 162.

38. Ethel P. Hill, *In Days to Come* (Los Angeles: New Age, 1957), 16.

39. *Ibid.*, 18–21.

40. *Ibid.*, 23–24.

41. *Ibid.*, 27.

42. *Ibid.*, 34.

43. Christopher Helland, "From Extraterrestrials to Ultraterrestrials: The Evolution of the Concept of Ashtar," in *UFO Religions* (London: Routledge, 2003), 170.

44. George King, *You Are Responsible!* (Los Angeles: The Aetherius Society, 1961), 12–13 and 19–20.

45. *Ibid.*, 30.

46. *Ibid.*, 40–41.

47. *Ibid.*, 42.

48. *Ibid.*, 45–46.

49. *Ibid.*, 48–52.

50. *Ibid.*, 61–67.

51. *Ibid.*, 83–84.

52. Simon G. Smith, "Opening a Channel to the Stars," in *UFO Religions* (London: Routledge, 2003), 89–90.

53. John A. Saliba, "The Earth Is a Dangerous Place — The World View of the Aetherius Society," *Marburg Journal of Religion* 4, no. 2 (December 1999).

http://www.uni-marburg.de/fb03/ivk/mjr/pdfs/1999/articles/saliba1999.pdf, 4.

54. "On Hale-Bopp, Cults, and Spirituality," *The Aetherius Society* (cached page via Archive.org), n.d. http://web.archive.org/web/19980205101504/http://www.aetherius.org/hale.htm.

55. "About the Aetherius Society," *The Aetherius Society*, n.d. http://www.aetherius.org/index.cfm?app=content&SectionID=28&PageID=1.

56. "Landing in South Africa," *Flying Saucer Review* (December 1956): 2–5.

57. Howard Menger, *From Outer Space to You* (Clarksburg, WV: Saucerian Books, 1959), 26–32.

58. *Ibid.*, 36.

59. *Ibid.*, 46.

60. *Ibid.*, 120–125.

61. *Ibid.*, 160–162, 164.

62. *Ibid.*, 163

63. Long John Nebel, *The Way Out World* (Englewood Cliffs, NJ: Prentice-Hall, 1961), 66.

64. Buck Nelson, *My Trip to Mars, the Moon, and Venus* (Mountain View, MO: The Author, 1956), 2.

65. *Ibid.*, 6.

66. *Ibid.*, 11.

67. *Ibid.*, 8.

68. *Ibid.*, 22.

69. *Ibid.*, 23.

70. *Ibid.*, 26.

71. *Flying Saucer Review* (December 1957): 1.

Chapter 5

1. Jacques Vallee, *Messengers of Deception: UFO Contacts and Cults* (New York: Bantam, 1979), viii.

2. *Ibid.*, 74.

3. *Ibid.*, 77–78.

4. *Ibid.*, 79.

5. *Ibid.*, 85–89.

6. *Ibid.*, 240–242.

7. *Ibid.*, 246.

8. Wendelle C Stevens, ed., *Message from the Pleiades: The Contact Notes of Eduard Billy Meier* (Tucson, AZ: UFO Photo Archives, 1988–1995), vol. 4, 11–12.

9. *Ibid.*, 49.

10. Stevens, vol. 1, 36–37.

11. *Ibid.*, 38.

12. Stevens, vol. 4, 13.

13. Stevens, vol. 1, 38

14. "The Talmud of Jmmanuel," *The Future of Mankind: A Billy Meier Wiki,* June 7, 2011.

15. "Attempts on Billy's Life," *The Future of Mankind: A Billy Meier Wiki,* December 8, 2011. http://futureofmankind. co.uk/Billy_Meier/Attempts_on_Billy%27s_Life.

16. "The Giza Intelligences." *The Future of Mankind: A Billy Meier Wiki,* May 11, 2012. http://www.futureofmankind. co.uk/Billy_Meier/Giza_Intelligences.

17. Stevens, vol. 3, 259.

18. Christian Frehner, "We Condemn All Racism," *They Fly!,* October 16, 2006. http://www.theyfly.com/newsflash4/frhnr01.htm.

19. "Contact Report 215." *The Future of Mankind: A Billy Meier Wiki,* February 24, 2012. http://futureofmankind.co.uk/Billy_Meier/Contact_Report_215.

20. "Special: Petition." *The Future of Mankind: A Billy Meier Wiki,* n.d. http://futureofmankind.co.uk/Billy_Meier/Special:Petition?p=121.

21. Tuella, *Project: World Evacuation,* 3rd ed. (Aztec, NM: Guardian Action, 1982), viii.

22. *Ibid.*, x.

23. *Ibid.*, 7–8

24. *Ibid.*, 10.

25. *Ibid.*, 95–96

26. *Ibid.*, 97.

27. *Ibid.*, 4.

28. *Ibid.*, 36.

29. *Ibid.*, 95.

30. Tuella, *Ashtar: A Tribute* (Durango, CO: Guardian Action, 1985), iv, v.

31. *Ibid.*, 26–27.

32. *Ibid.*, 29.

33. Gyeorgos C. Hatonn, *Space — Gate: The Veil Removed,* 3d ed. (Las Vegas: Phoenix Source, 1993), 1.

34. *Ibid.*, 12.

35. *Ibid.*, 40.

36. *Ibid.*, 2–3.

37. *Ibid.*, 6–38

38. *Ibid.*, 49.

39. *Ibid.*, 38.

40. *Ibid.*, 76.

41. Gyeorgos C. Hatonn, *Destruction of a Planet: Zionism IS Racism* (Phoenix Source, 1992), back cover copy.

42. *Ibid.*, 9

43. *Ibid.*, 13.

44. Michael Ellegion, index page, *Channel for the Masters,* n.d. http://www.channelforthemasters.com.

45. Michael Ellegion and Aurora Light, *Prepare for the Landings* (Sedona, AZ: Vortex Network, 2009), 1.

46. *Ibid.*

47. *Ibid.*, 30–33.

48. *Ibid.*, 3.

49. *Ibid.*, 117–123.

50. "PLEIADIAN MESSAGE FROM PETER: SHUT THEM DOWN," *Freer Spirit,* May 26, 2012. http://freerspirit.com/2012/05/26/pleiadian-message-from-peter-shut-them-down/.

51. Michael Salla, "About this Site," *Exopolitics,* July 6, 2009. http://exopolitics.org/about.htm.

52. Steven Greer, "The Disclosure Project — Steven Greer Credentials," *The Disclosure Project,* June 12, 2008. http://www.disclosureproject.org/sgbio.htm.

53. Steven Greer, "CSETI Homepage." CSETI Homepage. http://www.cseti.org/.

54. Steven Greer, "CSETI Ambassador to the Universe and Consciousness Trainings — 2008." CSETI Homepage. http://www.cseti.org/programs/Trainings2008.htm.

55. Jon Ronson, *The Men Who Stare at Goats* (New York: Simon & Schuster, 2006). Ronson's book is an excellent introduction to the people and ideas behind the U.S. government's explorations of psychic and paranormal phenomena during the Cold War.

56. Steven Greer, "CSETI Training Guidelines." CSETI Homepage. http://www.cseti.org/programs/trainingguidelines.htm.

57. *Ibid.*

58. Steven Greer, "CSETI — The CE-5 Initiative." CSETI Homepage. http://www.cseti.org/ce5.htm.

59. Steven Greer, "The Disclosure Project — Briefing Points." The Disclosure Project, 2001. http://www.disclosureproject.org/briefingpoints.htm.

60. *Ibid.*

61. Dean, 54–55.

62. Steven Greer, "Executive Summary." The Disclosure Project, April 5, 2001, cached page. http://web.archive.org/web/20010502113229/www.disclosureproject.org/execsummary/execsummarynonames.htm

63. *Ibid.*

64. *Ibid.*

65. *Ibid.*

66. *Ibid.*

67. *Ibid.*

68. *Ibid.* Greer describes these devices as tapping "zero-point" energy. Though zero-point energy (which stems from physical reactions on the quantum level) is acknowledged and studied by physicists, few believe that it can be converted into a usable form. The Calphysics Institute has produced a good summary of this topic at http://www.calphysics.org/zpe.html.

69. Dean, 55.

70. Greer identifies an extra-governmental organization as the major enemy: "PI-40 is a quasi-governmental, USAPS (*Unacknowledged Special Access Programs*) related, quasi-private entity operating internationally/transnationally. The majority of operations are centered in private industrial 'work for others' contract projects related to the understanding and application of *advanced extraterrestrial technologies.*" For more on this topic, see Greer, "The Covert Organization Responsible for the UFO/ET Issue: PI-40," May 1996. http://www.bibliotecapleyades.net/sociopolitica/esp_sociopol_mj12_20.htm.

71. Michael Salla, "Dennis Kucinich, Bill Richardson & UFOs: The 'other' Alien Question in the 2008 Presidential Election," *OpEdNews.com*, November 2, 2007. http://www.opednews.com/articles/opedne_michael__071102_dennis_kucinich_2c_bil.htm.

72. Stephen Bassett, "Open Letter to Barack Obama and John McCain," October 17, 2008. http://www.paradigmresearchgroup.org/Press_Releases/Press_releases.html#10–17–08.

73. Michael Salla, "Podesta influence in Obama White House extends to UFO disclosure," http://www.examiner.com/x-2383-Honolulu-Exopolitics-Examiner-y2009m1d26-Podesta-influence-in-Obama-White-House-extends-to-UFO-disclosure.

74. Michael Salla, "Senate confirmation of Panetta opens door to CIA X-Files," http://www.examiner.com/x-2383-Honolulu-Exopolitics-Examiner-y2009m2d14-Senate-Confirmation-of-Panetta-opens-door-to-CIA-XFiles.

75. Steven Greer, "Media Response to May 9th Event," www.disclosureproject.org. http://www.disclosureproject.org/May9response.htm.

76. Daniel Fromson, "Disclosed Encounters: Why UFO buffs think Barack Obama is their best hope for the truth about ET," *Washington Monthly*, February 2010. http://www.washingtonmonthly.com/features/2010/1001.tms-fromson.html#Byline.

77. "Nathan," "Disclosure Comments — 11," Comments Section, January 13, 2009, http://www.paradigmresearchgroup.org/Citizens_Briefing_Book_Comments/UFO_Disclosure-1.htm.

78. Tom Fife, "The First Time I Heard of Barack (with additional info)," *Free Republic*, September 19, 2009. http://www.freerepublic.com/focus/bloggers/2344042/posts?page=66.

79. Spencer Ackerman, "Barack Obama Converts to German," *Washington Independent*, June 26, 2009, http://washingtonindependent.com/48926/barack-obama-converts-to-german.

80. "Immediately Disclose the Government's Knowledge of and Communications with Extraterrestrial Beings × The White House." *The White House*, September 22, 2011. /petitions#!/petition/imme-

diately-disclose-governments-knowledge-and-communications-extraterrestrial-beings/bGWkJk9Y.

81. "Formally acknowledge extraterrestrial presence × The White House." *The White House*, September 22, 2011. /petitions#!/petition/formally-acknowledge-extraterrestrial-presence-engaging-human-race-disclosure/wfYDlmlG.

82. "Searching for ET, But No Evidence Yet × The White House." *The White House*, November 4, 2011. /petitions#!/response/searching-et-no-evidence-yet

83. Bassett.

Chapter 6

1. Albert K. Bender, *Flying Saucers and the Three Men* (London: Neville Spearman, 1963).

2. *Ibid.*, 134–135.

3. "About Gray Barker," Clarksburg Public Library, December 2011. http://clarksburglibrary.info/gbarker.html.

4. John Sherwood, "Gray Barker: My Friend the Myth-maker," *Skeptical Inquirer*, June 1998. http://www.csicop.org/si/show/gray_barker_my_friend_the_myth-maker/

5. Gray Barker, *They Knew Too Much About Flying Saucers* (Atlanta: IllumiNet Press, 1997), 114.

6. Albert K. Bender. "Letter to August C. Roberts," September 14, 1953. Gray Barker UFO Collection, Clarksburg-Harrison Public Library.

7. Albert K. Bender. "Letter to August C. Roberts," October 18, 1953. Gray Barker UFO Collection, Clarksburg-Harrison Public Library.

8. Albert K. Bender. "Letter to August C. Roberts," November 12, 1953. Gray Barker UFO Collection, Clarksburg-Harrison Public Library.

9. Albert K. Bender. "Letter to August C. Roberts," December 20, 1953. Gray Barker UFO Collection, Clarksburg-Harrison Public Library.

10. August C. Roberts. "Letter to Albert K. Bender," August 2, 1954. Gray Barker UFO Collection, Clarksburg-Harrison Public Library.

11. Albert K. Bender. "Letter to August C. Roberts," August 4, 1953. Gray Barker UFO Collection, Clarksburg-Harrison Public Library.

12. Bender, 16.

13. *Ibid.*, 30.

14. *Ibid.*, 84

15. *Ibid.*, 85.

16. *Ibid.*, 86.

17. "Project Description," The Gray Barker Project: Center for Literary Computing, n.d. http://clc.wvu.edu/projects/gray_barker_project/project_description.

18. Peter M. Rojcewicz, "The 'Men in Black' Experience and Tradition: Analogues with the Traditional Devil Hypothesis," *Journal of American Folklore* 100, no. 396 (June 1987): 148–160.

19. Bender, 125.

20. *Ibid.*, 91.

21. *Ibid.*, 125–127

22. *Ibid.*, 187.

23. *Ibid.*, 188–189.

24. Greg Bishop, "Albert K. Bender's Contactee Experience," *Radio Misterioso*, May 14, 2012. http://radiomisterioso.com/2012/05/14/albert-k-benders-contactee-experiences.

25. *Ibid.*

26. Moseley, 121.

27. Barker, 93.

28. "Contact Report 424," *The Future of Mankind: A Billy Meier Wiki*, May 3, 2009. http://futureofmankind.co.uk/Billy_Meier/Contact_Report_424.

29. Nelson, 26.

30. Melton, 10.

31. Saliba, 36–37.

32. John Weldon and Zola Levitt, *UFOs: What on Earth Is Happening?* (Irvine, CA: Harvest House, 1975), 15–16, 45.

33. *Ibid.*, 116–118.

34. "About Bob Larson," *Bob Larson*, n.d. http://boblarson.org/html/about_bob_larson.html.

35. *Ibid.*, 78–79.

36. *Ibid.*, 12.

37. *Ibid.*, 192, 200–201

38. Chuck Missler and Mark Eastman, *Alien Encounters: The Secret Behind the*

UFO Phenomenon (Coeur d'Alene, ID: Koinonia House, 1997), 116–117.

39. *Ibid.*, 124.

40. Serge Monast, "Project Blue Beam," *The Greatest Hoax*, n.d. http://www.sweet liberty.org/issues/hoax/bluebeam.htm.

Chapter 7

1. Barbara J. Risman, "Gender as a Social Structure: Theory Wrestling with Activism," *Gender and Society* 18, no. 4 (2004): 429–450, 431.

2. Bethurum, *Aboard a Flying Saucer*, 39.

3. *Ibid.*, 40.
4. *Ibid.*, 56.
5. *Ibid.*, 69.
6. *Ibid.*, 35, 40.
7. *Ibid.*, 96.
8. *Ibid.*, 187–190.

9. Helen Mitchell and Betty Mitchell, "We Met the Space People: Helen's Story," n.d. http://sacred-texts.com/ufo/wmsp/wmsp02.htm. *We Met the Space People* is one of the rarest publications from this early contactee era. It has, like many others, however, passed into the public domain. My references to the work are from the electronic copy hosted by the repository at the Internet Sacred Text Archive (http://www.sacred-texts.com).

10. *Ibid.*
11. *Ibid.*

12. Helen Mitchell and Betty Mitchell, "We Met the Space People: Betty's Account," n.d. http://sacred-texts.com/ufo/wmsp/wmsp02.htm.

13. *Ibid.*

14. Coral E. Lorenzen, *Flying Saucers: The Startling Evidence of Invasion from Outer Space* (New York: Pocket Books, 1966), 64–74.

15. Bender, 150–152.
16. Bender, 154–155.

17. Nick Redfern, *The Real Men In Black* (Pompton Plains, NJ: New Page Books, 2011), 150–151.

18. Elizabeth Klarer, *Beyond the Light Barrier: The Autobiography of Elizabeth Klarer* (Flagstaff, AZ: Light Technology Publishing, 2009), 2, 12.

19. *Ibid.*, 15.
20. *Ibid.*, 18.

21. A.J. Christopher, "Partition and Population in South Africa," *Geographical Review* 72, no. 2 (April 1, 1982): 127–138, 128.

22. Klarer, 17.
23. *Ibid.*, 24.
24. *Ibid.*, 29.
25. *Ibid.*, 28–29.
26. *Ibid.*, 30.
27. *Ibid.*, 88.
28. *Ibid.*, 89.
29. *Ibid.*, 30.
30. *Ibid.*, 42–43
31. *Ibid.*, 50–52.
32. *Ibid.*, 71–72.
33. *Ibid.*, 116–117.
34. *Ibid.*, 73.
35. *Ibid.*, 148–150.
36. *Ibid.*, 184.

Chapter 8

1. Mac Tonnies, *The Cryptoterrestrials* (San Antonio: Anomalist Books), 2010, 19.

Bibliography

Aartsen, Gerard. *George Adamski—A Herald for the Space Brothers*. Amsterdam: BGA, 2010.

"About Bob Larson." *Bob Larson*, n.d. http://boblarson.org/html/about_bob_larson.html.

"About Gray Barker." Clarksburg Public Library, December 2011. http://clarksburglibrary.info/gbarker.html.

"About the Aetherius Society." *The Aetherius Society*, n.d. http://www.aetherius.org/index.cfm?app=content&SectionID=28&PageID=1.

"About Us." *Share International*, April 1999. http://share-international.org/aboutus/aboutus.htm.

Adamski, George. *Behind the Flying Saucer Mystery*. New York: Warner Paperback Library, 1960.

_____. *Cosmic Philosophy*. N.p.: 1961.

_____. *Inside the Spaceships*. New York: Abelard-Schuman, 1955.

_____. "The Kingdom of Heaven on Earth," 1937. http://www.gafintl-adamski.com/html/heaven.html.

_____. *Pioneers of Space: A Trip to the Moon, Mars, and Venus*. Los Angeles: Leonard-Freefield, 1949.

_____. "Time Will Tell." *Saucerian Bulletin* 6 (Spring 1955): 33.

"Attempts on Billy's Life." *The Future of Mankind: A Billy Meier Wiki*, December 8, 2011. http://futureofmankind.co.uk/Billy_Meier/Attempts_on_Billy%27s_Life.

Barker, Gray. *Men in Black: The Secret Terror Among Us*. CreateSpace, 2012.

_____. *They Knew Too Much About Flying Saucers*. Atlanta: IllumiNet Press, 1997.

Barker, Gray, ed. *Gray Barker's Book of Adamski*. Clarksburg, WV: Saucerian Publications, n.d.

Bassett, Stephen. "White House Response to the Disclosure Petition." *Paradigm Research Group*, November 8, 2011. http://www.paradigmresearchgroup.org/Press_Releases/Press_releases.html#11-8-11.

Battaglia, Debbora. *E.T. Culture: Anthropology in Outerspaces*. Durham, NC: Duke University Press, 2005.

Baxter, Marla. *My Saturnian Lover*. New York: Vantage, 1958.

Bender, Albert K. *Flying Saucers and the Three Men*. Neville Spearman, 1963.

_____. "Letter to August C. Roberts," August 4, 1953. Gray Barker UFO Collection, Clarksburg-Harrison Public Library.

_____. "Letter to August C. Roberts," September 14, 1953. Gray Barker UFO Collection, Clarksburg-Harrison Public Library.

_____. "Letter to August C. Roberts," October 18, 1953. Gray Barker UFO Collection, Clarksburg-Harrison Public Library.

_____. "Letter to August C. Roberts," November 12, 1953. Gray Barker UFO Collection, Clarksburg-Harrison Public Library.

_____. "Letter to August C. Roberts," December 20, 1953. Gray Barker UFO

Collection, Clarksburg-Harrison Public Library.

Berliner, Don, and Stanton T. Friedman. *Crash at Corona: The U.S. Military Retrieval and Cover-up of a UFO*. New York: Marlowe, 1997.

Bethurum, Truman. *Aboard a Flying Saucer*. Los Angeles: DeVorss, 1954.

_____. *Facing Reality*. Prescott, AZ: The Author, 1959.

_____. "Truman Bethurum to Gray Barker," November 16, 1953. Gray Barker UFO Collection, Clarksburg-Harrison Public Library.

_____. October 4, 1954. "Truman Bethurum to Gray Barker." October 4, 1954, n.d. Gray Barker UFO Collection, Clarksburg-Harrison Public Library.

"Biography of Dr. George King." *The Aetherius Society*, n.d. http://www.aetherius.org/index.cfm?app=content&SectionID=29.

Bishop, Greg. "Albert K. Bender's Contactee Experience." *Radio Misterioso*, May 14, 2012. http://radiomisterioso.com/2012/05/14/albert-k-benders-contactee-experiences.

Boyer, Paul. *By the Bomb's Early Light: American Thought and Consciousness at the Dawn of the Atomic Age*. New York: Pantheon, 1985.

Brick, Howard. *Age of Contradiction: American Thought and Culture in the 1960s*. Ithaca, NY: Cornell University Press, 2000.

Brinkley, Alan. "The Illusion of Unity in Cold War Culture." In Peter J. Kuznick and James Gilbert, ed., *Rethinking Cold War Culture*. Washington, D.C.: Smithsonian Institute Press, 2001.

Butler, Smedley. *War is a Racket*. New York: Round Table Press, 1935.

Childress, David Hatcher, and Richard S. Shaver. *Lost Continents & the Hollow Earth*. Kempton, IL: Adventures Unlimited Press, 1999.

Christopher, A.J. "Partition and Population in South Africa." *Geographical Review* 72, no. 2 (April 1, 1982): 127–138, 128.

"Contact Report 215." *The Future of Mankind: A Billy Meier Wiki*, February 24, 2012. http://futureofmankind.co.uk/Billy_Meier/Contact_Report_215.

"Contact Report 424." *The Future of Mankind: A Billy Meier Wiki*, May 3, 2009. http://futureofmankind.co.uk/Billy_Meier/Contact_Report_424.

Cooper, William. "The Origins, Identity, and Purpose of MJ-12." *Bibliotecapleyades*, May 23, 1989. http://www.bibliotecapleyades.net/sociopolitica/esp_sociopol_cooper11.htm.

Curran, Douglas. *In Advance of the Landing*. New York: Abbeville Press, 1985.

Dean, Jodi. *Aliens in America: Conspiracy Cultures from Outerspace to Cyberspace*. Ithaca, NY: Cornell University Press, 1998.

Denzler, Brenda. *The Lure of the Edge: Scientific Passions, Religious Beliefs, and the Pursuit of UFOs*. 1st ed. Berkeley, CA: University of California Press, 2003.

Dibitonto, Giorgio (trans. John T. Sherwood). *Angels in Starships*. Sedona, AZ: Sedona Visions, 1990.

Edwards, Frank. *Flying Saucers, Serious Business*. New York: Lyle Stuart, 1966.

Ellegion, Michael. *Channel for the Masters*, n.d. http://www.channelforthemasters.com.

Ellegion, Michael, and Aurora Light. *Prepare for the Landings*. Sedona, AZ: Vortex Network, 2009.

Ellwood, Robert S. "Spiritualism and UFO Religion in New Zealand: The International Transmission of Modern Spiritual Movements." In *The Gods Have Landed: New Religions from Other Worlds*, edited by James R. Lewis. Albany: State University of New York, 1995.

Ferguson, Marilyn. *The Aquarian Conspiracy: Personal and Social Transformation in the 1980s*. 1st ed. Los Angeles: J.P. Tarcher, 1981.

Frehner, Christian. "We Condemn All Racism." *They Fly!*, October 16, 2006. http://www.theyfly.com/newsflash4/frhnr01.htm.

"The Giza Intelligences." *The Future of Mankind: A Billy Meier Wiki*, May 11,

2012. http://www.futureofmankind.co. uk/Billy_Meier/Giza_Intelligences.

Greer, Steven. "The Covert Organization Responsible for the UFO/ET Issue: PI-40," May 1996. http://www.bibliotecapleyades.net/sociopolitica/esp_sociopol_mjl2_20.htm.

_____. "CSETI Ambassador to the Universe and Consciousness Trainings — 2008." *CSETI Homepage*, n.d. http://www.cseti.org/programs/Trainings2008. htm.

_____. "CSETI Homepage." *CSETI Homepage*, n.d. http://www.cseti.org/.

_____. "CSETI — The CE-5 Initiative." CSETI Homepage. http://www.cseti. org/ce5.htm.

_____. "CSETI Training Guidelines." *CSETI Homepage*, n.d. http://www. cseti.org/programs/trainingguidelines. htm.

_____. "Disclosure and 9/11/01—An Analysis." www.disclosureproject.org, 2001. http://www.disclosureproject. org/disclosure911.htm.

_____. "The Disclosure Project — Briefing Points." The Disclosure Project, 2001. http://www.disclosureproject.org/briefing points.htm.

_____. "Executive Summary — No Names." *The Disclosure Project*, April 5, 2001. http://web.archive.org/web/200 10502013212/www.disclosureproject.org /execsummary/executivesummary nonames.htm.

_____. "Media Response to May 9th Event." www.disclosureproject.org, n.d. http://www.disclosureproject.org/ May9response.htm.

Hatonn, Gyeorgos C. *Destruction of a Planet: Zionism IS Racism*. Las Vegas: Phoenix Source, 1992.

_____. *Space — Gate: The Veil Removed*. 3rd ed. Las Vegas: Phoenix Source, 1993.

Haynes, Gerald K. "A Die-Hard Issue: CIA's Role in the Study of UFOs, 1947–90." *Studies in Intelligence* 1, no. 1 (1997): 2.

Helland, Christopher. "From Extraterrestrials to Ultraterrestrials: The Evolution of the Concept of Ashtar." In *UFO Religions*, 162–178. London: Routledge, 2003.

Henriksen, Margot A. *Dr. Strangelove's America: Society and Culture in the Atomic Age*. Berkeley: University of California Press, 1997.

Hill, Ethel P. *In Days to Come*. Los Angeles: New Age Publishing, 1957.

"History of the Integratron." *The Integratron*, n.d. http://integratron.com/2 History/History.html.

Hynek, J. Allen. *The UFO Experience: A Scientific Inquiry*. New York: Marlowe, 1998.

"Immediately Disclose the Government's Knowledge of and Communications with Extraterrestrial Beings × The White House." *The White House*, September 22, 2011. /petitions#!/petition/ immediately-disclose-governments-knowledge-and-communications-extraterrestrial-beings/bGWkJk9Y.

Jacobs, David M. *The Threat: Revealing the Secret Alien Agenda*. Simon and Schuster, 1999.

_____. *The UFO Controversy in America*. Bloomington: Indiana University Press, 1975.

King, George. *You Are Responsible!* Los Angeles: The Aetherius Society, 1961.

Klarer, Elizabeth. *Beyond the Light Barrier: The Autobiography of Elizabeth Klarer*. Flagstaff, AZ: Light Technology Publishing, 2009.

Knight, Peter. *Conspiracy Culture: From Kennedy to the X-Files*. New York: Routledge, 2000.

Koresh (aka C.R. Teed). "The Ark of the Covenant." *The Flaming Sword* 28, no. 2 (1914): 347.

Lade, John. "Adamski — A Reasoned Support." *Flying Saucer Review*, October 1956.

"Landing in South Africa." *Flying Saucer Review*, December 1956.

Larson, Bob. *UFOs and the Alien Agenda: Uncovering the Mystery Behind UFOs and the Paranormal*. Nashville: Thomas Nelson, 1997.

Lear, John. "Lear's Aliens: Original Statement." *Bibliotecapleyades*, December 29, 1987. http://www.bibliotecapley ades.net/vida_alien/esp_vida_alien_180. htm.

Leslie, Desmond, and Alice Wells. "Go in Peace!" In *Gray Barker's Book of Adamski*, edited by Gray Barker. Clarksburg, WV: Saucerian Publications, n.d.

Leslie, Desmond, and George Adamski. *Flying Saucers Have Landed.* London: British Book Centre, 1953.

Leslie, Stuart W. *The Cold War and American Science: The Military-Industrial-Academic Complex at MIT and Stanford.* New York: Columbia University Press, 1993.

Lhamon, W.T., Jr. *Deliberate Speed: The Origins of a Cultural Style in the American 1950s.* Washington, D.C.: Smithsonian Institution Press, 1990.

Lily (aka Louisa Evans Lombe). *Golden Thoughts in Quiet Moments.* London: J. Burns, 1882.

Lorenzen, Coral E. *Flying Saucers: The Startling Evidence of Invasion from Outer Space.* New York: Pocket Books, 1966.

Melley, Timothy. *Empire of Conspiracy: The Culture of Paranoia in Postwar America.* Ithaca, NY: Cornell University Press, 2000.

Melton, J. Gordon. "The Contactees." In *The Gods Have Landed: New Religions from Other Worlds*, edited by James Lewis. Albany: State University of New York Press, 1995.

"Men in Black." *The Future of Mankind: A Billy Meier Wiki*, August 7, 2009. http://futureofmankind.co.uk/Billy_Meier/Men_in_Black.

Menger, Howard. *From Outer Space to You.* Clarksburg, WV: Saucerian Books, 1959.

Miles, Christopher. *Science Report: Alternative 3.* UK: Anglia Television, 1977.

Missler, Chuck, and Mark Eastman. *Alien Encounters: The Secret Behind the UFO Phenomenon.* Coeur d'Alene, ID: Koinonia House, 1997.

Mitchell, Helen, and Betty Mitchell. "We Met the Space People: Betty's Account,"

n.d. http://sacred-texts.com/ufo/wm sp/wmsp02.htm.

_____. "We Met the Space People: Helen's Story," n.d. http://sacred-texts.com/ufo/wmsp/wmsp01.htm.

Monast, Serge. "Project Blue Beam." *The Greatest Hoax*, n.d. http://www.sweet liberty.org/issues/hoax/bluebeam.htm.

Moseley, James W. "Some New Facts about 'Flying Saucers Have Landed.'" *Nexus* 2, no. 1 (January 1955): 7, 12–13.

Moseley, James W., and Karl T. Pflock. *Shockingly Close to the Truth_: Confessions of a Grave-Robbing Ufologist.* 1st ed. Amherst, NY: Prometheus, 2002.

Moylan, Tom. *Scraps of the Untainted Sky: Science Fiction, Utopia, Dystopia.* Boulder, CO: Westview Press, 2000.

Nebel, Long John. *The Way Out World.* Englewood Cliffs, NJ: Prentice-Hall, 1961.

Nelson, Buck. *My Trip to Mars, the Moon, and Venus.* Mountain View, MO: The Author, 1956.

Oakley, Ronald. *God's Country: America in the Fifties.* New York: Dembner, 1986.

"On Hale-Bopp, Cults, and Spirituality." *The Aetherius Society* (cached Page via Archive.org), n.d. http://web.archive.org/web/19980205101504/http://www.aetherius.org/hale.htm.

Partridge, Christopher. "Understanding UFO Religions." In *UFO Religions*, 3–42. London: Routledge, 2003.

Partridge, Christopher, ed. *UFO Religions.* London: Routledge, 2003.

"Past Issues Revisited." *George Adamski Foundation*, n.d. http://www.adamski-foundation.com/html/issues.htm.

Peebles, Curtis. *Watch the Skies! A Chronicle of the Flying Saucer Myth.* Washington, D.C.: Smithsonian Institution Press, 1994.

Pierce, John J. *Foundations of Science Fiction: A Study in Imagination and Evolution.* New York: Greenwood, 1987.

"PLEIADIAN MESSAGE FROM PETER: SHUT THEM DOWN." *Freer Spirit*, May 26, 2012. http://

freerspirit.com/2012/05/26/pleiadian-message-from-peter-shut-them-down/.

Randle, Keven, Russ Estes, and William Cone. *The Abduction Enigma*. New York: Forge, 1999.

Redfern, Nick. *The Real Men in Black*. Pompton Plains, NJ: New Page Books, 2011.

Risman, Barbara J. "Gender as a Social Structure: Theory Wrestling with Activism." *Gender and Society* 18, no. 4 (2004): 429–450.

Roberts, August C. "Letter to Albert K. Bender," August 2, 1954. Gray Barker UFO Collection, Clarksburg-Harrison Public Library.

Rojcewicz, Peter M. "The 'Men in Black' Experience and Tradition: Analogues with the Traditional Devil Hypothesis." *The Journal of American Folklore* 100, no. 396 (June 1987): 148–160.

Ronson, Jon. *The Men Who Stare at Goats*. New York: Simon & Schuster, 2006.

Roth, Christopher. "Ufology as Anthropology: Race, Extraterrestrials, and the Occult." In *E.T. Culture: Anthropology in Outerspaces*, edited by Debbora Battaglia, 38–93. Durham, NC: Duke University Press, 2005.

Ruppelt, Edward J. *The Report on Unidentified Flying Objects*. Garden City, NY: Doubleday, 1956.

Saliba, John A. "The Earth Is a Dangerous Place — The World View of the Aetherius Society." *Marburg Journal of Religion* 4, no. 2 (December 1999). http://www.uni-marburg.de/fb03/ivk/mjr/pdfs/1999/articles/saliba1999.pdf.

Salla, Michael. "Dennis Kucinich, Bill Richardson & UFOs: The 'Other' Alien Question in the 2008 Presidential Election," n.d. http://www.exopolitics.org/Exo-Comment-60.htm.

Samuel, Lawrence R. *Future: A Recent History*. Austin: University of Texas Press, 2009.

Schulman, Bruce J. *The Seventies: The Great Shift in American Culture, Society, and Politics*. Cambridge, MA: Da Capo Press, 2002.

Shaller, Michael, Virginia Scharff, and

Robert D. Schulzinger. *Present Tense: The United States Since 1945*. Boston: Houghton Mifflin, 1996.

Sherwood, John. "Gray Barker: My Friend the Myth-maker." *Skeptical Inquirer*, June 1998. http://www.csicop.org/si/show/gray_barker_my_friend_the_myth-maker/.

Smith, Simon G. "Opening a Channel to the Stars." In *UFO Religions*, 84–102. London: Routledge, 2003.

"Special: Petition." *The Future of Mankind: A Billy Meier Wiki*, n.d. http://futureofmankind.co.uk/Billy_Meier/Special:Petition?p=121.

Steiger, Brad, ed. *Project Blue Book*. New York: Ballantine, 1976.

Stevens, Wendelle C., ed. *Message from the Pleiades: The Contact Notes of Eduard Billy Meier*. 4 vols. Tucson, AZ: UFO Photo Archives, 1988–1995.

"The Talmud of Jmmanuel." *The Future of Mankind: A Billy Meier Wiki*, June 7, 2011.

Tate, Nancy. "Hatonn Obama Update Feb 17/09." *Tree of the Golden Light*, February 17, 2009. http://www.treeofthegoldenlight.com/Freedom%20Empowerment/hatonn_obama_update_feb_1-7-09.htm.

Tonnies, Mac. *The Cryptoterrestrials*. San Antonio: Anomalist Books, 2010.

Tuella. *Ashtar: A Tribute*. Durango, CO: Guardian Action, 1985.

_____. *Project: World Evacuation*. 3rd ed. Aztec, NM: Guardian Action, 1982.

Vallee, Jacques. *Messengers of Deception: UFO Contacts and Cults*. New York: Bantam, 1979.

Van Tassel, George. *I Rode a Flying Saucer*. 1st ed. Los Angeles: New Age Publishing, 1952.

_____. *Into this World and Out Again*. N.p., 1956.

Wang, Jessica. *American Science in an Age of Anxiety: Scientists, Anticommunism and the Cold War*. Chapel Hill: University of North Carolina Press, 1999.

Watkins, Leslie. *Alternative 3*. Nantwich: Archimedes Press, 2010.

Weldon, John, and Zola Levitt. *UFOs:*

What on Earth Is Happening? Irvine, CA: Harvest House, 1975.

"Who Is Benjamin Crème?" *Share International*, April 1999. http://share-international.org/background/bcreme/bc_main.htm.

Williamson, George Hunt. "A Message from Our Space Brothers," n.d. http://webcache.googleusercontent.com/search?q=cache:http://www.bibliotecapleyades.net/bb/williamson.htm.

_____. *Other Tongues, Other Flesh.* Amherst, Wisconsin: Amherst Press, 1957.

_____. "Project Scroll." *Flying Saucer Review* (December 1957): 18–19.

_____. *Secret Places of the Lion.* London: Neville Spearman, 1958.

Williamson, George H., and Alfred C. Bailey. *The Saucers Speak.* London: Neville Spearman, 1963; reissue, Pomeroy, WA: Health Research Books, 1996.

Index

Numbers in **bold italics** indicate pages with photographs.